Readings and Cases
in Business Commun

Steven P. Golen
Louisiana State University

Ross Figgins
California State Polytechnic University

Larry R. Smeltzer
Louisiana State University

John Wiley & Sons
New York   Chichester   Brisbane   Toronto   Singapore

WILEY SERIES IN BUSINESS COMMUNICATIONS

The manuscript for this book was developed under the guidance of C. Glenn Pearce, Consulting Editor for Business and Organizational Communication. Dr. Pearce is a professor at Virginia Commonwealth University.

Library of Congress Cataloging in Publication Data:

Readings and cases in business communication.

   (Business communications series)
   Includes index.
   1. Communication in management—Addresses, essays,
lectures.   2. Communication in management—Case studies.
I. Golen, Steven.   II. Figgins, Ross.   III. Smeltzer,
Larry.   IV. Title: Business communication.   V. Series.

HF5718.R4   1984   658.4'5   83-17066
ISBN 0-471-86953-8

Printed in the United States of America

10 9 8 7 6 5 4 3 2 1

Preface

The development of skill in the various areas of communications—writing, speaking, listening, and reading—and the problems associated with this development greatly affect organizations today. Numerous studies of people within various organizations show the importance of and need for effective communications. Those who can communicate effectively in an organizational setting can approach their jobs with understanding, satisfaction, and confidence.

To succeed at communicating effectively, one must recognize the areas that need improvement and then work to develop better skills in those areas. This book is designed to help with this improvement. The purpose of the book is to help you improve your business communication skills by providing you with an overview of some major communication concerns facing those who work in an organizational setting. The readings and cases in the book have been carefully selected to ensure a meaningful and consistent approach to identifying and dealing with important communication issues.

Each reading in the book had to satisfy four criteria before it was included: (1) *relevant content*—the contents of each article must apply to the study of business communications; (2) *readability*—the article must be written in a way that is understandable to a general audience; (3) *timeliness*—the article must contribute to the current thinking in the field; and (4) *usefulness*—the article must add depth to the topics usually presented in a business communications course. To help meet these rigorous criteria, several original essays were written especially for this book; these and the other articles assure that a comprehensive coverage of the critical topics is offered for your use and enjoyment.

To help select appropriate articles to include in the book, a six-member review board was formed. Some members work in business, and others are business educators. The result is a compilation of articles from a wide range of sources. The authors extend their gratitude to the review board members who not only evaluated articles for inclusion but also made valuable suggestions that have made this a better book. The members of the review board are William Buchholz, Bentley College; Arthur Cornwell, The Boardroom Training Consultants; Jack Eure, Southwest Texas State University; Edward Goodin, University of Nevada, Las Vegas; Thomas Inman, Southwest Missouri State University; and Mike Spalding, Kaiser Aluminum and Chemical Corporation. We would also like to thank the publishers, authors, and case study writers whose cooperation made this project possible.

The book begins with a discussion of techniques for use in case analysis that will aid both the student and the instructor in using the cases effectively in the classroom. This discussion is followed by eight parts of readings, together with individual discussion questions for each article and selected cases for each part.

Part I contains four articles dealing with basic communication principles. Improving business writing, the theme of Part II, contains five articles on various aspects of fundamental writing principles. In Part III, three articles on business correspondence issues are presented. Part IV contains three articles on effective report writing.

With the advancement of technology that affects business communications, four articles on this topic are included in Part V. Interpersonal communications is the theme of the five articles in Part VI. Closely related to the articles in Part VI are the five articles in Part VII dealing with communications in different business situations. The three articles in Part VIII deal with the employment process.

This book can serve as a supplement to any business communication textbook at the university, college, and community college level. In addition, the book can be used in upper-division collegiate courses in managerial, organizational, and interpersonal communications. To make it easy for you to coordinate the contents of this book with those of textbooks in the field, the table on the following pages has been prepared

Steven P. Golen
Ross Figgins
Larry R. Smeltzer

TABLE

CROSS-REFERENCE BY PARTS IN *READINGS AND CASES IN BUSINESS COMMUNICATION* TO CHAPTERS IN MAJOR BUSINESS COMMUNICATION TEXTBOOKS

	Part I Planning	Part II Writing	Part III Correspondence	Part IV Reports	Part V Automation	Part VI Interpersonal	Part VII Meeting	Part VIII Job Search
Pearce (1984)	1, 21	2, 3, App. A	4–7, App. D	8–13, Apps. B, C	14	15, 18	16, 17	19, 20
Figgins (1984)	1, 2, App. A	1, 2, App. A	3–6, App. D	7–12, Apps. B, C	13		17	14, 15
Aronoff (1981)	1, 2	3, App. B	4–6	7–11, 18, App. C		14, 15	12, 13, 16, 19	App. A
Borman (1982)	5, 6, 14					2, 8, 9, 12, 13	3, 4, 7, 10, 11	1
Bowman (1980)	1, 2, 20	3, 4, App. A	5–11	12–15, App. B		19–20	16	17, 18
Brown (1982)	1, 2, 13	3, 4, App. B	5, App. A	7, 8	Epilogue, Apps. C, D	2, 9	10–12	6, Epilogue
Feinberg (1982)	1, 2	4–7	8–12	13, 14	15, 21, App. A	1, 20	3, 16	17–19
Haggblade (1982)	1, 11	3–6, 12	7	8–10	4	2	14, 15	13
Himstreet (1981)	1, 17	2–4	5–8	11–15			16	9, 10
Huseman (1981)	1–4, App. B	6	7–9	10, 11	App. A	5	13, 14, 16	15, 17, 18
Lee (1980)	1–4, 15	5–7	8	9, 10	14, 16, App. G	2	13	11, 12
Leonard (1979)	1	2–5	6–12	13–19		22	21	12

	Part I Planning	Part II Writing	Part III Correspondence	Part IV Reports	Part V Automation	Part VI Interpersonal	Part VII Meeting	Part VIII Job Search
Lesikar (1980)	1–6	7, 8, App. D	9–11, App. B	12–15, Apps. A, C		16	16	11
Level (1980)	1–3, 16	4	5–7	8–10		13	11, 12	14, 15, Apps. A, B
Lindauer (1979)	1, 2	App. E	3–6, 8–10	11, 12	15	15	13, 14	7
Lord (1983)	1	2, 3	4, 5	6–10				12
Murphy (1980)	1, 2, App A	3–6, App. B	7–10	15–17		19	18	11, 12
Persing (1981)	1–6	7	8–12	13, 14	7	15	16	17, 18
Quible (1981)	1, App. F	2, 3, Apps. A–E, G	4–7, 13	10–12	16	17	15, 17	8, 9
Rosenblatt (1982)	1–5	13	14	9, 15, 16		7, 8	6, 9, 11, 12	10, App.
Sigband (1982)	1, 2, 24	4, 5, App. B	18–22, App. C	6–10, App. A	23	3	11–15	16–17
Treece (1983)	1, 2, App. A	4, 5, App. D	6–8, App. B	9–14, Apps. B, C	18	3	3, 17	15–16
Wells (1981)		1–4, App. F	5–12	13, 15–18	19	19	19, 20	14
Wilkinson (1980)	App. A	1, 2	3–12	13–16		17	17	10
Wolf (1979)	1–3	4–6	8–10, 13–17	18, 19	7	7	7	11, 12

Contents

Readings and Cases
in Business Communication

Communicating with a Purpose

The resolution of problems is the test of any profession. Who would you go to, for example, to get advice about real estate law or corporate accounting? The most experienced person you know is the likely answer. And how did that person gain his or her knowledge and become someone you would seek out for advice? Hmmm! That's a little bit tougher. Through school? Partly, but can a person become a master chef simply by reading many cookbooks? Not really, so let's expand the answer to include the process of application—that is, taking experience from one situation and using it in another.

The broader a person's range of experience, the greater the potential to unearth a successful solution, especially when faced with *new* or *unusual* situations. From this viewpoint, then, difficulties should not be viewed as annoyances or setbacks but as opportunities and chances to learn. This viewpoint is especially appropriate in communications, because by its very nature communications becomes effective in application. By this time, you have probably studied the principles of business communications and used them in "textbook" problems. Here is an opportunity to adapt the communication skills you have developed to practical ends. The readings and case studies will be especially helpful in applying what you know now and in increasing your understanding of how communication works in business.

In case studies, solutions to problems are viewed on a different scale. For example, the answers to a spelling test are either right or wrong. But in a professional situation, right or wrong may not be effective. Just sending a letter is not enough; you must send an appropriate letter, one designed to meet the needs of particular circumstances.

In the following pages, you will read about how the communication process works and, through various problem applications, have the opportunity to test your professional skills. But before beginning with the readings and case studies themselves, let's spend a little more time discussing the nature of *problem solving*.

The Why of Case Studies

Several important reasons to concentrate on cases exist in the study of business communications. First, knowing about communications is of little value unless you learn to apply that knowledge. For example, memorizing the rules for letter writing is useful only when you can also analyze a situation, determine that a letter should be written, and then proceed to write an appropriate letter. The relationship between knowledge and application can be compared with the young man who was courting a young woman. He didn't know how to tell her how beautiful he thought she was. A friend suggested that he look at her and say lovingly, "When I'm with you and look into your eyes, all time stops." At the first opportunity he tried just that, but because he was a little nervous, he gazed at her and blurted, "Looking at your face could stop a clock." He had a good idea, but the results were less than successful.

The use of business communication cases also provides an opportunity to prepare for the various challenges a person faces on the job. The opportunity for practice is not often provided professionals; there is little or no allowance for errors or "guesses" when on the job.

A well-developed ability to analyze complex situations is required in business. Cases such as these that follow provide practice in developing the analytical skills necessary to communicate in complex situations. If a person develops a habitual way of responding, effectiveness is low. For instance, some people use the telephone by habit regardless of the purpose of the message. A study of communication barriers indicates that in many situations correspondence is more effective, whereas in other situations face-to-face or telephone communication might be preferable.

The final reason for using case studies is related directly to all of the others. Business requires creative employees who can analyze difficult situations and find appropriate solutions. Creativity, finding a fresh and valuable new association, is not automatic but requires practice.[1] Creativity probably is present in all human decision and problem-solving processes. However, the use of explicit creative techniques has the potential to improve those processes.[2] The difference in communication as a result of creativity is demonstrated in a story about two priests. The first priest asked his superior if it was all right to smoke while praying. His request was denied emphatically. The second priest asked the same superior if it was all right to pray while smoking. This request was granted gladly.

Flexibility, independence, freedom, and *satisfaction* are the four components of creativity that case studies can help develop.[3] Flexibility is the ability to change when business conditions change; case studies require that you adapt to changing situations. People are independent in their judgment when they do not automatically yield to pressure or criticism. Because pressure and criticism can be minimized in the classroom, case analysis allows freedom and uninhibited thought. The ability to be independent and free of the fear of criticism results in satisfaction.

The How of Case Studies

A systematic case analysis strategy can be employed to meet these different purposes. Regardless of the particular strategy you choose, it should be similar to what would be used in managing an actual communication problem. When developing this strategy, it is important to use what Edward de Bono terms "Lateral Thinking."[4] The critical element in Lateral Thinking is the examination of existing assumptions. In any business situation, or in a case study, it is impossible to know all the facts. Pertinent information is often unavailable to you in actual business situations. Consequently, your first step in finding a solution is to analyze the available facts and establish realistic assumptions based on them.

Once the initial situation has been reviewed, W. H. Newman, Charles E. Summer, and Warren E. Kirby suggest that most business decisions can be divided into a four-part process.[5] First, make a diagnosis and define the problem. This problem statement is generally the most critical step. Many managers can cite situations where the wrong problem has been solved! To avoid this mistake, it is wise to *write* out a statement of the problem. This provides others an opportunity to review it and share their ideas with you.

Next, arrive at alternative solutions to the problem. In some situations good alternatives are readily apparent but at other times a high level of creativity may be required. Group interaction can help develop this required creativity by using either the brainstorming or Nominal Group process. Brainstorming is probably the best known creativity technique. Alex F. Osborn, its developer, recommends a group of about six individuals who follow these rules:

1. Judgments are withheld until later evaluation.
2. Wild ideas are encouraged as they can be modified later if required.
3. Numerous ideas are solicited.
4. Participants are urged to use the input of others to develop additional tasks.[6]

In the Nominal Group process the group does not interact vocally, so the group is termed *nominal*—a group in name only. The Nominal Group process is implemented as follows:

1. Without discussion, group members write what they consider to be the viable alternatives.
2. Each person reads his or her list. The items from each person's list are recorded in clear view of all as they are read.
3. The alternatives are then discussed and the best possibilities are identified by a voting system.[7]

The third step in making a business decision is to determine the best alternative. This step actually is part of the second step when the Nominal Group process is used. When working alone or when brainstorming, however, it is a separate step. When working alone, it is a good idea to discuss your selected alternative with someone else. Everyone has a different viewpoint, which can often provide valuable insights.

The final step is to implement the solution. When doing this, consider the steps involved between choosing the correct solution and actually doing it. For instance, after analyzing a problem, listing alternatives, and selecting the best choice, you may determine that the problem requires that you write a letter of reprimand to a subordinate. Once a well-written letter is composed and delivered, the final step in the process will be completed. The process is complete only when the solution you decide is best is implemented.

In summary, the case method can be a valuable technique to foster effective communication. In working with the cases in this book, you can improve your analytical skills, creativity, and ability to apply your knowledge. To obtain these results, however, a systematic and realistic analysis must be used to achieve the goal of *communicating with a purpose*.

References

1. David Oates. "The Boom in Creative Thinking." *International Management,* 18, December 1972.

2. Irvin Summers and David E. While. "Creativity Techniques Toward Improvement of the Decision Process," *Academy of Management Review* (April 1976), pp. 99–107.

3. Evelyn W. Mayerson, *Shoptalk: Foundations of Managerial Communication.* Philadelphia: Saunders, 1979, p. 261.

4. Edward de Bono. *Lateral Thinking: Creativity Step by Step.* New York: Harper & Row, 1970.

5. W. H. Newman, Charles E. Summer, and Warren E. Kirby. *The Process of Management,* 3rd ed. Englewood Cliffs, N.J.: Prentice-Hall, 1972, p. 357.

6. Alex F. Osborn. *Applied Imagination.* New York: Scribner's, 1953.

7. Andre L. Delbecq and Andrew H. Van de Ven. "A Group Process Model for Problem Identification and Program Planning," *The Journal of Applied Behavioral Science,* 7 (1971), pp. 466–492.

Planning Effective Business Communication

All complex business functions require planning. To explore the complex nature of planning for business communication, this first part presents several articles related to the planning process.

Joe G. Thomas, in his article, "Communication: New Thoughts on an Old Subject," states that the subject of communication has been so widely discussed that we sometimes feel there is no need to consider it further. However, he presents evidence which indicates that most people are not as proficient as they think they are, or at least not to the extent that their employers would like them to be.

To increase communication proficiency, one needs to consider barriers to communication and make plans to overcome them. Gene E. Burton discusses the most prevalant barriers and techniques for managing them in his article, "Barriers to Effective Communication."

Communication is becoming even more complicated with the growing complexity of modern organizations. Thomas H. Inman presents organizational communication factors that one must plan for when communicating upward and downward in an organization. His article, "Effective Management Needs Upward and Downward Communication," presents four different suggestions to integrate into the planning process.

Legal considerations are becoming more and more important in all aspects of business, and communication is no exception. In their article, "Legal Aspects of Communication: Sexism to Slander," Sandra M. Robinson and Larry R. Smeltzer discuss defamation, privacy, and copyright concepts that a writer must consider when communicating today.

Communication: New Thoughts on an Old Subject

Joe G. Thomas

Northeast Missouri State University, Kirksville, MO

Everyone has seen cartoons showing an individual or a group in some awkward predicament with the accompanying caption, "What we have here is a lack of communication." While these incidents may be amusing in a cartoon, when they happen in organizations the consequences may not be so funny. Poor communications, for instance, may result in employees who are not certain what their job is or how to do it or how their work will be evaluated. This may encourage a lack of interest and low morale in the entire work group. The supervisor may blame subordinates for being disinterested, lazy, ignorant, or incompetent, when the real reason for poor performance may be poor communications.

What follows is based on the results of a survey that was conducted to identify the abilities most needed by middle-level managers in a cross-section of industries. One thing that is readily apparent from the results is the importance of communication skills. More is required to carry out instructions than just clear communications but it should also be apparent that one cannot follow the instructions unless they are transmitted in an understandable manner.

The competency statements used in this survey were developed from a literature review and from suggestions by employers. A list of 500 activities was developed and submitted to a panel of consultants who examined the items for validity. The consultants chose a list of 115 abilities for inclusion in the final questionnaire, which was then sent to a random sample of firms from various industries. Responses were received from 96 firms. The majority of the respondents were from manufacturing (46), banking and finance (20), and wholesale and retail related (10) industries. An index value was computed for the competencies based upon the number of respondents returning the questionnaire and the relative importance attached to each competency statement by each respondent. The 20 most highly ranked competencies are reported here. They have been grouped to show the competencies related to communications with subordinates, superiors, and individuals outside of the normal chain of command (for example, peers and labor union representatives).

Communications with Superiors

The major source of communication is one's superior in the chain of command. Table 1 shows the competency statements that involve communicating with one's boss. Of all the abilities desired of a middle-level manager, the two that were ranked highest were following instructions and exchanging information with superiors. These two skills are clearly related to communication and are prerequisite to satisfactory performance. It is therefore important that an environment exists in the organization in which supervisors feel free to talk with their superiors. If the supervisor has a question, opportunities for clarification should be available. This could be achieved by holding regular meetings or by scheduling appointments with superiors to allow for questions. In either case, it is necessary that superiors have time to develop answers to the questions that supervisors may raise.

Informal exchanges between the superior and the supervisor are also chances for discussion of problem areas. However, they generally do not provide the right kind of interaction because they usually occur at the convenience of the initiator. The supervisor, for example, may have time to talk, be relaxed, and have his thoughts well developed while his boss may be busy with something else, and not have had the opportunity to organize her thoughts. She may recognize that there is a problem that needs to be discussed but may be unable to speak tactfully and succinctly on such short notice. Formal, scheduled meetings allow the supervisor and superior to prepare questions that address the issues and make better use of their time. This also gives the superior an opportunity to inform the supervisor of changes in plans and objectives.

Meetings and conversations with superiors give the supervisor an opportunity to make certain that he or she has read and understood company

TABLE 1

COMMUNICATIONS WITH SUPERIORS

Overall Rank	Competency Statement
1	Follow instructions from superior.
2	Exchange information with superiors.
11	Follow proper channels of authority in the business organization.
13	Read company memorandums and reports.
20	Inform superiors of plans and objectives.

memorandums and reports. The superior can repeat essential information and ask the supervisor if there are any questions. This accomplishes two things. First, it should impress upon the supervisor that written communication is important and should be read. Second, it provides the superior with an opportunity to clarify any issues and to reinforce the key points made in the communication. If any misunderstanding has occurred, it's also a chance to correct the error.

The Subordinate

The middle-level manager must also develop competencies in communicating with his or her subordinates. The competency statements that concern communications with subordinates are shown in Table 2.

A number of the statements in our sample involve communicating the requirements of a job to the subordinate. Such competencies include setting an example of performance and behavior, defining the duties of the subordinate, and explaining the standards by which employee performance is going to be evaluated. It is at this point in the supervisor's job that a clear understanding of the assignments from one's own superiors becomes very important. If one does not fully understand the instructions of one's boss, it is very difficult to pass them on to one's subordinates.

Assuming that one does understand the task being assigned, how should that assignment be communicated? There are many techniques that could be used to relay the assignment to the subordinate. These could include written

TABLE 2
COMMUNICATIONS INVOLVING SUBORDINATES

Overall Rank	Competency Statement
6	Tactfully identify mistakes employees have made and help them constructively correct them.
8	Set example of optimum performance, attitude, and behavior.
9	Create an environment in which organizational members feel that their contributions are important.
12	Effectively handle the complaints of subordinates.
14	Clearly define the duties and standards of performance for each employee.
15	Define duties and responsibilities of each subordinate.
16	Identify any deviation from plans and take appropriate steps to correct them.
16	Give praise to subordinates for personal achievement and accomplishments.
19	Develop and maintain control so that an orderly group effort results.

and verbal media. No single technique is always effective, and a thorough understanding of a complex message is not likely to occur with just one transmission of the message. People wrongly assume that once individuals are told something, they understand it completely and can accomplish the task without further instruction. Managers may not always understand instructions the first time around, yet they often forget that subordinates may not either.

A skill closely associated with the explanation of the employee's job seems to be the evaluation of performance. In our survey, tactfully identifying employee mistakes was the sixth most highly prized ability desired of middle-level managers. Two other valued skills—the ability to identify and correct deviations from plans and the ability to praise subordinates for personal achievements—tied for sixteenth place. The value placed on these three skills should prompt the supervisor to think more about his or her approach to subordinates. It is too easy, when someone is observed making a mistake, to become so intent on correction that the feelings of the employee are ignored. Unless the mistake is intentionally made or represents a serious safety hazard, the supervisor should make the effort to phrase carefully the criticism so that it does not seem harsh. This may be accomplished by asking the employee about the mistake rather than taking the offensive in an accusatory manner. The criticism may be equally effective but less objectionable if it is phrased with humor.

Regardless of how the criticism is phrased, the subordinates' feelings should be considered. Criticism is more palatable if recognition is also given for previous achievements and good work. Too often managers concentrate solely on problem solving and forget to mention good performance, and that can lead to morale problems. The failure to give praise is apparently a serious problem since the participants in our survey ranked it sixteenth out of 115 competencies.

Good Feeling

The final items relating to communications with subordinates concern the creation of a productive work environment. These involve making employees feel that their contributions are important to the company and their department.

Skills like handling employee complaints, especially when they involve other subordinates, need to be cultivated. This area also requires the supervisor to be aware of the feelings of subordinates. One way to achieve this is through frequent contact with them. As in relations with one's superior, it may be helpful to have regularly scheduled meetings with subordinates to allow them to discuss their problems and answer questions.

Informal contact with employees may also allow the manager to identify potential problems before they seriously damage the work environment.

While this advice may seem to be a matter of common sense, it is very easy in the course of day-to-day problems to overlook the simpler aspects of human relations. From the employees' perspective, brisk behavior may be interpreted as a lack of concern.

Other Communication Skills

The final group of managerial abilities are skills that require relating to individuals outside of the normal chain of command—peers, representatives of the labor union, customers, suppliers, and the like. Four of the seven most frequently mentioned competencies in our survey were included in this group.

The third most frequently mentioned concerned working with union representatives on labor problems. This requires that the supervisor be able to explain management's point of view clearly and concisely to a union representative. To be effective in this area, the supervisor needs a thorough understanding of the labor agreement.

Another skill that those we surveyed desired of middle-level managers was the ability to use the experience of others in addition to one's own judgment. This requires an understanding of fellow workers' abilities in order to know who has the knowledge that would be helpful. Establishing an open communications network with one's peers is an integral part of this understanding. The individual manager can take some steps to make the necessary contacts, but the primary responsibility for creating this cooperative work environment rests with top management, which must make all supervisors aware of the special skills of others in the organization so that they will know the best person to contact. If one's superior does not do an adequate job of providing this information, it is up to the supervisor to seek out these sources of information.

The fifth most frequently mentioned skill is the use of the telephone for business communications. Telephone etiquette is another one of those com-

TABLE 3

COMMUNICATIONS OUTSIDE CHAIN OF COMMAND

Overall Rank	Competency Statement
3	Deal with labor union representative on labor problems.
4	Utilize the experience and knowledge of others as well as one's own judgment.
5	Use telephone for business communications.
7	Select the right person to perform a task.
18	Coordinate company effort through interdepartmental communications.

mon sense skills with which we too often assume that everyone is familiar. The importance of such things as identifying one's self on the telephone, taking clear messages, and remembering to pass the messages to the intended recipient seems perfectly obvious.

Unfortunately, it is difficult to identify the consequences of poor telephone manners. The missed message is often simply lost and the manager never knows that the call came in until he hears from an irate customer who waited in vain for the return call. It might help if a brief note outlining good telephone habits is circulated periodically to remind people about the correct way to answer the phone, take messages, and conduct themselves in general. Many companies use a note pad for taking messages that reminds the person taking the call to get the caller's name, number, date of call, message, and any other pertinent information.

Another communication skill that those in our survey ranked as important was the ability to select the right person to perform a task. If a new employee is being hired for the job, interviewing the prospect will require explaining the features of both the job and company to the potential employee. If a current employee is being considered for a job, he or she will probably be already aware of these things, but the supervisor must still determine the employee's interest and ability, and be ready to answer any questions that may arise about the job. A clear understanding of job responsibilities and standards for evaluation are needed both to ask and to answer questions. Especially when recruiting a person in a specialized area, the ability to answer questions well may be necessary to *sell* the applicant on the company and the job. A disorganized interviewer may cause a good prospect to lose interest in the job and go elsewhere.

Taken for Granted

Everyone agrees that good communications skills are an essential part of a manager's job, but the subject has been so widely discussed that sometimes we feel there's no need to consider it further. Yet the frequent mention of communications ability in our survey would indicate that most people are not as proficient as they think they are, or at least not to the extent that their employers would like them to be. It would be worth a supervisor's time to reexamine his or her performance in this area to make certain that communications skills are not being shortchanged by other problems that seem more pressing.

Discussion Questions

1.   The author states that informal exchanges between the superior and the supervisor are also chances for discussion of problem areas. Why does

this generally not provide the right kind of interaction? Explain what can be done to improve this situation.

2. What are the advantages of formally scheduled meetings between a supervisor and a subordinate?

3. Different competencies are required when communicating with superiors than when communicating with subordinates. Summarize these differences.

Barriers to Effective Communication

Gene E. Burton
California State University, Fresno, CA

Most managers agree that effective communication is essential for the successful performance of organizations. In fact, communication is the key to all interpersonal activity, whether in organizations such as business, government, education, and service institutions or in the individual's private and family relationships. Man's ability to think and to transmit human thought has opened the door for the development of man and his environment.

Unfortunately, it has only been in recent times that man has devoted any meaningful attention to the development of communication skills. Despite tremendous advances in technology, man's failure to improve interpersonal communications is evidenced by cold wars, racial intolerance, the moral decay of the political system (Watergate), the deterioration of the traditional family structure, and the ever-present conflict between management and labor.

In recent times, managers have implemented a variety of organizational strategies to improve operational effectiveness. The more popular strategies include matrix structures, organization development (OD), management by objectives (MBO), sensitivity training, and profit sharing. However, managers seem to be generally indifferent to the important role that organizational communication plays in the success or failure of any management technique. Of all the complexities of administration, perhaps the key to success lies in the manager's ability to communicate.

The Basics of Communication

The word *communication* comes from the Latin word *communis*, which means common. Therefore, when man communicates, he is trying to establish a degree of commonness with someone else. That is, there is conscious effort to transmit and share information or an attitude. Thus, communication

Source: Gene E. Burton. "Barriers to Effective Communication." Reprinted, from *Management World,* March 1977, by permission of the Administrative Management Society.

is a two-way street by which one communicates *with* people, not *to* people. Similarly, each person communicates constantly, by what he says or doesn't say, and by what he does or doesn't do.

Organizational communication is a highly complex process having certain key characteristics with which the successful manager must deal more effectively. First, organizational communication is a part of the total organization that interacts with its environment. In this manner, the organization is influenced by its environment and, in turn, the organization exerts an influence on that environment.

Second, organizational communication is a flow of messages through channels known as communication networks. These are composed of networks for problem solving, work-flow, information flow, and socializing. In effect, the communication network is an arterial system interwoven throughout the organization, touching everyone within its sphere of influence.

Third, organizational communication for the business firm has two basic purposes. First is the need to furnish information required for decision-making and control. Second is the desire to influence and motivate people in order to bring individual behavior more in line with the needs of the total organization.

Last and most important, organizational communication is a people-oriented process that encompasses all the behavior sciences. As such, it is more than a collection of communication devices such as telephones, closed-circuit TV, intercoms, and newsletters. Even AT&T has experienced the sting of failure associated with organizational communication:

Within the greatest communications organization in the world we are hurt and puzzled by a seeming communication failure—the problem of talking with our employees. By all odds, with the media and money at our command, we of all companies should be the case history of successful internal communications. . . . (John Howard, from Bell Telephone Magazine.)

Communication Barriers

There are many reasons why communication between two people can fail. Barriers to the communication process are called *noise*. Examples of common noise between a manager and an employee are described below.

Physical noise   Often, miscommunication is the natural result of physical noise which obstructs the process of communication. For instance, many factory environments produce such intense noise levels that verbal communication is difficult, if not impossible. Other times, the volume or clarity of the message may be inadequate, or the receiver's hearing may be impaired.

In the same manner, written communications are often unsuccessful due to inadequate lighting, glare, poor vision, color-blindness, etc.

Distance and Time   A good case could probably be made for the hypothesis that miscommunication can result from the distance between the sender and the receiver. It would seem logical that face-to-face communications have greater impact and clarity than messages filtering down from some remote facility. Managers also experience time barriers to communication, such as the difficulty in achieving good communications between employees who work different shifts.

Spatial Arrangements   Many times, effective communication is hindered by office partitions, desk arrangements, equipment positions, and walkways. Eye contact is often necessary for fidelity of communication. Therefore, any spatial arrangement which limits eye contact will also limit the effectiveness of communication.

Spatial arrangements can also cause emotional disturbances which, in turn, become barriers to communication. For instance, American men find it uncomfortable to work too close with other men. They also prefer to work where there is a minimum of activity behind them. Basically, the male worker in this country prefers to protect his rear, to keep his back to the wall, to keep the activity of others within his line of sight, and to keep other men at a comfortable distance, at least an arm's length away. Thus, if male workers must occupy desk chairs or workbench stools that are back to back with little room, managers can expect ineffective communications and poor job performance.

In much the same manner, if there are specific desks, work benches, or machine positions that acquire some form of status in the group, the manager can expect some unique patterns of miscommunication to develop among those who aspire to those work stations possessing status.

Organizational Distance   Other cases of miscommunication occur between people who fill positions in the firm that are separated by considerable organizational distance, especially with respect to the managerial hierarchy. For example, it would not be wise to expect clear understanding to result from communication between the president of a large corporation and one of the firm's janitors. Not only would these two men have difficulty finding a mutual base for communicating, but the president's position of power and prestige would probably overwhelm the janitor, leaving him so uncomfortable that his receptiveness to communication would be impaired. This distance barrier is often compounded by a credibility gap that seems to widen as the hierarchical distance is increased.

Source   The source of the message, along with the receiver's attitude toward the source, will have considerable impact upon the degree of the communication's success. For example, if the receiver does not like the sender or feels that the sender does not like him, he will tend to "read into" the communication those messages which support that opinion. In effect, we tend to distort the communication until we hear what we want to hear. Other times, we tend to be selective listeners, extracting bits of the total message, out of context, to support our own views.

Distractions Sometimes messages are not received or are improperly translated because of the myriad of distractions that surround the communicators. The receiver may misunderstand a communication because his listening was interrupted by the distraction of an attractive woman walking down the hallway. Other times, the listener finds that his attention is drawn, not to the sender's verbal message, but by some mannerism that is annoying or fascinating to the receiver. Each of us has experienced occasions when we could not focus on the sender's words, because we were almost hypnotized by the wart on the sender's chin or by his nervous facial tic.

Lack of Concentration A most common form of noise in the communication process is the lack of concentration on the part of the listener. Every schoolboy has experienced the inability to concentrate on a dull lecture, allowing his thoughts to stray out the window to the sounds of spring, to the crack of a hickory bat on a hanging curveball, or to the smell of "fresh-mowed" grass. Even the most seasoned executive suffers from the same frailty, allowing his or her lack of concentration to become a serious barrier to communication.

Lack of Common Knowledge The lack of a common body of knowledge leads to all kinds of communication errors. This is especially true among those who tend to use technical jargon, shop-talk, buzz-words, coined words, acronyms, or million-dollar words. Such diction might impress one but cause utter confusion for others.

Gobbledygook Gobbledygook, coined by William Haney in his book, *Communication and Organizational Behavior,* is a smoke screen type of communication which is designed to overwhelm the receiver through the use of technical jargon, involved sentences, and polysyllabic words. The "Systematic Buzz Phrase Projector," originated by the Royal Canadian Air Force, helps one construct verbose phrases to impress and confound associates. Simply think of a three-digit number and select the corresponding buzz-words from the three columns shown in the chart that follows. For example, 230 produces "systematized reciprocal options," an expression that is bound to bring instant respect—and confusion.

Perceptual Readiness Perception is the way man experiences his universe. However, it is necessary to keep in mind that we do not experience

"SYSTEMATIC BUZZ PHRASE PROJECTOR"		
Column 1	**Column 2**	**Column 3**
0. integrated	0. management	0. options
1. total	1. organizational	1. flexibility
2. systematized	2. monitored	2. capability
3. parallel	3. reciprocal	3. mobility
4. functional	4. digital	4. programming
5. responsive	5. logic	5. concept
6. optical	6. transitional	6. time-phase
7. synchronized	7. incremental	7. projection
8. compatible	8. third-generation	8. hardware
9. balanced	9. policy	9. contingency

the world as it is but as we interpret it. Therefore, man does not react to the real situation that confronts him, but to his unique perception of reality. Because of individual perceptual differences, no two people experience the world in the same way. Likewise, none of us experiences the world as it really is. Some of the factors which cause each person's perceptual processes to be unique are inner needs, prejudices, past experience, status, moods, roles, and cultural influences.

Man's perceptual process selects from a myriad of stimuli those events and ideas that will be "seen" or "remembered." Certain events or details of events are ignored as unimportant or are dismissed because they conflict with existing values or beliefs. Other events or details are accentuated or sharply ingrained in one's memory. These perceptual distortions are a primary cause of miscommunication.

Semantics   One of the most severe barriers to effective communication is the complexity of semantics, or the meanings of words and the changes in those meanings. For instance, to the Kansas farm boy in the 1930's, a "pig" was a four-legged animal that required "slopping." Later, in a World War II bootcamp, that farm boy soon learned that a "pig" was a certain kind of female to be avoided by a seventeen-year-old sailor while on leave. Today, that same veteran discovers, when communicating with his teen-age son, that a "pig" is a law enforcement officer. This piling-on of meanings is a common form of communication noise as well as a main cause of the generation gap.

What does a word really mean? Why does a word mean one thing to one person but something entirely different to someone else? Why do we stand a good chance of miscommunicating when we use such loaded words as *hippy, hard-hat, red-neck, democrat, republican, communist,* or *Watergate?*

The problem involves' the meaning of the word *meaning.* If we assume that no two people think exactly alike, we should not be surprised to find that words have different meanings to different people, resulting in faulty communication. For instance, the word *chair* holds special meaning for the convicted murderer waiting on death row. How different that meaning must be from that of the amputee for whom a wheelchair is the solution to his immobility problem! Or consider Johnny Carson's line when he is playing the role of old Aunt Flabby, "Never say *old* to an old person!"

Improving Communications

Despite the many problems inherent in the communication process, there are many ways an organization can minimize the adverse effects of miscommunication.

Consider the Source   Receivers tend to judge the credibility of a message on the basis for their evaluation of its source. Such characteristics as appearance, mannerisms, and status contribute to the believability of the communicator. A manager's credibility is often determined by his track record. That is, has he proven to be a man of his word? Subordinates are also more prone to be responsible to the communications of a manager who creates a hospitable environment built on trust, integration of goals, and supportive leadership.

Create Two-Way Communications   Everyone is constantly sending and receiving messages at the same time. In this manner, we influence the behavior of others who, in turn, exert influence on us. Two-way communication provides the opportunities to explore all sides of every issue and to allow for those questions and interactions that are necessary to achieve both mutual understanding and satisfaction.

Choose the Correct Channel   Oral two-way communication has been found to be superior to the written message in achieving understanding. Oral communications, while permitting questions and other input on the part of the receiver, tend to be time-consuming unless adequately controlled. Followed by a written memorandum, oral two-way communication is probably the most effective approach, as it provides the advantages discussed above plus a statement in writing which may prove to be invaluable for future reference.

Avoid Surprises and Rumors   By continually providing subordinates with accurate and up-to-date information, the manager can prevent "surprises" and "rumors," both of which can have a damaging effect on employee morale. Rumors, once identified, should be squelched immediately.

Semantics   A number of semantic barriers must be overcome. First and foremost, managers should refrain from using explosive or emotional words such as *rate-buster, deadbeat, punishment,* and *discharge.* One must also be sensitive to the fact that some words have many meanings depending on usage, context, education, and environment. Such words are baited traps just waiting to ensnare the unsuspecting communicator. A good manager also avoids shop jargon, big words, and other forms of gobbledygook that impress only the uninformed and confuse everyone.

Stereotyping is another common communications trap for the manager. Although stereotyping appears to be a convenient and time-saving technique, it is actually oversimplified classifying that is used by the Archie Bunkers of the world. It can also narrow one's perceptions and blind the manager to the real differences in people and events.

Spatial Arrangements The innovative manager will also discover that communications can be improved by making certain adjustments in communication patterns. Harold Leavitt studied patterns of communication in groups. Leavitt found that the mere existence of a communication center in a group made it likely that the position would become a decision center. Thus, authority in decision-making would come to be located in the central position of the communication pattern. It is interesting to note that the degrees of satisfaction expressed by members of groups were in reverse relationship to their performances and the presence of decision centers. Satisfaction was positively correlated with the amount of communication generated. Enjoyment was highest for those in the central positions.

Alex Bavelas conducted research that supported the findings of Leavitt and also determined that central positions were perceived by participants to be positions of leadership. Therefore, the manager can create communication structures that provide for communication centers which become positions for decision-making and leadership. However, if this role is too centralized, employee morale will deteriorate.

Horseshoe arrangements have been found to encourage more open communications than any other group seating arrangement. Robert Sommer determined that the presence of a strong leader causes participants to communicate only with people seated next to them. However, under minimal leadership, participants tend to become more involved and to speak out to those seated across from them.

Managers can also improve the communications efficiency of their organization by keeping work groups to a relatively small size. As groups grow numerically, they tend to require a good deal more messages in order to accomplish tasks. There is also an inverse relationship between the group's size and its efficiency and morale.

Perhaps the central problem for managers today is not inflation, recession, material shortages, or consumerism, but a simple matter of poor interpersonal relationships resulting from ineffective communications. Executives seem to agree to this premise in principle, but they tend to do little about it. Communication programs are given lip service while billions of dollars are spent on innovative technologies and new human relations gimmicks that will not realize their full potential due to failures to remove the noise from communication networks. Now more than ever, today's managers need to recognize that programs for improving organizational communications require comparatively small allocations of resources while promising the greatest possible pay-off potential.

Discussion Questions

1. Eleven different barriers are mentioned in this article. For purposes of discussion place each of these barriers in one of two categories: physical and psychological. Explain why you placed each barrier in that category.

2. One way to improve communications is to select the correct channel. Name three different channels. As you name the channel, indicate which barrier seems to be a special problem with that channel of communication.

3. This article suggests that managers should refrain from using explosive or emotional words. List at least five emotional words that are not presented in the article.

Effective Management Needs Upward and Downward Communication

Thomas H. Inman
Southwest Missouri State University, Springfield, MO

The growth and complexity of modern industry have placed pressure upon management at all levels to develop effective techniques of communication to lower echelons. The communication of policies, practices, and plans necessary to modern industrial life is the backbone of efficient management. Misinformation and the ensuing misunderstanding decreases work efficiency. Sharing information with subordinates at all levels tends to diminish the fears and suspicions about top management that often exist. Moreover, effective communication helps subordinates to understand, accept, and cooperate in the frequent changes that occur in a dynamic business setting. It can be concluded, then, that downward communication is a significant part of the business organization and is therefore accepted and used by management.

Unfortunately, some managers seem to consider communication a one-way street: the authoritarian point of view is: "It is my job to make decisions and to issue directives based on these decisions to subordinates. It is their job to carry out the directives." This view ignores the value that may be gained from encouraging employees to offer ideas, suggestions, and reactions to the policies and plans of the company. There is little, if any, opportunity to tap the imagination and creativity of subordinates even though there may be outstanding expertise among them.

There are dividends that accrue to managers who listen willingly and who encourage subordinates to speak openly and honestly. This flow of communication upward tells top management how well information that is passed down is understood and received. The open participation of subordinates

Source: Thomas H. Inman. "Effective Management Needs Upward and Downward Communication." Reprinted from *Arizona Business,* May 1977. Published by the Bureau of Business and Economic Research, College of Business Administration, Arizona State University, Tempe, Arizona.

encourages people to become more actively involved in departmental and company activity, which gives them a greater feeling of team spirit. Since they are more interested in the company, they tend to become more productive and loyal. The opportunity for upward communication encourages employees to contribute ideas for improving efficiency within the company. Additionally, it is upward communication that enables top management to take the pulse of the organization, to know the appropriate time for instituting a change, to know when to announce a pay raise (or cut), and to avoid what may be a potentially explosive situation in certain critical times.

Barriers to Upward Communication

§ The superior-subordinate relationship contains an innate barrier to effective communication. Regardless of the relationship between the two, it is extremely difficult for the subordinate not to fear, to some extent, his superior. When the superior has the authority to hire, fire, promote, raise, and recommend action relating to the subordinate, it is inevitable that some fear will be present.

The manager who wishes to minimize this built-in barrier to effective upward communication, must convince subordinates that such communication is in their own best interests. The boss who is open with employees, who shares goals and objectives, and who informs the staff of how they fit into the picture, will receive a supportive attitude and effort from subordinates. Top managers who are closed and secretive about what is happening in the company will not elicit strong support. Subordinates who are uncertain about corporate affairs become suspicious and unproductive.

Although it is impossible to eliminate the barrier caused by the difference in position—and perhaps it would be unwise to try to eliminate it—the barrier can be minimized by a boss who has a strong, positive self-concept, and is unafraid and willing to relate to employees. Workers who observe competence and confidence in superiors are stimulated and motivated by the strength of this leadership. They aspire to greater heights. They are more enthusiastic and creative in their work; their efforts reflect favorably on the boss, who is rewarded for his effective leadership. The cycle is completed but does not end there. This cycle continues in an unending process.

§ The subordinate who is not overly concerned about success tends to be more open with superiors and will probably expose his real thoughts. The greater the desire for upward mobility, the less likely it is that a subordinate will disclose honest feelings. The challenge for the boss is to dispel the subordinates' fear of speaking candidly. Managers who reward subordinates for telling the boss only what the boss wants to know will develop an organization driven by mediocrity. It is a fact of organizational behavior that people will learn to "play the game." This translates to mean that employees will seek to do that which yields reward. If the boss rewards positive candor and honesty, then candor and honesty will be forthcoming. If the boss encourages and rewards "yes men," then "yes men" will develop.

The desire to move up and to exploit opportunity in the business world is an admirable trait, which should be sought and nurtured. The individual who has reached his goal and has nothing further for which to strive, is probably going to be marginally productive. That is, eagerness to "climb the ladder" is not inherently bad; the manner in which that need and drive is channeled is the critical factor.

§ The physical distance between subordinate and superior impairs the flow of communication upward and downward. As organizations grow in size and complexity, communication becomes ineffective. It is not unusual in today's business world for many workers at various levels to have a distant attitude toward top management simply because they have no occasion to be in touch with them. There is a strong tendency to work in isolation without a feeling and attitude of teamwork. In some instances, top management projects an inaccessible posture. Because of this "distant attitude," subordinates conclude that the boss is not interested in them except for their hours of work.

The effective manager closes the gap between himself and his subordinates by developing a planned communication system that assures that his message travels down the line and is understood. Additionally, he includes as a part of the system, a procedure for providing feedback and follow-up to the communication. It is not simply assumed that the message is received and understood. Further, the efficient communication structure provides a direct line of communication for workers at all levels to have an audience with the appropriate management person. Any employee who feels isolated and out of touch with what is going on within the company, becomes disenchanted and unhappy. Top management must exercise skill in ferreting out the facts and eliminating bottlenecks in the organizational communication. One responsibility of subordinate managers is to filter messages and decide what should be passed on; this must not be done, however, at the expense of sparing the boss the truth—which he needs to know if he is to be effective.

§ Listening is a significant part of upward and downward communication. In studies completed in 1927 and 1929, it was discovered that people in various levels of management spend approximately 40 percent of their work day listening to employees.[1] A study in 1975 showed essentially the same results.[2] Managers are paid a large portion of their salary for listening.

Yet, a fact uncovered by Ralph G. Nichols in some of his outstanding work at the University of Minnesota is that the average manager listens at only 25 percent of efficiency. At Loyola University, Chicago, a research study designed to identify the most important single attribute of an effective manager concluded that attribute is listening skill. The most common response received from thousands of workers in that study was, "I like my boss; he listens to me." "I can talk to him."[3]

§ The manager's self-awareness is an outstanding factor in organizational communication.[4] The manager who knows his mind, is aware of his own needs, interests, strengths, and weaknesses, is in a better command position to relate to others. Because of his self-awareness, he is not caught up in the problems of his own ego and is able to get to the heart of problems and ignore the surface matters, which are insignificant. He is able to relax and be himself in an open and confident manner, knowing that his competence and integrity as a manager will be adequate for the occasion.

When managers are open and candid with associates, their behavior tends to elicit a similar reaction. In a study completed by Northwestern Bell Telephone Company, D. C. Wilcox and R. J. Burke pursued the proposition that open two-way communication is associated with a satisfying and effective superior-subordinate work relationship.[5] The results indicated that greater openness of communication by one or both members of the relationship was associated with increased satisfaction. In addition, openness of one member of the pair was significantly related to openness of the other member. The research also indicated that fostering open communication would yield a satisfying and productive work atmosphere. The boss holds the key to establishing this climate.

It is apparent from study of group dynamics that the superior-subordinate relationship makes communication difficult. Whether the two are having coffee together, playing golf, or enjoying a night on the town—one is still the boss, and the other is only the subordinate. Vogel found this to be true among 2,000 employees of eight companies. As he stated in *Personnel Administration* (May–June, 1967) they believed that if a subordinate told his immediate superior everything he felt about the company, he would probably get into "a lot of trouble," and that the best way to gain promotion was not to disagree very much with a superior.

Factors Contributing to Upward Communication

Although it is recognized that upward communication is difficult, there are some measures that, if implemented wisely, will promote better understanding and more effective communication.

- There must be an atmosphere of trust and honesty. Subordinates must feel that their expressions will be received with an open mind, and that they need not fear reprisal.
- Internal communication must be recognized as a vital tool of effective management. The flow of information within the organization cannot be left to chance. As William K. Allen pointed out, "today's managers are quickly discovering that their large organizations are either enhanced or limited to the extent of the effectiveness of the communication."[6]

Arthur M. Wood, of Sears, Roebuck and Company, said it unequivocally in discussing how Sears has been able to go from a gross of $5 to $10 to $15 billion. "We learned many years ago that there is only one way you can go in bigness—better communication."[7]

There must be a willingness to listen without quick evaluation and premature judgment. The subordinate must feel that top management will hear him out. The higher a person goes in management, and the more authority wielded, the less that person is *forced* to listen to others. Yet the *need* to listen is even greater. The farther a manager gets from the firing line, the more he has to depend on others for the accurate information so necessary for correct decisions. If he has not formed the habit of listening—carefully and intelligently—he is not going to get the facts he needs.

There is another good reason for listening carefully, especially to subordinates. They *want* to talk to someone about their problems. And it is important to their effectiveness and job satisfaction to know that someone is really listening, not just going through the motions.

It is very natural for people in management positions to become impatient listeners. With all the pressure for deadlines and budgets, no one wants to waste time listening to something that may not be worth hearing. Yet the very act of listening to people, regardless of the insignificance of what they are saying, is important in itself.

Nothing hinders progress in managerial positions faster than people who will not listen. The hardening of management opinions is as detrimental to a company's health as hardening of the arteries in the human body.

- There must be a plan for action when suggestions, ideas, or complaints warrant it. The subordinate who is persuaded that quick and decisive action will be taken relative to a suggestion, a problem, or an idea, is stimulated to contribute and to be open. One of the strongest deterrents to upward communication is the failure of management to act on matters that justify action. The result is that workers lose faith in management's ability to be decisive. They tend to lose faith in communication. Their conclusion is, "What's the use?" Managers must be ready to have policies and practices questioned. They must be prepared to reexamine and change policies, to tell employers facts that had not been known or shared. Fast, candid, visible, and sensitive response by top managers is the key.

- The internal communications program must be planned with specific responsibility and authority assigned to appropriate persons. Such a program cannot be left to chance or be handled as a part-time responsibility by just anyone. As Bruce Harriman, vice president and general manager of the Massachusetts area of New England Telephone, pointed out in *Harvard Business Review*, "Absolutely essential to the success of the program is the full-time coordinating staff, made up of a few management people selected on the basis of proven human relations skills and strong personal commitment to the program. This staff should be in a location that permits private, face-to-face discussions with employees at all levels."[8]

Improving Employee Communication

There are many techniques that may be used to enhance internal communication but the most important, yet frequently overlooked, is the usual day-to-day activity. If there is a pleasant atmosphere with the firm, the casual conversations among workers, whether during coffee breaks, at lunch, or during planned meetings and conferences, provide excellent opportunities for keeping in touch with everyone. In order to support and augment this daily communication activity, there are some other strategies that should be considered.

First, social gatherings provide a pleasant and satisfying way of improving company communication. Whether it is a company tennis tournament, such as Pfizer Corporation sponsors, where employees and managers are invited to play together, or a round robin golf tournament such as several firms have established successfully, activities of this nature can be very effective in breaking down the barriers. Many potential problems have been solved in the locker room or over refreshments after a good physical workout.

Southland Corporation designed a lounge on the top floor of their Dallas offices, and it is opened immediately after work each day. They are delighted with the results. Employees talk freely in this leisurely setting.

Second, there should be staff and line contact daily. The boss cannot wait for subordinates to come to him; the boss must take the initiative and be visible about the premises. Most people are more comfortable and more responsive on their own territory. When they are in the boss' office, they are on foreign soil and tend to be more guarded and closed. The boss who is available stimulates subordinates by demonstrating a special interest in them. Such contact must be made on a regular basis in order for employees to feel comfortable and responsive; sporadic, occasional contact may appear to be spying and snooping. Daily line and staff contact will provide an awareness of employee morale and enable managers to stay abreast of what goes on down the line.

Third, company publications must be used effectively and skillfully. In many instances, house organs or company newsletters are nothing more than a feeble attempt to disseminate information from the top down. Too often, the employee down the line, sees no reason to read what is printed. Thus, he does not get the message, or understand what is going on. Company publications must involve everyone in order to provide input for print that will include information of interest to employees. Interest may develop by including special items about selected employees. Specific persons may be featured occasionally with a short article; this may include citation of a special achievement or an item on production. Certain departments may be singled out for distinction because of efficiency, high production, perfect attendance, receipt of a contract, or some similar item. The kind of news that results in employee involvement will command a broader and more concerned readership.

Fourth, a suggestion system that works will improve employee communication. It is a device for making clearly known management's interest in having employees help with ideas and creative suggestions. The key to the success of any suggestion system is responsiveness. Managers must respond to suggestions however ridiculous or outstanding they appear to be, and the response must be prompt. Employees must be able to see that management is interested in their ideas and will consider each one. Additionally, there must be an appropriate reward system for productive suggestions. The more constructive suggestions and ideas are rewarded, the more likely it is that they will be made. Rewards might take the form of a bonus (a cash gift), recognition of some kind within the company or in local news media, or it might be a simple but sincere word of praise.

Many companies have used several other methods to improve internal communication. Pitney-Bowes has found Personnel Councils effective. Bendix and IBM have been successful with the ombudsman approach. Bank of America has used Task Teams successfully in improving communication up and down the company ladder.

Benefits from Effective Communication

In companies where management encourages, promotes, and rewards free expression, there is a better understanding of subordinates at all levels. The more democratic leadership yields greater satisfaction among workers and more intense loyalty and respect for the company. Logically, this translates into increased productivity with efficiency.

Fred T. Allen, Chairman of the Board and President of Pitney-Bowes, reports his company has used many of these ideas with success. In 1974, productivity increased 17.3 percent over the previous year, as measured by revenue per employee. The average absenteeism rate is 3 to 4 percent, and the turnover rate in all departments is 12 percent; both figures are low for the industry.

It is often difficult to measure the results of an effective communication system; nevertheless, it is clear that several purposes are achieved, including growth of democracy and leadership in the work place, strengthening of individuals through the satisfaction of the human need for self-expression and participation, and promotion of loyalty and respect for the firm. Management has a clearer picture of the accomplishments, plans, problems, attitudes, and feelings of subordinates at all levels. Managers are able to spot potential problems before they materialize and become unmanageable. By encouraging upward communication, many excellent ideas are found among employees that are often overlooked. This gives management a better perspective toward its problems. Further, when those at the top begin to listen, those down the line tend to listen also and to respond with creative interest.

Notes

1. Paul Rankin, "Listening Ability," *Proceedings of the Ohio State Educational Conference,* 9th Annual Session, Columbus, Ohio, 1929, pp. 172–183.

2. J. Donald Weinrauch and John R. Swanda, Jr., "Examining the Significance of Listening: An Exploratory Study of Contemporary Management," *ABCA Journal,* Vol. 13, No. 1, Fall, 1975, pp. 25–32.

3. Ralph G. Nichols, "Listening is a Ten-Part Skill," *Nation's Business,* 45 (July 1957), pp. 56–60.

4. Thomas H. Inman, "The Role of Self Awareness in Interpersonal Communication." *Management World,* May 1976, pp. 12–16.

5. R. J. Burke and D. C. Wilcox, "Effects of Different Patterns and Degrees of Openness in Superior-Subordinate Communication on Subordinate Job Satisfaction," *Academy of Management Journal,* September 1969, pp. 319–326.

6. William K. Allen, "An Integral Part of the Process of Managing," *Perspective,* July–August 1968, p. 62.

7. Arthur M. Wood, "How Giant Sears Grows and Grows," *Business Week,* December 15, 1972, pp. 52–57.

8. Bruce Harriman. "Up and Down the Communications Ladder," *Harvard Business Review,* September–October 1974, pp. 143–151.

Discussion Questions

1. List and explain the barriers to upward communication that are presented in this article.

2. Three different studies on listening are presented by Inman. Summarize the results of these studies and explain how they relate to upward and downward communications.

3. What different strategies have been presented for improving employee communication?

Legal Aspects of Communications: Sexism to Slander

Sandra M. Robinson
Larry R. Smeltzer
Louisiana State University, Baton Rouge, LA

Introduction

Increased government regulation, higher levels of employee awareness, and a willingness to pursue litigation mean that business professionals need to be aware of the legal implications of their communications. Records that must be made available if subpoenaed include: copies or tapes of internal or external letters, telephone conversations, and minutes of meetings. With the increased ability to store and duplicate such documents, what is recorded can now be saved for long periods of time; consequently, the margin of error in communication has been greatly reduced in recent years.

Legal problems that arise in business communication can often be traced to problems of perception. If a message is not received in the same light in which it was sent, the message is subject to misinterpretations that could lead to legal problems. And to complicate the situation the law itself can often lead to misinterpretation.

All the legal problems that may arise from business communications are beyond the scope of this article; the topics covered here are those with which employees should be familiar. An important guideline to remember is that whenever there is a question about the legality of a situation, legal counsel should be consulted.

Defamation

Defamation is a public statement that is injurious to an individual's character or reputation. In order to be considered a public statement, the words must be "communicated to, and understood by, at least one person other than the one of whom they are spoken or written."[1] Therefore, an argument between

Source: This is an original essay prepared for *Readings and Cases In Business Communication.*

two people, if no one else hears it, is not a defamatory action regardless of what is said. If a third party is present, however, defamation becomes a possibility. The same is true for letters and telegrams. If the letter is seen by a third party, the receiver may have grounds to file defamation charges against the sender. In this case, if the letter were marked "personal," the receiver would have to prove that the sender knew that the letter might be intercepted.

A distinction is made between defamation that is written—libel—and that which is spoken—slander. The letter mentioned above could lead to libel charges, whereas the argument could result in charges of slander.

Any written record may contain libelous statements. Letters, memos, and other written business records can be subpoenaed and used against a company in court. If such records are in the hands of someone outside the company, such as the plaintiff in a libel case, that individual can produce the records as evidence in the case.

Slander per se is the legal term meaning slanderous because a third party heard the statement. To win a case of slander, only the testimony of the third party is needed by the plaintiff. One or more of the following categories qualifies a statement as slander per se:

(1) words imputing the commission of a crime; (2) words imputing infection by a loathsome or contagious disease that excludes the person from society; (3) words proclaiming unfitness for office or employment or words derogatory of a person's fitness for a trade or profession; (4) words imputing unchastity (spoken of a woman).[2]

The best defense against defamation, slander, or libel is the truth. When the statements in question are true, the plaintiff will have a hard time proving defamation. However, truth is sometimes difficult to prove, particularly in a court of law.[3] The exception to this defense of truth is if malice can be proved. The term *malice* refers to "knowledge that the statements were false or circumstances showing a reckless disregard for whether they were true or not."[4] Even if the statements in question in a defamation case are factual, if they are communicated to at least one other person and malice can be proven, the courts probably will rule in favor of the plaintiff.

Successful defamation cases show that the following words may be considered libelous and might well be avoided or used with extreme caution:[5]

bankrupt	forger	profiteer
communist	fraud	quack
corrupt	hypocrite	shyster
crook	incompetent	swindler
dishonest	inferior	thief
disreputable	insolvent	unchaste
drug addict	kickbacks	unworthy of credit
falsified	misappropriation	worthless

An example of libel would be a situation in which an employee is being considered for a new position within the company. A committee is formed to review all the applicants, and during a meeting they decide to ask a former supervisor about one of the applicant's credentials. The supervisor writes a memo to the committee chairperson saying that the applicant is a hypocrite who is incompetent and cannot be trusted due to falsifying information. This may be a libelous statement because it is a public statement (the entire committee may read the memo); it is potentially injurious to the applicant's reputation; it is a written statement; and it may be difficult to prove the truthfulness of these statements so malice could be a factor. This would be an example of slander instead of libel if the supervisor verbally reports these comments to the committee rather than writes a memo.

The idea that perception would be a factor in libel and slander cases is not surprising. Often such statements are not intentional, and meanings are misinterpreted. However, the statements are no less defamatory when they are unintentional.

Privacy

The Privacy Act of 1974 deals with records kept by federal agencies about individuals. According to this, individuals have the right to inspect files containing data collected about them by federal government, and to correct any inaccuracies. Although such practices are not yet required by law of businesses in the private sector, many organizations have established them voluntarily.

The Business Roundtable, a group representing American business, recommends the voluntary incorporation of privacy practices for employees of American business. The American Management Association (AMA) refers to these practices as "employee fair information practices." According to a 1980 AMA survey, managers felt that the following rights of employees should be protected:

1.   The right to inspect personal information as held by their employers, to suggest corrections to their records, and to file written disputes in those records if any item is not resolved to their satisfaction.
2.   The right to be told whom an employer will contact to obtain information about them and what sort of questions will be asked.
3.   The right to restrict the dissemination of information about them outside their organizations.

In addition, those managers responding to the survey agreed that the major problems they had experienced in protecting the confidentiality of employee information were unauthorized internal release and release (whether authorized or not) outside the corporation to persons who had no legitimate business seeing the information.[6]

Although adherence to the practices mentioned here is not regulated by the government, businesses and their managers are still responsible for protecting the privacy of employees. Dissemination of highly objectionable, private information about an individual can lead to a charge of invasion of privacy. Even if such information is true, the person holding the information is responsible for its protection from disclosure.

Imagine that a claims processor in the benefits department told a friend in the company that a production manager was receiving treatment from a psychiatrist. This friend, who has no legitimate business pertaining to benefits, tells others in the company about the production manager. Such dissemination of information would be an invasion of privacy.

Agency

The principal-agent relationship describes the employment situation where the employee (the agent) has the power to contract for the employer (the principal). The law of agency deals with questions of contractual liability when an agent enters into a contract on behalf of a principal. The word *contract* here is generally defined as any legal business agreement.

The agency relationship is necessary in business, for it permits the manager to act for the company. To qualify as an agent, the individual needs to be a manager—an exempt employee not subject to hourly wage regulations. For large organizations, this relationship can become a problem because the law of agency assumes that the manager is under the control of the company. Therefore, the company is liable for the contracts made by its agents. An especially important feature of the agency concept regarding communications is that the correspondence of the manager is the company's correspondence.

Use of the company's letterhead is effective in establishing the principal-agency relationship. Company stationery signifies that the company is in agreement with the message. Even if the message contains a statement denying the agency relationship, the agency concept still holds because it is contained in the letterhead. Therefore, only company business, never personal business, should be conducted on the company's letterhead.

The firm's name does not necessarily have to be part of the signature portion of a letter when using company stationery. The agency concept is established as long as the company letterhead is being used. In order to establish the agency relationship when using nonletterhead stationery, however, the company name must appear as part of the signature portion of the letter. Once this concept is established, the manager cannot deny responsibility for acting on behalf of the company. The company is also bound by the agency relationship to agree with the correspondence.

Agency or contract law can have disastrous effects when managers are careless with their communication. An overzealous sales manager may follow up a meeting with a client company by writing a letter to it. In this letter, the manager indicates that 100 cases of green widgets for $2 each can be delivered by the end of the month. The manager may be attempting to show only what excellent services and prices can be provided by the company; however, if the client surprisingly accepted the offer, a contract may be established. Problems may result if production cannot deliver on this offer!

Harassment

Sexual harassment as an area of discrimination has drawn increased attention in recent years. Part of the business communication problem with sexual harassment is its many definitions. A few of the different definitions offered are:

1. Working Women's Institute states that sexual harassment is any repeated or unwanted verbal or physical sexual advances; sexually derogatory statements; or sexually discriminatory remarks made by someone in the workplace which are offensive or objectionable to the recipient, or cause the recipient discomfort or humiliation, or interfere with the recipient's job performance.[7]
2. Lin Firley states that sexual harassment is best described as unsolicited nonreciprocal male behavior that asserts a woman's sex role over her function as a worker.[8]
3. Bureau of National Affairs concerned with Labor Relations states that defining sexual harassment broadly, the (EEOC) guidelines states that "unwelcome sexual advances, requests for sexual favors, and other verbal or physical conduct of a sexual nature" will be considered harassment . . .[9]

The idea of perception is extremely important in harassment cases. Some incidents of harassment are totally unconscious acts that are a result of sex roles learned at a very early age. According to a survey conducted by the Bureau of National Affairs (BNA), the type of sexual harassment that is hardest to define consists of comments, innuendos, and jokes of sexual nature. This type of harassment is also the most prevalent type cited by employers. Many claims of sexual harassment which have led to federal court decisions involve suggestive remarks as the offensive activity rather than sexual contact.[10]

Because sexual harassment is so difficult to define, it is open to different interpretations by different individuals. Physical contact may be meaningless to one person and objectionable to another. A joke may be offensive to one person and humorous to another.

Just as some incidents of sexual harassment are unconscious acts, some are intentional with a specific purpose of gaining power or forcing compliance. If evil intent can be proved in a discrimination case, the employer's position could be impossible to defend. The implications of harassment claims are being recognized by employers and steps are being taken to protect organizations and their employees.

Copyright

Most employees generally know that certain material is protected from duplication; however, the Copyright Act of 1976 is very specific in regard to photocopying and duplicating material. This act becomes rather complicated, but a few guidelines generally ensure that no law is broken when duplicating copyrighted material:

1. Single copies of material may be made for personal files or posting on a bulletin board.

2. Multiple copies of material may be made if a notice of copyright permission is included on the material, the timing renders it unreasonable to wait for permission, or it is to be used for one-time classroom use.

3. Unlimited use may be made of U.S. government works and "fair use" items such as tables, slogans, formulas, and so on.

4. Publishing an original work, text tables, and illustrations requires formal permission from the copyrighted author. The simple acknowledgment of the source in the manuscript cannot substitute for formal permission when: (a) prose quotations of 400 words or more from a full-length book are used, and (b) a table, diagram or illustration (including cartoons, photographs, or maps) are reproduced exactly or adapted only slightly.

Employees who are in a position to do extensive duplicating can avoid any potential problems by simply asking the original authors for permission to use the material. Most authors are extremely cooperative and often consider it a compliment to have their materials reproduced.

Solutions

Organizations are finding ways to deal with the legal problems of business communications. For example, many have developed guide letters for their employees. The writer composes an individual letter from several optional sentences and paragraphs prescribed in the guide. These guide letters may stifle the creativity of a young professional, but they serve to keep the organization and its employees out of court.

Every business entity is unique, and each will find its own way of handling communcation problems. In order to avoid such problems, employers need to become familiar with the laws that affect them. This discussion has only briefly reviewed several of the many legal implications of business communication.

Depending upon a person's job, it may be necessary to be familiar with the provisions of the Civil Rights Act (1964) when interviewing; certain employees in financial institutions must be aware of the Truth in Lending Act (1968); and those in sales should know what constitutes fraud and a legally binding warranty. If there is a legal question, it should be answered by a legal counsel before action is taken.

Notes

1. Alice K. Heom, ed., *The Family Legal Advisor,* 2nd ed. New York: Greyston Press, 1978, p. 235.

2. Ibid, p. 234.

3. Lillian O. Feinberg, *Applied Business Communication.* Sherman Oaks, Calif.: Alfred Publishing Co., 1982, p. 490.

4. Robert N. Corley, Robert L. Black, and O. Lee Reed, *The Legal Environment of Business,* 5th ed. New York: McGraw-Hill, 1981, p. 123.

5. Zane K. Quible, Margaret H. Johnson, and Dennis L. Mott, *Introduction to Business Communication,* Englewood Cliffs, N.J.: Prentice-Hall, 1981, p. 420.

6. Jack Lester Osborn, *Fair Information Practices for Managers and Employees,* AMACOM, 1980.

7. Dail Ann Neugarten and Jay M. Shafritz, eds., *Sexuality in Organizations.* Oak Park, Ill.: Moore Publishing, 1980, p. 3.

8. Lin Farley, *Sexual Shakedown.* New York: McGraw-Hill, 1978, p. 14.

9. *Sexual Harassment and Labor Relations.* Washington, D.C.: Bureau of National Affairs, 1981, p. 3.

10. Ibid., p. 5.

Discussion Questions

1. Why are the legal implications of business communications becoming increasingly important?

2. What is the difference between slander and libel? Give an example of each.

3. Why is the individual perception so important when considering sexual harassment?

Part I

Cases

Taming of the Shrew

William J. Buchholtz

Bentley College, Waltham, MA

The following incident contains numerous communications barriers. These illustrate how failed communication results in failed management at Anascom, Inc, a research and development corporation. Identify and classify these barriers. Be prepared to present possible solutions.

Description of Participants

Sarah Jones: *Title: manager, Environmental Impact Group.* Sarah holds an MS in biological sciences from Yale. She has just started working for Anascom, Inc. Under her supervision are five men, all with BS degrees in the biological sciences from various colleges, none as impressive as Yale.

Ralph Johnson: *Title: biologist, Environmental Impact Group.* Ralph has a BS degree from State U. He is 5 years older than Sarah and has been with Anascom for 3 years. Ralph was the prime candidate to become head of the environmental group; in fact, Jack Danils, the former group manager, looked upon Ralph as a son, and groomed him for the manager's position. Anascom, however, decided to hire from outside the company and thus brought in Sarah Jones.

Background

Jack Danils, the previous manager, was a good friend to all the men in the Environmental Group, but under his supervision, the department was sometimes inefficient and occasionally error prone. The men felt, however, that Jack had been let go without cause. No one in management had ever explained to them why he was transferred. The change was simply ordered from the top. (Jack wasn't even sure why he was being moved.) The group had done some very good things in the past, but management wanted to upgrade performance in anticipation of a huge government chemical waste disposal contract.

The Setting

Sarah Jones is seated behind her large desk in a huge padded executive chair. Ralph Johnson is sitting in a low slung wooden guest chair directly in front of Sarah's desk. The window behind Sarah emits a rather bright light, making it difficult for Ralph to look directly at Sarah. As the meeting begins, Sarah offers Ralph coffee, hands it to him brusquely, forgetting that he uses cream and sugar. The wooden chair is far enough from Sarah's desk that Ralph has no convenient place for his cup and saucer; he must awkwardly balance the coffee on his knee throughout their discussion.

Discussion

Sarah begins. "Tell me, Ralph, why has this department failed so miserably in the last 2 years?"

Ralph looks at her puzzled. She continues, "You know what I mean, Ralph. You guys are always late with your reports. The travel vouchers are never filled out right; nothing is ever turned in on time. The last proposal you guys sent out just before I got here was so lousy the client sent it back to us. I just got done looking at it. . . . You know what, Ralph?"

"What?"

"It was *lousier* than lousy. The client took a red pen and marked it up. Just like a flunked exam. How do you explain that, Ralph?"

"My God, Sarah, I don't know anything about the final draft of that report. Fweep and Birdstone put that together. Do you want me to talk with them?"

"Will that do any good, Ralph? I mean, if they can't write, do you think they'll be able to listen any better?"

"Now look, Sarah, I know you're angry about the report, but really . . ."

"You guys screwed up. Anascom lost a quarter of a million dollar contract because of you guys."

"Sarah, I didn't have anything to do with that report."

Seeing that she was getting nowhere with Ralph, Sarah shot up from her chair, whirled over to Ralph, and glowered down into his face. She snapped that she expected five grown men to do a better job for her than they'd done for Jack Danils. Jack didn't really know what he was doing, but she did and they'd better get that straight right from the start. And if she didn't get action right away, all of them would be gone before the month was out. Sarah told Ralph she'd call them in one-by-one for interviews to get to the bottom of the mess in this group. He could pass the word along to the others: "Dismissed."

Questions

The following questions will help you pinpoint some of the barriers in this case:

1. What role do participant description, setting, and background play in this situation?
2. What messages are being sent from Sarah to Ralph over and above those being spoken?
3. How would you assess Sarah's tone?
4. Is she correct in assuming that private interviews are the answer to her problem? What might be more effective?
5. What do you predict will be the men's reactions to Sarah's threats? Why?
6. In what critical ways has Sarah failed in interpersonal communication?
7. Speculate on the future of the group under Sarah's leadership. Speculate as well on Sarah's future with Anascom.
8. In your discussion of this case, try to use the following terms:
    *   moralistic evaluation
    *   defensiveness
    *   feedback failure
    *   self-esteem
    *   blame placement
    *   nonverbal negative messages
    *   ultimatum
    *   threatening stance
    *   distancing (spatial, emotional, and organizational)
    *   distraction
    *   one-way communication
    *   surprise
    *   status gaming
    *   absolutism

What Just Went Wrong?

Judie Cochran

Management Consultant, Scottsdale, AZ

Mark Lockwood had just sat down at his desk one Monday morning when his boss, Terry Livingston, entered the office.

"Mark, have you finished that report I asked you to do?"

"Report? What report was that?"

"Yes, a report. I asked you for a short report on the Crane factory personnel problem. Remember? I assigned it to you last week."

"Oh, yeah . . . I think I remember it."

"Think you remember it? I need it now! I have a meeting in 30 minutes with the personnel director of Crane and some very important managers. Don't tell me you don't have it ready!"

"Well, why didn't you tell me that you needed it this morning?"

"I told you I needed it soon. 'Soon' means this morning!"

"Well, how was I supposed to know that 'soon' meant now?"

"Any moron could have understood what I meant. Doesn't 'soon' mean to complete an assignment in a couple of days?"

"Well, when I was working for Mr. O'Connell in the purchasing department, he always told me the exact date he wanted a report. And he never called me a moron!"

With that remark, Terry turned red and charged for the door, pausing just long enough to say, "Well, you're not working for Mr. O'Connell any longer, and don't you forget it."

No, Mark didn't quit his job after this little encounter, nor did he try to transfer back to Mr. O'Connell's department. What he did try to do was analyze the situation. He took out a sheet of paper and listed on it what he thought were the major barriers of communication between his boss and himself. He then listed the various steps each could take to help overcome the existing communication problems.

Questions

1. List at least three barriers to communication that Mark may have listed about *himself.*

2. List at least three barriers to communication that Mark viewed about *his boss.*

3. How do the words used in conversation affect the barriers (example: the use of "moron" by Mark's boss)?

4. Does sexism cause barriers to change in the conversation? If Terry Livingston is a male, would the barriers listed above be altered?

   If Terry Livingston is a female, would the barriers listed above be altered?

5. Does age cause barriers to change in the conversation? If Terry is 30 years old, Mark 35 years old, and Mr. O'Connell 50 years old, would the barriers listed above be altered?

   If Terry is 23 years old, Mark is 30 years old, and Mr. O'Connell is 45 years old, would the barriers listed above be altered?

   If Terry is 50 years old, Mark is 25 years old, and Mr. O'Connell is 30 years old, would the barriers listed above be altered?

6. Could Mark's remarks have been changed substantially had Mr. O'Connell been a female?

7. List three possible solutions so that Mark and Terry can eliminate this type of problem from occurring again.

How Much Not To Say!

R. Jon Ackley
Virginia Commonwealth University, Richmond, VA

You have just received a letter from Wingo Products requesting information about George Smith, one of your former employees. George, who has just made application for employment at Wingo, worked for your firm for 2 years before you fired him.

Prior to his being terminated, George had performed well in his capacity as clerk. He was seldom late for work and missed few days due to illness. The quality of his work was above average. However, you let George go after he repeatedly ignored your warnings that personal business was not to be conducted during working hours or completed using company supplies or equipment. George had continually used company stationery and other supplies during his regular working hours to complete tasks for a local charitable organization. In addition, although there was never any proof, you had also suspected that George had been taking supplies from the company and selling them. This suspicion seemed to be confirmed because little pilferage of supplies has occurred since George left.

Wingo Products has indicated that George told them the reason for his termination was his continuing to do outside work during working hours even after your warnings.

Questions

1. Because Wingo Products already knows why George was terminated, would you find it necessary to discuss his termination in your letter? Why or why not?

2. How would you handle the problem of suspected theft of company supplies?

3. Respond to Wingo's request for information about George by writing a letter. Wingo's address: 2375 Valencia Lane, Richmond, VA 23731.

4. What other legal aspects do you need to be aware of when you write or speak?

Ideas on Improving Business Writing

A high level of proficiency is critical to a person's success in business. This part provides a number of practical suggestions to use to improve business writing proficiency. Each of the five articles provides informative guidelines that are both easy to apply and easy to remember for future application.

John Louis DiGaetani suggests a conversational test in his article, "Conversation: The Key to Better Business Writing." He states that the conversational test will eliminate the mechanical business jargon and clichés that can make business writing so embarrassing.

Writing may be like "Wrestling Alligators" for some, but Yvonne Lewis Day presents seven errors that business people commit when wrestling with their writing tasks. Writing becomes easier and more effective when authors avoid genteelisms, obfuscations, and euphemisms.

Ten simple steps for composing a message are presented by Tom Stapleton. He advocates the use of these steps to avoid fog and improve the tone of the communication. His article, "Why Use Ten Words Instead of Two?," emphasizes that practice is required to master these suggestions.

The last two articles in this part, "Musings of an Old Infinitive-Splitter," by Hap Frances and "The Fumblerules of Grammar," by William Safire, use humor to demonstrate typical writing errors that should be avoided. Frances emphasizes that we all seem to have one or two "favorite" errors, whereas Safire demonstrates errors while discussing them.

Conversation: The Key to Better Business Writing

John Louis DiGaetani
Hofstra University, Hemstead, NY

Your writing as a manager goes to your subordinates, your colleagues and your superiors. If your memos and business letters make you sound like a pompous illiterate, they may make you the laughing stock of the office.

To avoid this, a useful way to revise your business writing is called the Conversational Test. As you revise, ask yourself if you would ever say to your reader what you are writing. Or imagine yourself speaking to the person instead of writing. If you were talking to a business colleague, would you ever say: "In response to your memo of 11/18/81"? If you did, he would probably laugh.

If you were speaking to a customer, would you ever say: "Enclosed please find your order for three (3) replacement keys"? If you did, your customer would surely think you were weird.

The Conversational Test, while a valid method for revising business writing, is not a mandate for slang. If you were speaking to that colleague, you would maintain a certain formality unless you were friends. If you were speaking to that customer, you might be talking to a total stranger and would certainly not use slang.

But using the Conversational Test will eliminate the mechanical business jargon and cliches that can make your business writing so embarrassing. It will, instead, let your own humanity add color and interest to your writing.

Thus, if you were speaking to a colleague, you would probably say, "I am writing about the question you raised in your last memo." If you were speaking with that customer, you would probably say, "Here are the three replacement keys you ordered." Using the Conversational Test will enable you to write as naturally and persuasively as you speak.

Source: John Louis DiGaetani. "Conversation: The Key to Better Business Writing." Reprinted from *The Wall Street Journal,* February 8, 1982, by permission of *The Wall Street Journal,* copyright © Dow Jones & Company, Inc., 1982. All rights reserved.

You might imagine a regional sales manager calling up one of his district managers to say, "We don't have the final figures yet for the quarter, but word of mouth has it that they're bad. Inventories are too high again and we might be cutting out some dealerships soon. Just wanted to let you know. I'll send you the figures as soon as I can."

Too often such a person's follow-up memo will read like this: "Re our telephone conversation of July 8, final sales totals for the quarter ending in June are enclosed herewith. A planning conference for all sales personnel will be scheduled for the near future and these figures will be discussed. It is hoped that all district managers will be aware that the figures are such that reductions in the total number of retail units may be indicated. Thank you for your cooperation."

Why does the man who seems so direct and clear on the phone make himself sound mechanical, pompous and stilted in his writing? First, he is probably insecure about his writing skills. He doesn't trust his own use of language enough to write naturally. And he thinks that somehow jargon, wordy expressions, the passive voice and puffy sentences will make him appear more educated or more polished than he fears he really is. Second, he may be under the impression that business writing is supposed to seem stuffy, roundabout and impersonal since so many of the memos he gets read that way. Finally, he may be timid about putting certain information—in this case bad news—too bluntly, especially in writing.

All of these reasons are equally bad. Chances are your command of English is plenty good enough if you just write things down as naturally as you say them. Trying to puff things up and give added heft to your everyday thoughts only makes you seem like a blowhard. It impresses only the naive. Lots of business people adopt such a stilted style when writing, but the truly savvy are not impressed.

And direct, clear writing which approximates the way reasonable people speak will never embarrass you. Trying to hide bad news in a fog of wordiness just doesn't work. The reader of the memo cited above, once he manages to figure out its content, is going to be annoyed and maybe amused. If you're the writer, you might as well state your message as simply and clearly as you can and spare your reader the added burdens of trying to puzzle out its meaning. And the Conversational Test will help you here.

But one warning: The test will work best if your parents did not speak a foreign language or a dialect of English at home. If you did not learn standard American English at home, you will have to be more careful to revise according to the rules of grammar and usage.

But for most business people, the key to better writing is as close as their mouths. Using the Conversational Test will vastly improve the quality of their business writing. It will make their writing as interesting and human as they are.

Discussion Questions

1. What is the conversational test?
2. Why does the person who seems so direct and clear on the phone sound mechanical, pompous, and stilted when writing?
3. What is some jargon that you or your colleagues may be inclined to use?

Wrestling Alligators

Yvonne Lewis Day

Consultant, Baton Rouge, LA

Writing is the hardest way of earning a living, with the possible exception of wrestling alligators.

If writers were good businessmen, they'd have too much sense to be writers.

Irvin S. Cobb

I was an embarrassment to my family from the beginning, but the fault was not mine, you see.

I was born a writer.

The obstetrician broke the news gently to my father. "It's a girl, 7 pounds, 4 ounces. She has your hair, your wife's eyes, and a No. 2 lead pencil already showing signs of wear."

Before I could form the sounds "ma-ma" and "da-da," I could say, "All characters in this book are fictitious, and any resemblance to persons living or dead is purely coincidental."

In 1963, I entered LSU as a freshman in journalism.

Later, with a bachelor's in hand, I began work as technical writer and editor at a leading research institute. I didn't know a bluntnose minnow from a gas chromatograph. "Not to worry," said my supervisor. His grammar never did improve, but my self-confidence took wing. I soon learned that you don't need a degree in spectroscopy to see through murky prose.

Though not so lucrative as robbing stagecoaches, technical writing does have its rewards. There is one problem, however. When one reads as much copy as a writer/editor does, it's easy to feel that the English language is falling apart, that we are reverting to arrows in the dust. Abuses of the language abound. Some blunders are so minor that only an editor would notice them; others are so appalling that they spoil the effect of the material entirely.

No one will question that the state of grammar and word usage is on the

Source: Yvonne Lewis Day. "Wrestling Alligators." Reprinted from *The Regents Report*, Vol. 6, 1981. Reprinted by permission of the author.

decline in this nation. The average score among high school students on the verbal section of the Scholastic Aptitude Test has declined 51 points since 1963.

Many professional writers, including newscasters, are beginning to sound semi-illiterate. On a local television channel, a reporter tells his listeners, "To you and I, this is a serious matter." To I?

Among some newscasters there is apparently a phobia about using the same word twice in a news story, even if it is the right word. In a story about the arrest of suspects, therefore, the villains first are arrested. Then they are seized. Then they are scooped up. Some newscasters nab them, corral them, round them up.

Sports announcers and the people who write commercials make up their own language. For some reason, the people who read ball scores hate the word *defeated.* So they wallop, trounce, devastate, bomb, humiliate, demolish, massacre, murder, and kill.

Governmental officials send messages like this in memoranda to unsuspecting (and uncomprehending) taxpayers:

> An organizational arrangement which establishes one component as a junior partner, or intersystem dynamics which tend to reduce one or the other partner to such status in the partnership, are highly likely to be programmatically dysfunctional.

Which means:

> An organization that does not treat equals equally is going to have problems.

And the disease is spreading. A firm seeking a government contract proudly asserts:

> Our proposal follows the sequential itemization of points occurring elsewhere in your RFP, wherever possible, to facilitate your review.

Which means:

> Our proposal follows your outline.

In academia, a professor of education blithely (or is it blightly?) states:

> There is a large loss of educational talent prior to the application of college entrance examinations; and the profession at large is not in agreement on or even well informed about why this loss occurs or under what varieties of circumstances it begins to occur.

Which means:

> Many bright students drop out of high school, and their teachers don't know why they do it.

Language is a tool. Its purpose is to communicate knowledge, ideas, and feeling. The more precise the tools, the better the communication. Hippocrates put it this way: "The chief virtue that language can have is clearness."

Lack of clarity is *the* major fault in most business and professional writing. Richard Mitchell *(The Underground Grammarian)* says the problem is one of misdirection and evasiveness. "In the timid language of evasive English," he states, "no one dares step forth and say that a turkey is a turkey. He might mutter, tentatively, that a turkey has been recognized as being a turkey, although not necessarily by him."

Dr. Fred. H. MacIntosh of the University of North Carolina recently asked 182 senior professionals in science and industry if the technical writing they read is satisfactory. *Not one of the 182 people said the writing they see is properly prepared.* The main complaint, listed first by every one of those surveyed, was "generally foggy language."

Here is a partial list of their complaints (the number making the complaint is in parentheses).

1. "Generally foggy language" (182)
2. "Inadequate general vocabulary" (175)
3. "Failure to connect information to the point at issue" (169)
4. "Wordiness" (164)
5. "Lack of stressing important points" (163)
6. "All sorts of illogical reasoning" (163)
7. "Too much 'gobbledygook'"(160)
8. "Poor overall organization"(153)
9. "No clear overview"(143)
10. "No clear continuity"(142)

Poor grammar ranked twelfth; poor punctuation, fifteenth.

A moral is here (there has to be . . . somewhere). The point being made is this: a command of grammar and spelling, although important, is no guarantee of effectiveness in writing. Using language effectively is the sum of skills in four areas:

- Spelling and punctuation
- Grammar (the parts of speech)

- Usage (choosing the right word)
- Style

Of the four, style is least susceptible to classification. It is hardest to define. Its equivalent, in terms of being elusive, is "soul." How do you define soul? Someone once said, "Man, if you hafta ask, you ain't nevah gonna know!"

Style in writing is like style in anything else: some special quality that commands attention and gives pleasure, that makes you sit up and take notice. You are bored by the writer who makes his point laboriously, tediously, in dull and awkward langauge. The writer who makes the same point without apparent effort, in language that is as natural and easy as good conversation, will draw and hold your attention.

The air of effortlessness, whether in sports or writing, is deceptive. Its secret is *control* and control is a hard-won thing. The ballplayer doesn't have that perfect hook-shot handed to him; he learned it—and he learned it through hours of patient, disciplined practice on any empty court.

Because style in writing is not merely a matter of what's right or what's wrong, you can stay entirely "within the rules," and still sound sophomoric, pompous, or out-to-lunch.

The most common fault among professionals in education, government, and industry is overwriting—using too many words, especially those that duplicate or overlap meaning. The result is "clutter," which smothers ideas and stands in the way of reader comprehension (not to mention causing incoherent convulsions in lowly editors). Anyone who has peered over an editor's shoulder will verify that we spend 90% of our time deleting unnecessary words and shifting the remainder to their proper positions.

Sidney Smith had this bit of advice for writers of all species: "When you've finished writing, go through your manuscript and strike out every other word; you have no idea how much vigor it will give to your composition."

Recognizing the nearly uncontrollable impulse among human beings to pontificate with pen in hand, Samuel Johnson offered this advice: "Read over your compositions, and when you meet with a passage you think is particularly fine, strike it out."

The same sentiment was expressed by two American statesmen. According to Thomas Jefferson, "The most valuable talent is that of never using two words when one will do." (Samuel Goldwyn, the movie mogul, blatantly ignored the advice. Said he, "In two words: im possible.")

Goldwyn wasn't the only native out obfuscating. There were others. One Elucidator of Maximized Obfuscation verbalized operational difficulties with Abe Lincoln. "That fella," said Lincoln, "can compress the most words into the smallest idea of any man I ever met."

But there was no stopping them now. Pandora's Box grew pale in comparison (and was finally institutionalized to maximize amelioration). The doctor was speechless—but not for long. Oscar Wilde, with tongue in cheek, later actualized the optimum: "Nothing succeeds like excess."

Even by today's standards, the excess is excessive. Seven common writing faults contribute to Excessitis (aka Runoff-at-the-Mouth Syndrome).

1. *Redundancies* (repeating the same meaning in different words)

I have a ten-page list of these, which I call "dog puppies." Some typical examples:

Consensus (of opinion)	commute (back and forth)
(true) facts	(past) history
(free) gift	combine (together)
(fellow) partner	(new) innovation

Would any literate soul ever speak of false facts, a consensus of bubblegum, a gift on sale, or old innovations?

2. *Circumlocutions* (roundabout, indirect, evasive expressions)

of a generous nature	generous
in the field of economics	in economics
in a manner of speaking	in a way
due to the fact that	because
in the neighborhood of	about, nearly

Pompous vocabulary will not convince readers that you are intellectually superior. It will merely convince them that you are unpardonably dull.

3. *Obfuscations* (clouding the issue, throwing up a smoke screen, using words that mean everything and nothing at all)

considerable element of the unpredictable (a good chance)
individualized learning station (a desk)
substantive dialogue (a good talk)
unyielding propinquity for veracity (always honest)

Egregious obfuscators thrive in academia and government bureaucracy, where they perpetrate popularized technicalities such as *ambivalent, continuum, dichotomy, empathy, parameter, polariy, totality . . . ad nauseam.* Most have a propinquity for scientisms, as well; namely, *focus, impact, component, end-product, order of magnitude, spectrum, extrapolate.* In the vogue words of the obfuscator, any success must be viable, any connection whatsoever must be a tie-in, anything of magnitude or importance is massive, obnoxious characters are abrasive, items that don't clang are repercussive, and anything collected or compiled is developed.

4.   *Abstractions* (words that can be defined in a number of ways—most of them vague—leaving the reader with no earthly idea of your meaning)

relevant	nature
meaningful	feature
eventualities	aspect
structure	amenity
case	many
character	several
level	a few

To say that a large number attended an event is to say nothing, specifically. How many people does it take to make a large number? Six writers (in the same room, all of them awake) is a large number. Five thousand is a small number, however, if you're talking about rock fans at a Rolling Stones concert.

5.   *Clichés* (expressions worn out, bleached white, from long use; indicates lack of originality, freshness, vitality)

In a computer study of 400,000 words, the Associated Press identified these as the most tiresome:

hailed	racially troubled
backlash	jam-packed
in the wake of	grinding crash
informed	confrontation
violence flare	oil-rich nation
kickoff	no immediate comment
death and destruction	cautious optimism
riot-torn	limped into port
tinder dry	

My own list of tiresome expressions would fill the greater part of a book. My nominations for Most Tiresome include:

in the final analysis	last but not least
in this day and age	few and far between
by the same token	a crying (crucial, critical) need
first and foremost	as a matter of fact

6. *Euphemisms* (bland, inoffensive words used in place of more explicit term)

Most euphemisms concern body functions, sex, and death (the subjects that are taboo in "polite" conversation). Euphemistically, people don't die; they "pass on" or "enter into rest." The body becomes "the remains," which is "interred" in a "casket" in a "garden of rest." The trend toward prissiness is becoming more evident in technical writing. Students no longer fail; they underachieve. No one is poor anymore; he is merely disadvantaged. Used cars are now previously owned vehicles. At the turn of the century, nations were backward. Then they were undeveloped, later underdeveloped, and most recently developing (or Third World). Conditions in the countries have not changed, only the bureaucratic terminology.

At their worst, euphemisms hide or distort the truth and thus mislead the reader. In his drive to stamp out the nasty-nice, the late Senator Dirksen related the story of an applicant for a life insurance policy. One of the questions on the form was "How old was your father when he died and what was the cause of death?" The man's father had been hanged, but the applicant—after great deliberation—wrote this answer: "My father died at age 39 at a public function when the platform on which he was standing gave away beneath his feet." That's no lie (but it ain't the truth, neither).

7. *Genteelisms* (expressions of overrefinement, artificiality, pretension)

Genteelisms are like the practice of extending your pinkie when you sip tea. They are equally absurd. Two examples are the misuse of *advise* and *appreciate.* To advise is to offer guidance, counsel, or legal assistance. A police officer advises you of your rights, but you simply tell, notify, or inform an associate of a change in business plans. Don't advise unless you're offering advice. *Appreciate* has two meanings: to increase in value; to recognize the value or worth of a thing. It is not a synonym for "to be grateful" nor is it a synonym for "realize," as in "I appreciate your difficulties." Think about it.

Whatever your faults (stylistically), remember that in writing as in editing it is essential to maintain a sense of humor. In one of the old Marx Brothers' movies, Groucho's secretary comes into his office and says, "Your clients have been waiting in the outer office for an hour. They are waxing wroth." Groucho jiggles his brows and quips, "Send in Roth and tell the other two bums to wait."

We editors may wax wroth from time to time, but it's all in the hope of adding shine to the words we read.

Discussion Questions

1. According to this article, what is the major fault in most business and professional writing? What information can be used to support your answer?

2. Although style is not easy to define, try writing your own definition.

3. Discuss this comment: "A command of grammar and spelling, although important, is no guarantee of effectiveness in writing."

4. List and explain the seven common writing faults discussed in this article.

Why Use Ten Words Instead of Two?

Tom Stapleton

California State University, Los Angeles, CA

"It does not appear that there would be any need for us to continue owner-ship of this stock."

This statement, which ended a memo written by a bank vice president, seems simple enough on first reading. But look again. Isn't it merely saying, "We don't need this stock anymore"?

Of course! Why, then, did the writer not use just six words to convey a message that took eighteen? Is it possible that a direct, simple, uncluttered statement violates some "law" that says, "Where ten words will say the same as two, use ten"?

Most of us, whether in our written business communications or in profes-sional writing, needlessly inflate the English language. We often contradict the way we are in person by the way we come across on paper. All too often our letters, memos, reports, and essays are impersonal and mechanical—showing a stiff, sterile tone devoid of human contact.

Take for instance this statement written by a data processing chief, "Since the program began, it has become apparent that participation in the program is not economically feasible due to the low percentage of approval that has been realized on these applications." What he meant was, "The program isn't paying off for us because so few applications are approved." Thirteen words replace thirty-one. But writing is not merely a numbers game.

Ten Simple Steps

Effective communications—those the reader understands and therefore get the results the writer wants—demonstrate that the sender of the message is thinking about how and what he writes. Because we have been conditioned rather than taught how to write, remedies cannot be achieved with the wave

Source: Tom Stapleton. "Why Use Ten Words Instead of Two?" Reprinted with permission from *Business Forum*, Spring 1982, Vol. 7, No. 2, pp. 14–15. Copyright © School of Business and Economics, California State University, Los Angeles.

of a magic wand. But we can follow ten simple steps in composing any message:

1. For openers, collect your thoughts. Is your communication action oriented or information only? Know your objective for writing and outline your points, if only mentally. No matter how rushed you are, such preparation is time well spent. The payoff comes when your reader understands, and responds.

2. Regard your written communication as a conversation. Write the way you speak, provided you are careful. Ask yourself "How would I say this in person or over the phone?" Everyday language is what people are accustomed to hearing and what they use when they speak. So do not jar the "mind's ear" with business "bafflegab." Converse on paper.

3. Profile your reader. Other human beings, sharing much in common with you, read your communication. Keep in mind that they will react to what you write, picking up images and impressions you convey. Ask yourself how much the reader already knows about your subject, what his experience is in relation to it, and how you can best get him to do what you want.

4. Consider what tone, or attitude, you want to take—firm, friendly, humorous, or apologetic. Once you decide, stick to it; otherwise you will only confuse your reader.

Firm or Apolegetic

As an illustration of why consistent tone is important, a collection agency letter began by telling the reader about his arrears account, leading up to this statement, "You leave us no recourse but to take appropriate legal action." The writer then shifted gears and concluded the letter by saying, "Please call us about making arrangements to grant an extension."

What stand was the writer taking?

5. Open emphatically. People do not read your messages with the same effort or concern you put into composing them. An emphatic approach attempts to get the reader's attention immediately and hold it, to make your communication (whether to a customer or a coworker) stand out. Here is how an investment counselor began a letter to a client hesitant to invest a sum of money, "Pursuant to our conversation of the 30th, I shall endeavor to utilize fully the firm's expertise in regard to the investment amount you agree to forward in order to realize, at the earliest possible date, an equitable return."

Doesn't your brain shift into park as you try to read that? The message is lost. A better version would be, "As we discussed on the 30th, once you send the money we'll go to work to get you the best possible return."

6. Use short sentences (average maximum length: 20 words), active voice ("we *save* money" not "money *is saved* by us"), short paragraphs (about three or four sentences), and visual images. And be careful of using jargon in external communications. If a technical term is necessary, explain what it means; use language and images your reader will grasp immediately.

Brace yourself for this sentence from the *Journal of Politics,* one of the most prestigious publications in its field, "In an age of growing cynicism and declining interest in American politics, some have suggested that democratic decision making in the work place might represent a context within which people could engage and become familiar with forms of social interaction more appropriate to genuine democracy than those which are experienced in the distant, impersonal, and highly abstract system of electoral, representative politics that characterize our society."

Remove Fustian Fog

Who wants to read further? This type of professional writing obscures the substance of what the writer intended to get across. Although more formal than business writing, professional writing still needs clear, concise sentences and effective organization to hold reader's attention. Obfuscated academic prose locks readers out, thus reducing the chances that the essay will even be published. If you are composing a report, a monograph, or an article for publication, take heed; stack the deck in your favor by removing fustian fog from your writing.

7. Do not sag in the middle; add reader incentive by conveying benefits. What good will your message do the reader? Let the person on the other end know what is in it for him. Maybe you can point out a way to save time or money, to put human resources to better use, or to reach a decision. This is necessary information to help sell your points and motivate the reader.

8. Organize your thoughts in chronological order. Listing points in the body of the message helps give them impact. Proceed from background to present to future. You will find this helps you go from general to particular information, which is a deductive method of getting your ideas across. As people read, they subconsciously wonder whether you are emphasizing "where we've been, where we are, or where we're going." Effective organization is a key to getting reader reaction.

9. Explain what you want the reader to do. Look back over step one. Do you want action to result from your message, or are you dealing only with information? Use the closing to reinforce your objective. Do not just run out of ideas and stop or, nearly as bad, begin unnecessarily repeating yourself. We often water down our closings because we do not think about summing up. Readers cannot divine what you intend; spell it out. They should not have to play Sherlock Holmes in solving the "mystery" of your message. Put your concluding thoughts into one of three categories:

    Direct—"I'll call you within a week to set a meeting date."

    Suggestive—"I'm awaiting your call."

    Provocative—"Can we afford to delay in involving upper management?"

    Of these, the provocative closing is often the most effective approach. When you ask a question, you put a burden on the reader to respond. A closing such as "Let's meet to discuss this further" merely drifts off. In fact, such a vague and uncertain statement may detract from the information that went before it. People tend to remember first what they read last.

10. Review your communications regularly. Look for a slow time for going over copies of your various messages. This will not change what went out, but it may help you do better next time.

Note What Worked

As you evaluate, ask yourself whether you went through each of the preceding steps. Be honest. If you got the responses you wanted, note what worked and use those methods again. If you did not get the desired results, check what you have written. Usually you will find something left out or confusing. The time lapse between writing and reviewing will show you patterns in your writing that come to light only after some time has passed.

Take a tip from this anecdote. A farmer wrote to the Department of Agriculture asking if it was safe to use hydrochloric acid to clean his irrigation pipes and got this reply, "The efficacy of hydrochloric acid is indisputable, but the corrosive residue is incompatible with metallic permanence." Grateful, the farmer wrote back his thanks, saying he would order some acid. Fortunately, a resourceful clerk opened the farmer's message and shot back a telegram, "Don't use hydrochloric acid. It eats hell out of the pipes."

Finally, remember that very few people reach the top without cultivating useful communication skills. So when you take pen in hand, take care.

Discussion Questions

1. Explain what the author means in the following statement? "Because we have been conditioned rather than taught how to write, remedies cannot be achieved with the wave of a magic wand."

2. What are some of the questions you should ask yourself when profiling a reader?

3. List and explain the three categories of concluding thoughts that the author presents.

Musings of an Old Infinitive-Splitter

Hap Frances

One aspect to the seminomadic career of technical writers and editors is as fascinating as it is revealing of human nature. That is, the same people appear to be employed at each facility. From military contractors on the West Coast to contractors on the East Coast, these folks bend over their cluttered desks, frequently glancing at the wall clock, paper shuffling through one unexciting day after another. Let's meet some of these reappearing coworkers.

There's Faultless Flora. Her typing speed is 80 wpm and her error rate approaches that. But don't blame her. Responsibility for her errors rest with others. "I just couldn't read that handwritten manuscript," she explains. Or, "The lead writer didn't explain it to me that way." And Flora is happy to tell everybody about these grievous shortcomings during coffee break, at lunch, in the car pool, at the dinner table, at the family reunion, in the checkout line at the grocers, and before the PTA.

Every office has Hurricane Harry. He rushes in, creating air currents that sweep papers off nearby desks. Half typed, half hand written, his manual drops on your desk. "I'm sorry, truly sorry. But I've been so damned busy I haven't had time to get this document into better shape." Naturally, the document must be mailed Thursday, just two working days away. He departs, saying he'll return to discuss the manual after attending the important meeting to which he is rushing. Be he's fooling nobody. You know you won't see him again until mail time, Thursday.

No facility could operate without Castin Bronze. His words Must Never be Touched! Like the Ten Commandments etched in stone, Castin's words are sacred. When you point out ambiguities and shop talk that should be clarified in his paper, he glowers. "Anyone with an ounce of knowledge knows what that means," he says. You further suggest a little background information to help top management readers understand the paper, and he spurns that, too. "I would insult my colleagues and waste their time if I added such

Source: Hap Frances. "Musings of an Old Infinitive-Splitter." Reprinted from *Journal of Technical Writing and Communication,* Vol. 8 (3), 1978, pp. 251–252. Copyright © 1978, Baywood Publishing Co., Inc.

insignificant trivia." His farewell, friendly words are, "That paper does *not* need editing!"

And who has not worked with Gertie Guardian, the efficient, kiln-dried perennial who is the self-appointed guardian of the Company's assets? She is adamant in her refusal to give the requesting tech writer a pencil. "I gave you one a week ago," she admonishes. And a look of disgust crosses her face when asked for a Central Supply form. "What happened to the one I gave you yesterday?"

Every technical writing group is plagued with an Alphabet Al. He talks, writes, and thinks in acronyms. Over the years he has collected a ready supply of defenses against clarifying his prose. "Everyone knows that RFD means 'Raised Face Diameter'" he says. "We do *not* have to define it!" His face reflects disgust at having to talk to such uneducated fools. "The word SEX in that report title does not mean what you imply! It's an abbreviation for Selective Experimental X-ray unit. Any high school graduate knows that!"

And of course, there's the illustrator who never seems to get around to tracing the charts and graphs needed in a report. Robbie Rembrandt lets the world (including management) know that such menial tasks do not require talent of his caliber. His creativity is best used to draw clever illustrations for visual presentations at VIP meetings, or to produce graphic renderings of the proposed new building addition. Let a draftsperson or a compositor do those tracings!

Recently, when I shifted jobs, I found the folks all there. And then I heard about a new one. Faultles Flora asked Gertie Guardian if she had met the new technical editor. "Which one?" Gertie asked. "The old, fat, infinitive splitter who can't spell," Flora replied.

Now, I'll have to meet *him*.

Discussion Questions

1. What is the moral of the story about Faultless Flora?
2. What are the errors that Hurricane Harry is committing?
3. List some acronyms that are used by newspapers or by your colleagues that could result in communication errors.

The Fumblerules of Grammar

William Safire
The New York Times, New York, NY

Not long ago, I advertised for perverse rules of grammar, along the lines of "Remember to never split an infinitive" and "The passive voice should never be used." The notion of making a mistake while laying down rules ("Thimk," "We Never Make Misteaks") is highly unoriginal, and it turns out that English teachers have been circulating lists of fumblerules for years.

As owner of the world's largest collection, and with thanks to scores of readers, let me pass along a bunch of these never-say-neverisms:

- Avoid run-on sentences they are hard to read.
- Don't use no double negatives.
- Use the semicolon properly, always use it where it is appropriate; and never where it isn't.
- Reserve the apostrophe for it's proper use and omit it when its not needed.
- Do not put statements in the negative form.
- Verbs has to agree with their subjects.
- No sentence fragments.
- Proofread carefully to see if you any words out.
- Avoid commas, that are not necessary.
- If you reread your work, you will find on rereading that a great deal of repetition can be avoided by rereading and editing.
- A writer must not shift your point of view.
- Eschew dialect, irregardless.
- And don't start a sentence with a conjunction.
- Don't overuse exclamation marks!!!

Source: William Safire, "The Fumblerules of Grammar." Reprinted from *The New York Times Magazine,* Nov. 4, 1979. Copyright © 1979 by The New York Times Company. Reprinted by permission.

- Place pronouns as close as possible, especially in long sentences, as of 10 or more words, to their antecedents.
- Hyphenate between syllables and avoid un-necessary hyphens.
- Write all adverbial forms correct.
- Don't use contractions in formal writing.
- Writing carefully, dangling participles must be avoided.
- It is incumbent on us to avoid archaisms.
- If any word is improper at the end of a sentence, a linking verb is.
- Steer clear of incorrect forms of verbs that have snuck in the language.
- Take the bull by the hand and avoid mixed metaphors.
- Avoid trendy locutions that sound flaky.
- Never, ever use repetitive redundancies.
- Everyone should be careful to use a singular pronoun with singular nouns in their writing.
- If I've told you once, I've told you a thousand times, resist hyperbole.
- Also, avoid awkward or affected alliteration.
- Don't string too many prepositional phrases together unless you are walking through the valley of the shadow of death.
- Always pick on the correct idiom.
- "Avoid overuse of 'quotation "marks."'"
- The adverb always follows the verb.
- Last but not least, avoid clichés like the plague: seek viable alternatives.

Discussion Questions

1. Correct the grammar in the examples the author has presented.
2. What is the purpose of writing the article? Explain.

Part II

Cases

Filtering the Windy Memo

Judie Cochran
Management Consultant, Scottsdale, AZ

The following memo was sent from B. E. McGunn to J. R. Jones on December 1. Mr. McGunn tends to get very long-winded when it comes to writing; he believes that there is merit in *quantity* and *quality*. Mr. McGunn dictated this memo in rough draft form late yesterday afternoon before leaving the office. During the evening at home, he was rushed to the hospital with an apparent heart attack.

The physician believes that Mr. McGunn will not be able to return to work for several weeks. Therefore, someone will take over Mr. McGunn's work; you, along with others, will be responsible for his work load.

The rough draft, below, has returned to Mr. McGunn's desk from the word processing unit; it must be reworded and sent on its way to J. R. Jones as soon as possible. Because you are a good business writer, you realize that the rough draft of Mr. McGunn's memo could be changed substantially so that clarity, conciseness, and readability could be greatly enhanced. It is now your job to rewrite the memo.

From Word Processing Unit, No. 18, *Rough Draft*

TO: J. R. Jones, Building Superintendent
FROM: B. E. McGunn, Measurement Department
DATE: December 1
SUBJECT: Ineffective Sun Filtering on the South Side of Building

During the afternoons, especially in warm months of the year, offices on the South Side of the building become excessively hot. The employees have complained that when the curtains are fully drawn that they do not effectively filter out the sun's rays.

When the employees brought this problem to my attention some weeks ago, it initiated an investigation. Therefore, thermometers were placed in all of the 18 offices on the South Side of the building and the curtains were fully drawn throughout the entire afternoons. Readings were carefully recorded hourly. Heavy cloth was placed over the windows in two of the offices, which were chosen randomly, and the temperature was also recorded hourly during the afternoons. During the entire time of the investigation, all room thermostats were set at 72° and were left constant all day.

At the end of the working day, the following conclusions were drawn after the data were evaluated. The average temperature in the curtained offices was 82°, as recorded by the room thermostats and the test thermometers. However, the temperature in the control offices with the specially covered windows varied from 72° to 75°, as recorded by the room thermostats and the test thermometers. Therefore, the test data indicate that the curtains on the South Side of the building do not effectively filter out the rays of the sun.

On the basis of this conclusion, we initiated a search for curtain material that would prove effective in supplying the required protection for all the offices on the South Side of the building. There are two types of curtains presently on the market would could solve our problem with excessive heat. ABC Fabrics handles Filtra-Sun material for $9.95 per yard; XYZ Fabrics handles Block-Ray material for $11.95 per yard. Both materials would do a good job for our problem.

Questions

1. Is the subject line effective and to the point? If not, how could it be changed?

2. Is the topic sentence of the first paragraph adequate? If not, how could it be rewritten?

3. Do all paragraphs have topic sentences with sufficient developmental sentences to support clarity?

4. Are word choices, punctuation, and grammar usage correct?

5. Could any of the paragraphs be reduced by eliminating wordy phrases, repeated phrases or clauses, or trite expressions?

6. Does J. R. Jones need to have all of the information reported by Mr. McGunn? If not, what could be eliminated?

7. Could headings help to organize the information? If so, what headings might be appropriate?

8. If you are responsible for sending the memo to J. R. Jones, even though Mr. McGunn conducted the research and wrote a rough draft, whose name should appear on the "From" line in the memo heading?

9. When you rewrite the memo, would your memo be an effective one so that J. R. Jones could make a decision?

Removing Excess Baggage

Judie Cochran
Management Consultant, Scottdale, AZ

You have recently been hired by the Zippy Typewriter Company in the accounting department. Your boss, a fine accountant but not-so-fine business writer, wrote the following rough draft to Arizona Transit Company concerning payment for damaged typewriters.

Your boss left this with you to "spruce up" and to send out by tomorrow. You were told to use your own judgment on rewriting the letter so that it could be clear to Mrs. Adams at the Transit Company that your company wants a check sent promptly.

Rewrite this letter, eliminating the "excess baggage" and correcting the errors in sentence structure.

Rough Draft

Dear Mrs. Adams:

On the date of January 25, a shipment of a crate of seventy-five of our Zippy Typewriters to Trust-Us Insurance Company in the city of Houston, was made by Mr. Mark Lamb who is your shipping agent. Six days subsequent to the above date, damage to a vast majority of the machines was sustained when one of your Phoenix crane operators dropped the crate.

February 16 was the date that a Freight Damage Claim in the amount of the sum of $3,500.00 was sent by mail by men at my office to Mrs. Dorothy Richards, in your Claims division in your Phoenix office. Writing me in return, I was advised that she would give my claim special attention and the settlement, no doubt, being received by me at my office at the earliest possible date.

A period of two months passed by and on April 17, I sent an inquiry in regards to the claim to Mrs. Dorothy Richards in your Claims Division in your Phoenix office. A form postcard came by mail to me advising me, three weeks subsequent to my inquiry to your Phoenix office, that the processing of my claim was underway and that my patience would be appreciated. That was two months before the writing of this letter, and no further contact has been made or any remittance sent either.

It is my personal opinion that it ought to be brought to your attention that replacement of our Zippy Typewriters had to be made to our customer, Trust-Us Insurance Company in the city of Houston. And, the cost of repairing sixty-eight of the damaged typewriters was absorbed by our company. Therefore, it was necessary to get rid of these repaired typewriters at prices that were greatly reduced and that caused a loss to our company.

Very soon I would like to have your reply as to your action; or better yet, it would be greatly appreciated if you would send a check for the amount of $3,500.00 in remittance of your damage caused by your Phoenix crane operators.

Very truly yours,

Questions

1. What is the purpose of writing this letter?

2. Is the first paragraph adequate for Mrs. Adams' understanding of the purpose of the letter?

3. Is the information logically presented so Mrs. Adams can take action?

4. Are word choices, tone of voice, punctuation, and grammar usage correct in the rough draft?

5. Do all paragraphs have topic sentences with sufficient developmental sentences to support clarity and completeness?

6. Could the paragraphs be greatly reduced by eliminating wordy phrases, repeated phrases or clauses, or trite expressions?

7. Does Mrs. Adams need to know all of the information presented in the rough draft? If not, what can be eliminated?

8. If you are responsible for sending the letter to Mrs. Adams, should you mention that your boss had been the previous correspondent with her company? Or, should you write the letter and sign your boss's name?

9. When you rewrite the letter, would your letter encourage Mrs. Adams to take prompt action?

Thoughts About Business Correspondence

This part contains three articles: two about the business letter and one on memorandums. The first article, "Better Business Writing" by Edward Wakin, presents a three-part formula for improving business letters: open up, back up, and follow up. He discusses each component of this formula and presents techniques that will help the correspondence achieve its desired goal.

Malcolm Forbes presents an approach that he has found separates the winners from losers when writing business correspondence. In his article, "How to Write a Business Letter," Forbes says that several points characterize the winner: Know what you want, plunge right in, write so the reader will enjoy it, give it the best you've got, sum it up, and get out.

In her article, "Memorandums—An Effective Communication Tool for Management," Jo Ann Hennington states that the use of internal communications rivals the use of external communications in quantity. Hennington's major points include when to use memorandums, parts of the memorandum, margins, arrangement, and other time-saving features.

Better Business Writing

Edward Wakin

Fordham University, New York, NY

When a business letter "seeks viable alternatives to maximize the decision-making process" or a memo reports "not insignificant economies being effected by minimizing the time interval in opting for decisions," there's trouble afoot.

Whether dressed up and sent out as a fuzzy letter or distributed as a murky interoffice memo, such messages are virtually useless. Documents containing such highfalutin nonsense are either misread or, more often than not, not read at all. The result: wasted time and money. The remedy: letters and memos that are clear, informative and brief; in other words, well written.

Judging from the articles on better writing published by the business press and the increased demand for writing workshops, many companies are seeking this remedy. Business has recognized the problem of bad writing and is emphasizing to its executives the importance of well-written memos and letters. Recognition of this problem is the first step toward a solution.

Clarity in business writing depends on the thinking, as well as the writing, process. Therefore, the author should thoroughly think through the one central message of the piece. In some cases, the central message is obvious and will take only a moment to define. On other occasions, it is more complicated and will require some thought before the actual writing process begins. In rare instances, the central message will only become clear after a first draft has been completely revised.

Since the central message dictates the content and, therefore, the ordering of information, it keeps the piece on track. It also enables the writer to decide what to put in and what to leave out.

This is not always as easy as it sounds. As one consultant reported to the *Wall Street Journal*, "We get people who are swamped by their work because they need a whole hour to compose a simple one-page letter."

Helpful strategies for those who suffer and stumble with letters and memos come in many forms. But, basically, it boils down to a three-part formula: *open up, back up* and *follow up.*

Letters and memos (which are really just internal letters) have but one fleeting chance to catch the reader's attention. It's imperative, then, that you

Source: Edward Wakin. "Better Business Writing." Reprinted with permission from *Today's Office*, May 1982, Hearst Business Communications, Inc. UTP Division and the author.

open up with a direct statement of what the document is all about. In other words, tell them what you're going to tell them. Otherwise, you run the risk of not being read at all, given the volume of written material that arrives on desks every day.

Your piece is also in competition with phone calls, meetings, conferences, administrative duties and decision making. To be effective, your opening paragraph must be able to pass this simple test: Can the reader stop after reading it and know what the entire message is all about?

An effective opening does two things. It provides a context for the message and delivers the entire message in one, two or three concise sentences. A letter typically refers to a bond between sender and receiver, such as previous correspondence, a common concern, a common goal. A memo can assume more, since it goes to people in the same office or organization. In either case, the reader should be able to determine immediately why the letter or memo has been written and what it's all about.

Next, *back up* the opening with whatever details are necessary. Exclude the unnecessary. Tick off the main points in order of importance, magnitude, interest or urgency. The system of ordering does not matter as long as the writer has some sort of order in mind.

Usually, it's a good idea to allow one back up point to a paragraph. Bullets (•) or numbers can be used to identify each point. Indenting these back up details also works well, particularly in memos. To be effective, back up points must provide whatever information is needed in order for the reader to understand, react to and act on the message.

Follow up the main points by looking ahead to future action (a phone call, a visit, the deadline for a response), foreseeable consequences and the outcome.

Limit letters and memos to one page and one page only—unless a very good reason dictates otherwise. This is easily tested by looking through the nearest in-box. The one-page messages are no doubt gone, while other, lengthier documents remain untouched.

The appearance of a message also counts. Readers are put off by masses of written material, so use short paragraphs, abundant white space, indentation, underlining (through sparingly) and centering. The less work there is for the reader, the more likely it is that there will be a reader.

Use simple words, active verbs, specific details and short sentences. This not only makes letters and memos easier to understand, but it forces the writer to think more clearly about what is being written. Aim at a conversational tone and avoid stilted language and multisyllabic words.

As Mark Twain said of getting paid per word for his writing, "I never write 'metropolis' for seven cents a word because I can get the same price for 'city'." E. B. White also commented on this subject: "Avoid the elaborate, the pretentious, the coy and the cute. Do not be tempted by a twenty-dollar word when there is a ten-center handy, ready, and able."

Finally, business letters and memos reveal the style, attitude and competence of the writer as a manager and an executive. Read a manager's letters and memos for the past few months and you can discern, for instance, whether he or she: grasps what needs to be done; trusts the staff; gets cooperation; feels self-confident; meets deadlines; runs the show democratically or dictatorially; or has a future in the company.

The executive who continues to write about "maximized output with minimized input" increases the chances of not getting the message across, while decreasing the chances of getting ahead in business.

Discussion Questions

1. Because clarity in business writing depends on the thinking, as well as the writing process, the author makes certain recommendations. What are these recommendations?

2. In less than 100 words summarize the three-part formula: open up; back up; and follow up.

3. What are some of the techniques that a writer may use to make less work for the reader?

How to Write a Business Letter

Malcolm Forbes

Forbes Magazine, New York, NY

A good business letter can get you a job interview.

Get you off the hook.

Or get you money.

It's totally asinine to blow your chances of getting *whatever* you want—with a business letter that turns people off instead of turning them on.

The best place to learn to write is in school. If you're still there, pick your teachers' brain.

If not, big deal. I learned to ride a motorcycle at 50 and fly balloons at 52. It's never too late to learn.

Over 10,000 business letters come across my desk every year. They seem to fall into three categories: stultifying if not stupid, mundane (most of them), and first rate (rare). Here's the approach I've found that separates the winners from the losers (most of it's just good common sense)—it starts *before* you write your letter:

Know What You Want

If you don't, write it down—in one sentence. "I want to get an interview within the next two weeks." That simple. List the major points you want to get across—it'll keep you on course.

If you're *answering* a letter, check the points that need answering and keep the letter in front of you while you write. This way you won't forget anything—*that* would cause another round of letters.

And for goodness' sake, answer promptly if you're going to answer at all. Don't sit on a letter—*that* invites the person on the other end to sit on whatever you want from *him*.

Source: Malcolm Forbes. "How to Write a Business Letter." Reprinted by permission of International Paper Company, 1981.

Plunge Right In

Call him by name—not "Dear Sir, Madam, or Ms." "Dear Mr. Chrisanthopoulos"—and be sure to spell it right. That'll get him (thus, you) off to a good start.

(Usually, you can get his name just by phoning his company—or from a business directory in your nearest library.)

Tell what your letter is about in the first paragraph. One or two sentences. Don't keep your reader guessing or he might file your letter away—even before he finishes it.

In the round file.

If you're answering a letter, refer to the date it was written. So the reader won't waste time hunting for it.

People who read business letters are as human as thee and me. Reading a letter shouldn't be a chore—*reward* the reader for the time he gives you.

Write So He'll Enjoy It

Write the entire letter from his point of view—what's in it for *him?* Beat him to the draw—surprise him by answering the questions and objections he might have.

Be positive—he'll be more receptive to what you have to say.

Be nice. Contrary to the cliché, genuinely nice guys most often finish first or very near it. I admit it's not easy when you've got a gripe. To be agreeable while disagreeing—that's an art.

Be natural—write the way you talk. Imagine him sitting in front of you— what would you *say* to him?

Business jargon too often is cold, stiff, unnatural.

Suppose I came up to you and said, "I acknowledge receipt of your letter and I beg to thank you." You'd think, "Huh? You're putting me on."

The acid test—read your letter *out loud* when you're done. You might get a shock—but you'll know for sure if it sounds natural.

Don't be cute or flippant. The reader won't take you seriously. This doesn't mean you've got to be dull. You prefer your letter to knock 'em dead rather than bore 'em to death.

Three points to remember:

Have a sense of humor. That's refreshing *anywhere*—a nice surprise in a business letter.

Be specific. If I tell you there's a new fuel that could save gasoline, you might not believe me. But suppose I tell you this:

"Gasohol"—10% alcohol, 90% gasoline—works as well as straight gasoline. Since you can make alcohol from grain or corn stalks, wood or wood waste, coal—even garbage, it's worth some real follow-through.

Now you've got something to sink your teeth into.

<u>Lean heavier on nouns and verbs, lighter on adjectives. Use the active voice instead of the passive.</u> Your writing will have more guts.

Which of these is stronger? Active voice: "I kicked out my money manager." Or, passive voice: "My money manager was kicked out by me." (By the way, neither is true. My son, Malcolm Jr., manages most Forbes money—he's a brilliant moneyman.)

Give It the Best You've Got

When you don't want something enough to make *the* effort, making *an* effort is a waste.

<u>Make your letter look appetizing</u>—or you'll strike out before you even get to bat. Type it—on good-quality 8½" x 11" stationery. Keep it neat. And use paragraphing that makes it easier to read.

<u>Keep your letter short</u>—to one page, if possible. Keep your paragraphs short. After all, who's going to benefit if your letter is quick and easy to read? You.

For emphasis, <u>underline</u> important words. And sometimes indent sentences as well as paragraphs.

> **Like this. See how well it works? (But save it for something special.)**

<u>Make it perfect.</u> No typos, no misspellings, no factual errors. If you're sloppy and let mistakes slip by, the person reading your letter will think you don't know better or don't care. Do you?

<u>Be crystal clear.</u> You won't get what you're after if your reader doesn't get the message.

<u>Use good English.</u> If you're still in school, take all the English and writing courses you can. The way you write and speak can really help—or *hurt.*

If you're not in school (even if you are), get the little 71-page gem by Strunk & White, *Elements of Style.* It's in paperback. It's fun to read and loaded with tips on good English and good writing.

<u>Don't put on airs.</u> Pretense invariably impresses only the pretender.

<u>Don't exaggerate.</u> Even once. Your reader will suspect everything else you write.

<u>Distinguish opinions from facts.</u> Your opinions may be the best in the world. But they're not gospel. You owe it to your reader to let him know which is which. He'll appreciate it and he'll admire you. The dumbest people I know are those who Know It All.

<u>Be honest.</u> It'll get you further in the long run. If you're not, you won't rest easy until you're found out. (The latter, not speaking from experience.)

<u>Edit ruthlessly.</u> Somebody ~~has~~ said that words are ~~a lot~~ like inflated mon-

ey—the more ~~of them that~~ you use, the less each one ~~of them~~ is worth. ~~Right on.~~ Go through your entire letter ~~just~~ as many times as it takes. ~~Search out and~~ Annihilate all unnecessary words, ~~and~~ sentences—even ~~entire~~ *paragraphs.*

Sum It Up and Get Out

The last paragraph should tell the reader exactly what you want *him* to do— or what *you're* going to do. Short and sweet. "May I have an appointment? Next Monday, the 16th, I'll call your secretary to see when it'll be most convenient for you."

Close with something simple like, "Sincerely." And for heaven's sake sign legibly. The biggest ego trip I know is a completely illegible signature.

Good luck.

I hope you get what you're after.

Sincerely,

Malcolm L. Forbes

Discussion Questions

1. What does the author consider the "acid test" of a letter? What is the purpose of the "acid test"?

2. Give an example of the difference between the active and passive voice.

3. What does the author suggest as a possible reason that some people use completely illegible signatures on their letters? What do you think of this explanation?

Memorandums—An Effective Communication Tool for Management

Jo Ann Hennington,
Arizona State University, Tempe, AZ

In many business firms today, the use of internal communications rivals the use of external communications in quantity. The business memorandum (memo) is typically the format used most often for internal communication. The memo can flow vertically or horizontally within an organization. Because communication by memo is an integral part of almost all segments of management, business firms expect all managers to communicate effectively and efficiently with memos within an organization.

Professors of business communication contribute to the acquisition of the skill and the art of communication of the students they teach in communication classes. They have a responsibility to assist their students, who are or will become managers in an organization, in improving their competence in communicating effectively and efficiently with the business memorandum. To make memos work effectively, managers must know when and how to use them properly. A few words about the general use of preparation of business memorandums will assist business communication students in placing this useful business form in its proper setting.

When to Use Memorandums

Since the memorandum is an internal communication, it is more management-oriented than a business letter and is a more objective type of communication. As a memo writer, a manager may need to disseminate information concerning new policies and business decisions, relay asked-for information, present facts for decision making by others, report progress on what is happening within the organization, suggest ideas, justify or set responsibility

Source: Jo Ann Hennington. "Memorandums—An Effective Communication Tool for Management." Reprinted from *The ABCA Bulletin*, September 1978, by permission of the author.

for certain courses of action, or take a stand on an issue. Managers frequently use memos to communicate useful facts and data within their organization. Memos are especially useful if there is the possibility that information communicated verbally may be forgotten or misunderstood. Frequently, the identity of a manager who makes suggestions on the telephone or in a meeting may be confused or forgotten. Having one manager take credit for another manager's ideas does happen. When a manager has offered an important viewpoint verbally, it may be wise to prepare a memo for the record. Memos also can be used to confirm and recap points discussed in meetings or on the telephone.

A memo is an effective method of expressing appreciation and building good morale within an organization. A short memo to a staff member who has performed in an outstanding manner often has greater effect than a verbal compliment. Also, a memo acknowledging how a colleague has helped you or other members within your department not only benefits the relationship but also shows that a manager has one of the qualities of a good administrator–the ability to recognize superior performance.

Parts of the Memorandum

A well-organized memorandum ordinarily contains eight parts: (1) Memorandum Head, (2) To Line, (3) From Line, (4) Writer's Signature, (5) Date Line, (6) Subject Line, (7) Body, and (8) Reference Initials. Each of these eight parts, as well as various optional parts that may be needed, is described below. The order in which the parts of the memorandum are discussed is the same as that in which they appear in a memorandum.

Memorandum Head

Memorandum Head is used if available. If not, have the secretary create Memorandum Head by typewriting the word MEMORANDUM, in all capital letters, at the left margin on a sheet of plain bond paper, leaving a one inch top margin and a one-inch left margin. This format will save both time and expense for the organization as it can be set up quickly and efficiently by the secretary and eliminates the purchase of printed Memorandum Head.

To Line

This line consists of the name of the person to whom the memo is directed. It begins on the third line below the Memorandum Head. The TO notation begins at the left margin, is typed in all capital letters, and is followed by a colon. The name of the recipient is typed a double space after the colon. Multiple addresses are shown by typewriting each name in full and listing them in order of importance.

TO: Jon Rodgers, Ph.D.
Martha Heard, CPA
Dennis Headley

If the addressees are all on the same level, list them alphabetically. If rank of importance is unknown, ask someone who knows. Since the memo is an informal communication directed between offices within the organization, omit personal or official titles and departmental headings, unless some readers might not know them. Professional titles are often retained. Be especially careful to spell the names and professional titles of the recipients correctly. When copies of a memo are directed to several persons, the name of the person to whom it is to be forwarded is checked on each copy. This checkmark technique insures that each addressee receives a copy of the memo.

From Line

The typewritten name of the writer is shown in the FROM Line with only essential information included.

FROM: Byron Merritt, Ph.D.

Note that the official title and departmental heading are omitted in the From Line. However, a professional title such as Ph.D is often retained, as preferred by the writer or by organizational policy. If the memo is written to a number of readers who do not know the writer, include the official title. Usually the To Line and the From Line are parallel in content.

Writer's Signature

Since a memo is an internal communication, ordinarily it does not need the kind of authenticating signature an outgoing letter requires. If authentication is necessary or preferred, the usual practice is for the writer to initial the memo on the From Line following the typewritten name.

Date Line

For both reference and legal purposes, memorandums must be dated. The month, the day, and the year, in that order, should be typed in the Date Line and positioned after the word DATE, a double space below the From Line. The military style date line, which consists of the day, the month, and the year, in that order, is acceptable in memorandum writing and saves time since the comma is omitted.

DATE: October 17, 1977 *or*
DATE: 17 October 1977

Never abbreviate the month or write the date entirely in figures—it increases the possibility of making a mistake when interpreting the date.

Subject Line

A Subject Line is used to let the reader know immediately what is discussed in the memo. It is typed a double space below the Date Line. Following the SUBJECT notation, the writer briefly states the topic of the memorandum.

SUBJECT: Joint Meeting with Patrick
            Corporation

A Subject Line, carefully and concisely phrased, will assist the writer in the development of the message of the memo. If it indicates the content of the memo accurately and specifically, it is also a valuable aid for the secretary in filing the communication. And maintaining the same Subject Line for all memorandums pertaining to the same item of business will facilitate filing and retrieval of correspondence.

Body

The most important part of the memorandum is the Body. The Body contains the message, the purpose of writing the memo. The message is typed in block form and single-spaced with double spacing between paragraphs. A triple space separates the Subject Line from the Body to the memo.

Style, tone, and content of the memorandum are governed to a great extent by standard procedures and practices of a particular organization. Some departments within an organization tend to be more formal than others. However, most memorandums are generally informal typewritten messages of things to be remembered, as in future action, and make great use of listings and itemizations, or are directives going down the chain of command and requests coming up the chain of command.

When composing memos, the manager should emphasize important facts—avoid undue emphasis on trivial details. Get to the point quickly by using terminology, sentence length and structure, and paragraph length and structure that make the memo easy to read and understand. Short words, sentences, paragraphs, and listings help keep the reader's interest. Long, detailed memos bog down and turn off the reader. Memos written in clear, concise language are more easily comprehended.

Before dictating or writing a memo, a manager should organize the thoughts to be transmitted. Articulate them as if explaining them verbally to a colleague. Then jot down a few main ideas in outline form. Use the outline as a guide when dictating, including only essential information. If the memo is to be of value to the reader, it should have these qualities: correctness, clearness, conciseness, courteousness, and convenience for the reader. A well-organized memo, with the above qualities, will accomplish the writer's mission.

When dictating, a manager has two options for arranging the information presented in the body of the memo. Either inductive or deductive arrangement of ideas may be used. When the inductive approach is used, facts and findings are presented before conclusions and recommendations. When the deductive approach is used, the memo begins with a short summary, which is followed by conclusions and recommendations. Facts and findings are then presented. Because many memo readers find conclusions and recommendations to be of greatest interest and value, and use facts and findings only if additional information is needed, the deductive arrangement is frequently used in memorandum writing. However, if negative information is involved, an inductive approach is used. No rigid rules govern the content and organization of memos, but most memo writers include at least these parts:

1. The introduction, which includes the purpose of the memorandum and the method used to obtain the information presented;
2. The body, which includes detailed information and presents facts and findings with accuracy (do not mix opinion with fact in this part of the memo); and
3. The conclusion, which includes plans or recommendations for future action. Personal comments and opinions are included in this part of the memo; however, conclusions must be supported by facts or other evidence presented in the memo.

Reference Initials

The initials of the secretary are typewritten a double space below the last line of the body of the memorandum. The manager's initials do not need to appear in the Reference Initials area as this is superfluous.

Enclosure Notation

If one or more items are enclosed with the memorandum, this fact is noted on the line below the Reference Initials. These styles are frequently used in the Enclosure Notation:

Enclosure
Enclosures
Enclosures: 1. Check, 2. Envelope
Enclosures (2)

Note that the word enclosure is spelled out, not abbreviated. Also, it is more informative to the reader to enumerate the enclosures if there are multiple enclosures.

Carbon Copy Notation

If a copy of the memo is to be directed to an individual other than the addressee and the addressee is to be notified of this fact, a carbon copy notation (cc) is typed flush with the left margin on the line below the Enclosure Notation or the Reference Initials, whichever is immediately preceding:

cc: James Ramsey

It is a wise idea to instruct the secretary to prepare a copy for the office files for both reference and legal purposes. Send the original of the memo to the person whom it most directly concerns and send copies to anyone else involved. Again, use the check-mark technique by the names in the Carbon Copy Notation area.

Blind Carbon Copy Notation

If a copy of a memorandum is directed to an individual other than the addressee and the addressee is not to be notified of this fact, a blind carbon copy notation (bcc) is typed in the lower left-hand corner of the copy, followed by the name of the individual to receive such a copy.

bcc: Patrick Hurley

This notation never appears on the original memorandum. It should appear, however, on the office file copy.

Multipage Headings

Since a one-page memo is far more effective than a multipage memo, a memorandum should be typed on a single sheet of bond paper, if possible. When this is not possible, a plain sheet of bond paper of the same quality as the Memorandum Head is used for subsequent pages. Use the same side margins on all pages of the memo. A Multipage Heading, arranged in pure block style, is typed at the left margin on the seventh line from the top of the paper in single spacing and includes the addressee's name, the page number, and the date.

Jon Rodgers, Ph.D.
Page 2
17 October 1977

The message resumes on the third line below the Multipage Heading. The pure block style is a time-saving arrangement for Multipage Headings.

Margins for a Memorandum

To save space and time in adjusting marginal stops on the typewriter, memorandums, regardless of length, should be typed with one-inch margins. Both side margins are always one inch. Since the top margin is one inch, begin the Memorandum Head on line seven. The bottom margin should be at least one inch on the first page of a multipage memo. A one-page memo may, of course, have a much deeper margin, depending on the length of the message.

Memo Arrangement

The most time-saving arrangement for a memorandum is pure block style using single space typewriting with double spacing between paragraphs. This arrangement is simple in appearance and saves the secretary time when typewriting the memo since every line begins at the left margin and the secretary has a minimum number of machine adjustments to make before and while typewriting the memo.

Other Time-Saving Features

The organizational title, department heading, salutation, complimentary close, and writer's complete handwritten signature are omitted in a memo in order to save time when communicating information within an organization. When an envelope is needed to transmit a memo, only the recipient's name and department is typewritten on an interoffice mail envelope. If a memo is of a confidential nature, it should be forwarded in a sealed envelope with the name of the person to whom it is going typed on the outside of the envelope. If a short memo is single spaced on a full sheet of bond paper, a reply to the message can be typewritten or jotted at the bottom of the page, resulting in a saving of both time and paper.

Conclusions

The memorandum, one of the most widely used pieces of correspondence within a business organization, is an informal, concise method of communication. It is an effective management tool used to simplify correspondence procedures and to improve communication as it carries written information rapidly and conveniently between members of an organization. The use of memorandums with headings illustrates simplicity in organization of internal correspondence, contributes to easy reading, makes quick messages between colleagues more businesslike, and provides a key to strong managerial communication. Communication by memorandum represents one of today's most important opportunities to save valuable managerial time. The effective manager knows when and how to use the following simplified memorandum format as a tool to improve written communication within an organization.

A MEMORANDUM EXEMPLIFIED

MEMORANDUM HEAD	MEMORANDUM
TO LINE	TO: Jon Rodgers, Ph.D.
FROM LINE	FROM: Byron Merritt, Ph.D.
DATE LINE	DATE: 17 October 1977
SUBJECT LINE	SUBJECT: Joint Meeting with Patrick Corporation
BODY	Jon, enclosed is a letter we received from the Patrick Corporation. They ask us to come to a joint meeting at their corporation on October 30.
	Please take over. Tell them we will be pleased to have a joint meeting with them, set up a company car to get us there, get the details of the meeting, and find out whether our company can help them in any way. Let me know when all details have been completed.
REFERENCE INITIALS	jh
ENCLOSURE NOTATION	Enclosure

Discussion Questions

1. Discuss three of the many uses of a memo.
2. What is the purpose of the Memorandum Head? the Date Line? the Subject Line?
3. What is a blind carbon copy notation and when is it used?

Part III

Cases

Fast Food: Slow Layoff

C. Glenn Pearce

Virginia Commonwealth University, Richmond, VA

Five years ago, you opened a Burger Heaven franchise outlet on a busy intersection in Falls Church, Virginia. Two investors joined you as limited partners, and you agreed to manage the business.

You began operations with eight employees and trained them well. To keep them, you give them good salaries, paid vacations, health insurance, and started a retirement plan for them. You wanted only full-time employees who would make a career of their jobs. As business grew, you added six employees the second year and six more the following year. Things were going very well, indeed.

Then the economy declined sharply in the fourth year and so did your sales. You fired no one, however. But when sales dropped sharply this year, you were forced to fire four people.

You estimate that sales next year will be down about $25,000. Your partners are angry because net profits are declining. Although they agree that nothing can be done to increase sales, they think labor costs are much too high. In fact, those costs do average about $2000 more yearly for each employee than those of competitors. You think that having a stable work force and no part-time help is worth the extra money, but you agree reluctantly to reduce labor costs by $50,000 next year. Rather than fire anyone else, you decide to cancel the health insurance, eliminate paid vacations, and ask employees to pay half the cost of their retirement plans. If you do not do this, you must fire four people and ask the others to work an additional two hours daily without pay.

You call a meeting of your employees to tell them the grim news. They know that they may have a hard time finding other jobs, so they accept the bad news. They ask you to put it in writing, though, and they especially want information on the company's net income. Your partners agree that you can supply some information but do not want to make a full disclosure of the partnership's finances. Here is what you can tell them:

Year	Sales	Number of Employees	Labor Costs	Percentage Change in Net Income
First	$208,672	8	$120,080	——
Second	420,790	14	224,500	+50.6
Third	675,560	20	340,112	+36.2
Fourth	405,220	20	256,776	−30.3
This Year	275,520	16	220,212	−30.4
Next Year*	250,000	16	170,000	−3.5

*Estimated

Exercise

Write a memorandum to your employees. Explain the cutbacks and give them enough information to convince them that your actions are necessary.

Crystal Ball Parking Limited

Judie Cochran
Management Consultant, Scottsdale, AZ

Kelly Nelson works for a small manufacturing firm called Christensen's Crystal Ball Shop. Recently, there has been a problem with inadequate parking spaces for the 140 plant and office employees at this location. The problem is supposedly caused by people who shop at nearby stores and some who work at nearby businesses—they are parking in the Crystal Ball Shop's lot.

The lot is not fenced; it has no sign designating that it is part of the Crystal Ball Shop's property. Kelly Nelson, assistant personnel director, has been receiving many complaints from the employees about the lack of parking spaces when they arrive for work. Other parking areas are at least two blocks away and most are metered areas owned by the city.

Part of Kelly's job description makes her responsible for the supervision of property maintenance, which includes the supervision of adequate parking spaces. Kelly understands the problem and decides to write "the boss" (Kelly's supervisor) with a request for funds pending approval of the recommendations Kelly includes in the written correspondence.

Questions

1. If you were Kelly, what written form of correspondence would you use to describe the problem and make a recommendation?

2. What major points would be essential in this message? In what logical pattern should these points be arranged?

3. If the recommendation is approved by Kelly's supervisor, what written form of correspondence would Kelly use to inform the employees about a change in parking lot procedures?

4. What major points would be essential in Kelly's written message to the employees? How would this written message be best distributed to all employees?

The Dollfuss Affair

Ross Figgins
California State Polytechnic University, Pamona, CA

Assume that you are the owner of a small stamp and philatelic supply store in Claremont, California. Three of your best customers have expressed interest in purchasing mint copies of the Austrian Dollfuss stamp of 1936.

You know of a retired dealer in the Midwest who has a number of excellent copies of this rarity. He will sell them to you at two thirds of the catalogue value (most dealers charge 75 percent for scarce items like these). But this dealer is a stubborn old man who refuses to be pressured now that he has retired; in fact, sometimes he doesn't even answer requests from those he feels are trying to take advantage of him.

On the other hand, your customers are aggressive, impatient people. If you can't produce this merchandise within a reasonable amount of time, they will probably cancel their orders and find another dealer. That would leave you with a large sum of working capital invested in expensive, slow-moving stock.

You have tried to contact your customers by telephone a couple of times, but they are either out, on vacation, or too busy to discuss their hobbies during working hours. You finally decide that the best way to handle the situation is to compose two letters, one to the dealer in the Midwest and the other to your prospective purchasers. (Remember that both messages must be persuasive.)

Here is some additional information you may require in preparing your solution to this problem:

1. Your clients are Dr. Earl Richards, Mrs. Eve Harold, and Rev. Charles Hamilton. (*Addresses for clients:* Dr. Earl Richards, 64 Apian Drive, Los Angeles, California; Mrs. Eve Harold, 3621 Stepple Avenue, Claremont, California; Rev. Charles Hamilton, 125 Darsey Street, Claremont, California.)
2. The dealer is James Earl Blackthread, 117 N.E. Halberd Road, Ames, Iowa.
3. The standard Scott Philatelic Catalogue description of the stamp is: Austrian, 1936, Dollfuss, #380, 10 shilling dark blue, $1200.00 mint.
4. You did not ask for a deposit when the customers asked you to see if you could find the stamps for them.
5. Your normal profit is cost plus 20 percent.

Suggestions About Business Reports

The three articles included in this part present techniques for writing business reports. Each article makes the point that report writing can be a difficult task, but it can be simplified when the writers use the appropriate strategies. Edward Wakin, in the article "Better Business Writing," suggests that the key to writing a report is to answer the "five Ws" not only in the summary or abstract but also in the body of the report. He also mentions that the writing in a report requires revision and unmerciful self-scrutiny.

Vincent Vinci's article, "Ten Report Writing Pitfalls: How to Avoid Them," does just that: It presents a series of errors and suggests how one may avoid them. Writers should keep this list of 10 pitfalls in a convenient place, and use it as a reference when writing a report.

It seems that computers affect every aspect of communication including report writing. Steven Golen and Gavin L. Ellzey review the various ways that computer graphics can assist a business report writer. Their article, "Communicating With Graphics: A Picture Can Be Worth a Thousand Words," presents suggestions for using bar, line, and pie graphs in reports.

Better Business Writing

Edward Wakin

Fordham University, New York, NY

If the typical executive could shed any single responsibility, report writing would probably be the first to go. Compared with letters and memos, reports take much more time to research, cover more territory in greater depth and call for more detailed analysis.

The time and effort invested in producing a report only make sense if the report passes this fundamental test: Is it useful to its audience? This will depend on the quality of the report's content and on its intelligibility to the reader—which depends, in turn, on how well the report is written.

The consequences of bad report writing can be disastrous: Such reports are often neither read nor used. For instance, one company invested heavily in developing a new product only to learn that one of its researchers had developed it five years earlier. Unfortunately, the researcher had buried the discovery twenty-five pages deep in his report. Horror stories such as this abound. For that reason, the importance of well-written reports cannot be overemphasized.

Different companies use different approaches to report writing. Some require that everyone follow the same format; others leave such matters up to the individual writer. Regardless of the approach taken, a report breaks down in four basic parts: summary, background, body, and conclusions or recommendations.

In writing each section, one law applies: Each paragraph should contain one topic sentence. The discipline of organizing a paragraph is the same discipline needed to organize an entire report. It requires a grasp of theme and idea, and the ability to bring facts together.

The key part of any report is the summary, or abstract, the part of a report in which you tell the reader what you're going to tell him. No longer than one page, the summary is the most difficult page to write; it is also the most important part of the report. It is basically the entire report in miniature.

For example, in a report recommending a new system for inventory control, the conclusion and the reasons supporting it constitute the heart of the summary. Descriptions of the present system and company requirements provide the background that puts the report in context.

Source: Edward Wakin. "Better Business Writing." Reprinted from *Today's Office*, Vol. 17, No. 1, June 1982, with permission from Hearst Business Communications, Inc. UTP Division and the author.

When carefully prepared, the summary guides both the writer and the reader through the body of a report by covering the "five Ws":

- *Who* is reporting—headquarters, a division, a section?
- *What* is the central message and theme, and what is the supporting information?
- *When* were the facts and findings gathered?
- *Where* did the research take place?
- *Why* is the content of the report important and significant?

After reading the summary, the reader should understand what the contents add up to.

Following the summary is the body, which covers the five Ws in more detail. Each of these areas should be given a clear heading and should include a description of the research in order to make the data believable. The reasons for the recommendations must be stated, in order of importance, because they sell the proposal.

When reviewing a report (or any piece of writing, for that matter), there are some key areas to examine.

Grammar, spelling and punctuation   Those with problems in these areas have known about them for some time. These people must be overly cautious and attentive, double checking everything and getting someone else to double check, as well.

Sentences and paragraphs   While no hard-and-fast rule governs the length of sentences and paragraphs, take a second look at any sentences that run over twenty-five words and paragraphs that run over two hundred and fifty words.

Do you have a tendency to be verbose? If so, assume that words can be cut and you will find them. Look for these words. Do your sentences run on and on? If so, avoid the passive voice wherever possible, as it adds unnecessary words.

Do your paragraphs get out of control? Find the topic sentence and make certain that the other sentences in the paragraph support it.

Organization   Do your paragraphs cluster together under one subtopic? Does one cluster lead to another? Is there a story line running through all the groupings of paragraphs? Careful attention to these questions will help you build a clear and meaningful document.

The writing in a report requires revision and unmerciful self-scrutiny. Once finished, a cooling-off period is essential before a final review of the work is done. Putting aside a report for a day or two allows the writer to review the end product with a cold and alert eye. The least effective time to revise is immediately after finishing a piece, for the writer is usually too close to the work.

The ultimate question in report writing is the same one facing all writers: Have you gotten the message across clearly and effectively? A yes answer justifies all the toil and trouble of writing a report.

Discussion Questions

1. Why are reports more difficult to write than letters or memos?
2. What are the key areas that should be examined when reviewing a report?
3. Why is the least effective time to revise a report immediately after completing the first draft?

Ten Report Writing Pitfalls: How to Avoid Them

Vincent Vinci

Lockheed Electronics Co., Inc., North Plainfield, NJ

The advancement of science moves on a pavement of communications. Chemists, electrical engineers, botanists, geologists, atomic physicists, and other scientists are not only practitioners but interpreters of science. As such, the justification, the recognition and the rewards within their fields result from their published materials.

Included in the vast field of communications is the report, a frequently used medium for paving the way to understanding and action. The engineering manager whose function is the direction of people and programs receives and writes many reports in his career. And therefore the need for technical reports that communicate effectively has been internationally recognized.

Since scientific writing is complicated by specialized terminology, a need for precision and the field's leaping advancement, the author of an engineering report can be overwhelmed by its contents. The proper handling of contents and communication of a report's purpose can be enhanced if the writer can avoid the following 10 pitfalls.

Pitfall 1: Ignoring Your Audience

In all the forms of communications, ignoring your audience in the preparation of a report is perhaps the gravest transgression. Why? All other forms of communication, such as instruction manuals, speeches, books and brochures, are directed to an indefinable or only partially definable audience. The report, on the other hand, is usually directed to a specific person or group and has a specific purpose. So, it would certainly seem that if one

Source: Vincent Vinci. "Ten Report Writing Pitfalls: How to Avoid Them." Reprinted from *Chemical Engineering*, December 22, 1975, with special permission from *Chemical Engineering*. Copyright © 1975, by McGraw-Hill, Inc., New York, N.Y. 10020.

knows both the "who" and the "why," then a report writer should not be trapped by this pitfall.

But it is not enough to know the who and why, you need to know "how." To get to the how, let's assume that the reader is your boss and has asked you to write a trip report. You are to visit several plants and report on capital equipment requirements. Before you write the first word you will have to find out what your boss already knows about these requirements. It is obvious that he wants a new assessment of the facilities' needs. But, was he unsatisfied with a recent assessment and wants another point of view, or is a new analysis required because the previous report is outdated—or does he feel that now is the time to make the investment in facilities so that production can be increased over the next five years? That's a lot of questions, but they define both the who and why of your trip and, more importantly, your report.

By this time you may get the feeling that I suggest you give him exactly what he wants to read. The answer is yes and no. No, I don't mean play up to your boss's likes and dislikes. I do mean, however, that you give him all the information he needs to make a decision—the pros and the cons.

I mean also that the information be presented in a way that he is acclimated to in making judgments. For example, usually, a production-oriented manager or executive (even the chief executive) will think in terms of his specialty. The president of a company who climbed the marketing ladder selling solvents will think better in marketing terms. Therefore, perhaps the marketing aspects of additional equipment and facilities should be stressed. You should also be aware that if you happen to be the finance director, your boss will expect to see cost/investment factors too.

A simple method for remembering, rather than ignoring, your audience is to place a sheet of paper in front of you when you start to write your report. On the paper have written in bold letters WHO, WHY and HOW, with the answers clearly and cogently defined. Keep it in front of you throughout the preparation of your report.

Pitfall 2: Writing to Impress

Nothing turns a reader off faster than writing to impress. Very often reports written to leave a lasting scholarly impression on top management actually hinder communication.

Generally, when a word is used to impress, the report writer assumes that the reader either knows its meaning or will take the trouble to look it up. Don't assume that a word familiar to you is easily recognized by your reader. I recall a few years ago, there was a word "serendipity" which became a fashionable word to impress your reader with. And there was "fulsome," and "pejorative," and more. All are good words, but they're often misused or misapplied. They were shoved into reports to impress, completely disregarding the reader. Your objective is that your reader comprehend your thoughts, and there should be a minimum of impediments to understanding—understanding with first reading, and no deciphering.

Unfortunately, writing to impress is not merely restricted to use of obscure words but also includes unnecessary detail and technical trivia. Perhaps the scientist, chemist, chemical engineer and others become so intrigued with technical fine points that the meaningful (to your audience) elements of a report are buried. And quite often the fault is not so much a lack of removing the chaff from the grain but an attempt to impress the reader technically. Of course there exist reports that are full of technical detail because the nature of the communication is to impart a new chemical process, compound or technique. Even when writing this kind of report, you should eliminate any esoteric technical facts that do not contribute to communication, even though you may be tempted to include them to exhibit your degree of knowledge in the field.

Pitfall 3: Having More Than One Aim

A report is a missile targeted to hit a point or achieve a mission. It is not a barrage of shotgun pellets that scatter across a target indiscriminately.

Have you ever, while reading a report, wondered where or what it was leading to—and even when you finished you weren't quite sure? The writer probably had more than one aim, thereby preventing you from knowing where the report was heading.

Having more than one aim is usually the sign of a novice writer, but the pitfall can also trip up an experienced engineer if he does not organize the report toward one objective.

It is too easy to say that your report is being written to communicate, to a specific audience, information about your research, tests, visit, meeting, conference, field trip, progress or any other one of a range of activities that may be the subject. If you look at the first part of the sentence, you will see that "specific audience" and "information" are the key words that have to be modified to arrive at the goal of your report. For instance, you must define the specific audience such as the "members of the research council," "the finance committee" or "the chief process engineer and his staff."

Secondly, you need to characterize the information, such as "analysis of a new catalytic process," "new methods of atomic absorption testing" or "progress on waste treatment programs." You should be able to state the specific purpose of your report in one sentence: e.g., "The use of fibrous material improves scrubber efficiency and life—a report to the product improvement committee."

When you have arrived at such a definition of your purpose and audience, you can then focus both the test results and analysis toward that purpose, tempered with your readers in mind.

The usual error made in writing reports is to follow the chronology of the research in the body of the report with a summary of a set of conclusions and recommendations attached. The proper procedure to follow is to write (while focusing on your report goal) the analysis first (supported by test essentials or any other details), then your introduction or summary—sort of reverse chronology. But be sure that your goal and audience are clearly known, because they become the basis of organizing your report.

Pitfall 4: Being Inconsistent

If you work for an international chemical firm, you may be well aware of problems in communicating with plant managers and engineers of foreign installations or branches. And I'm not referring to language barriers, because for the most part these hurdles are immediately recognized and taken care of. What is more significant is units of measure. This problem is becoming more apparent as the United States slowly decides whether or not to adopt the metric system. Until it is adopted, your best bet is to stick to one measurement system throughout the report. Preferably, the system chosen should be that familiar to your audience. If the audience is mixed, you should use both systems with one (always the same one) in parentheses. Obviously, don't mix units of measure because you will confuse or annoy your readers.

Consistency is not limited to measurements but encompasses terms, equations, derivations, numbers, symbols, abbreviations, acronyms, hyphenation, capitalization and punctuation. In other words, consistency in the mechanics of style will avoid work for your reader and smooth his path toward understanding and appreciating the contents of the report.

If your company neither has a style guide nor follows the general trends of good editorial practice, perhaps you could suggest instituting a guide. In addition to the U.S. Government Printing Office Style Manual, many scientific and engineering societies have set up guides which could be used.

Pitfall 5: Overqualifying

Chemical engineers, astronomers, geologists, electrical engineers, and scientists of any other discipline have been educated and trained to be precise. As a result, they strive for precision, accuracy, and detail. That tends to work against the scientist when it comes to writing. Add to that the limited training received in the arts, and you realize why written expression does not come easily.

Most reports, therefore, have too many modifiers—adjectives, clauses, phrases, adverbs and other qualifiers. Consider some examples: the single-stage, isolated double-cooled refractory process breakdown, or, the angle of the single-rotor dc hysteresis motor rotor winding. To avoid such difficult-to-comprehend phrases, you could in the first example write "the breakdown of the process in single-stage, isolated double-cooled refractories," and in the second, "the angle of the rotor winding in single-rotor dc hysteresis motors can cause . . .," and so on. This eliminates the string of modifiers and makes the phrase easier to understand.

Better still, if your report allows you to say at the beginning that the following descriptions are only related to "single-stage, isolated double-cooled refractories" or "single-rotor dc hysteresis motors," you can remove the cumbersome nomenclature entirely.

In short, to avoid obscuring facts and ideas, eliminate excessive modifiers. Try to state your idea or main point first and follow with your qualifying phrases.

Pitfall 6: Not Defining

Dwell, lake, and barn, are all common words. Right? Right and wrong. Yes, they are common to the non-scientist. To the mechanical engineer, dwell is the period a cam follower stays at maximum lift; to a chemical engineer, lake is a dye compound; and to an atomic physicist, a barn is an atomic cross-sectional area ($10-^{24}cm^2$).

These three words indicate two points: first, common words are used in science with other than their common meaning; and second, terms need to be defined.

In defining terms you use in a report, you must consider what to define and how to define. Of the two, I consider what to define a more difficult task and suggest that you review carefully just which terms you need defined. If you analyze the purpose, the scope, the direction and your audience (reader/user), you will probably get a good handle on such terms.

"How to define" ranges from the simple substitution of a common term for an uncommon one, to an extended or amplified explanation. But whatever the term, or method of definition, you need to slant it both to the reader and to the report purpose.

Pitfall 7: Misintroducing

Introductions, summaries, abstracts and forewords—whatever you use to lead your reader into your report, it should not read like an exposition of a table of contents. If it does, you might as well let your audience read the table of contents.

The introduction, which should be written after the body of the report, should state the subject, purpose, scope, and the plan of the report. In many cases, an introduction will include a summary of the findings or conclusions. If a report is a progress report, the introduction should relate the current report to previous reports. Introductions, then, not only tell the sequence or plan of the report, but tell the what, how and why of the subject as well.

Pitfall 8: Dazzling with Data

Someone once said that a good painter not only knows what to put in a painting, but more importantly he knows what to leave out. It's much the same with report writing. If you dazzle your reader with tons of data, he may be moved by the weight of the report but may get no more out of it than that.

The usual error occurs in supportive material that many engineers and scientists feel is necessary to give a report scientific importance. The truth is that successful scientific writing (which includes reports) is heavily grounded in reality, simplicity, and understanding—not quantity.

The simplest way to evaluate the relevancy of information is to ask yourself after writing a paragraph, "What can I remove from this paragraph without destroying its meaning and its relationship to what precedes and what will follow?" Then, ask another question, "Does my reader require all that data to comprehend, evaluate or make a decision with?" If you find you can do without excess words, excess description and excess supportive data, you will end up with a tighter, better and more informative report.

These principles should also be used to evaluate graphs, photographs, diagrams and other illustrations. Remember, illustrations should support or aid comprehension rather than being a crutch on which your report leans. The same should be kept in mind when determining just how much you should append to your report. There is no need to copy all your lab notes to show that detailed experimentation was performed to substantiate the results. A statement that the notes exist and are available will suffice.

Pitfall 9: Not Highlighting

Again, I believe the analogy of the painter applies. A good painter also knows what to highlight and what to subdue in a portrait or scene.

If you don't accent the significant elements, findings, illustrations, data, tests, facts, trends, procedures, precedents, or experiments pertinent to the subject and object of your report, you place the burden of doing so on your reader. As a result, he may consider the report a failure, draw his own conclusions, or hit upon the significant elements by chance. In any event, don't leave it up to your reader to search out the major points of your report.

Highlighting is one step past knowing what goes into your report and what to leave out (see Pitfall 8 above). All the key points of your report should define and focus on the purpose of your report. They must be included in your summary or conclusions, but these sections are not the only places to highlight. Attention should be called to key elements needed for the understanding of your material throughout the body of the report. Several methods may be used: you can underline an important statement or conclusion, you can simply point out that a particular illustration is the proof of the results of an experiment, or, as most professional writers do, you can make the key sentence the first or last sentence of a paragraph.

Pitfall 10: Not Rewriting

Did you ever hear of an actor who hadn't rehearsed his lines before stepping before an audience? An actor wouldn't chance it—his reputation and his next role depend on his performance. The engineer shouldn't chance it either. Don't expect the draft of your report to be ready for final typing and reproduction without rewriting.

Once you have judged what your report will contain and how it will be organized, just charge ahead and write the first draft. Don't worry about choosing the precise word, turning that meaningful phrase, or covering all the facts in one paragraph or section. Once you have written your first draft (and the quicker you accomplish this the more time you will have to perfect the text), you are in a better position to analyze, tailor, and refine the report as a whole. Now you are also able to focus all the elements toward your purpose and your audience.

As you begin the rewriting process simply pick up each page of your draft, scan it, and ask yourself what role the material on that page plays in the fulfillment of the report's objective and understanding. You will find that this will enable you to delete, add, change, and rearrange your material very quickly.

After you have completed this process, then rewrite paragraph by paragraph, sentence by sentence, and word by word. Your final step is to repeat the procedure of examining each page's contents. When you are satisfied with its flow and cohesion, then you will have a good report, one you know will be well received and acted upon.

Discussion Questions

1. Why is the audience analysis different for a report than for other forms of communication such as instruction manuals, speeches, and brochures?

2. To which of the three pitfalls is the statement, "Writing to Impress Rather than Express" most related?

3. Which of the ten pitfalls mentioned do you think would be the most difficult to avoid? Why?

Communicating With Graphics: A Picture Can Be Worth a Thousand Words

Steven Golen
Louisiana State University, Baton Rouge, LA

Gavin L. Ellzey
Hewlett-Packard, Jackson, MS

Currently, the computer industry is growing at a rapid pace. Because of the technological advances, the cost of computer hardware (equipment) and software (programs) is declining steadily. This cost decline enables even small businesses and individuals to use the computer.

An Increasing Need for Graphics

With technological advances comes the increased volume of data. Although managers find themselves buried under stacks of computer printouts containing important data, the volume often makes it difficult to identify certain trends or patterns in these data. Because these managers are decision makers, they are under a great deal of pressure and time constraints to read, evaluate, and interpret the data that are useful to them to make important decisions as quickly as possible.

Today, with graphics, even data on a 50-page computer printout can be condensed into one well-designed graph that fits on one page! Furthermore, when data are presented graphically, various trends and patterns can be recognized immediately. Obviously, this process greatly minimizes the mangers' decision-making time.

Before you can enjoy the benefits of computer or manually generated graphics, you need to understand the basic principles of graphic design. But how do you being? One way of approaching this design process is by answering the 5Ws and H—who, what, when, where, why, and how.

Source: This is an original essay prepared for *Readings and Cases in Business Communication.*

WHO   Who will be your intended audience? Vice-president of marketing? Shop foreman?

WHAT   What quantities do you want to measure? Inventory on hand? Sales?

WHEN   When is the time interval you want to show? Monthly or yearly comparisons? Daily trend analysis for a particular month?

WHERE   Where in your business do you want to center your analysis? One division? All the divisions?

WHY   Why do you want to analyze these quantities and their possible relationships? Do you have a purpose for the graph?

HOW   How will you present the data? Bar? Line? Pie or circle?

Matching the Graph to the Message

Managers who are very familiar with the various aspects of their businesses will probably not have too much difficulty in answering the 5Ws; however, answering the "how" question may be a little more difficult. Nevertheless, the one point to keep in mind in answering this question is that most reporting functions in business can be completed with the use of three basic types of graphs: (1) bar, (2) line, and (3) pie or circle. The computer can design and generate these and other types of graphics, such as flow charts, organizational charts, time charts, drawings, and diagrams; but these graphics are more specialized and are not used as often in business as the bar, line, and pie graphs.

The bar, line, and pie graphs depict a specific type of comparison or relationship that serves to illustrate the message you want to convey. Let's look at some examples of these types of graphs. Remember that tedious manual preparation of graphics is no longer required; incidentally, a computer generated all the graphics illustrated in these examples. Although these examples are in black and white, they could have been presented in color as well.

Bar Graphs

Bar graphs, whether horizontal or vertical, are used to show item size and quantity comparisons for two or more items. An example might be the comparison of sales of various equipment divisions for a particular company. Figure 1 is a simple, horizontal bar graph constructed from the following sales data:

SCIENTIFIC INSTRUMENT COMPANY
1981 SALES REVENUE

Division	Sales (in Millions of Dollars)
Computer systems	$374
Medical instruments	226
Calculators	109
Analytical instruments	342

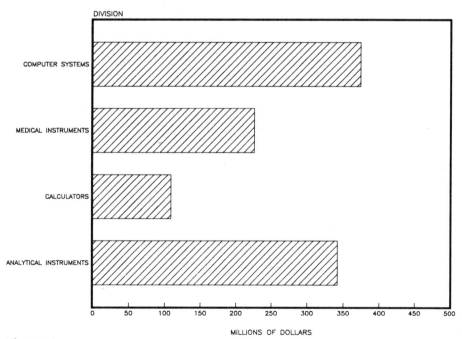

SCIENTIFIC INSTRUMENT COMPANY
1981 SALES REVENUES BY DIVISION

Figure 1

A simple horizontal bar graph.

Variations of the simple bar graph, such as grouped, subdivided, or paired, could be used to show comparisons of one or more items for a particular time series or interval. This time comparison can show how a particular quantity has changed or fluctuated over a period of time. An example of this type could be a comparison of quarterly sales over a 5 year period. Figure 2 is a grouped bar graph generated from the following sales history:

D.T.D. PERIPHERALS
5-YEAR QUARTERLY SALES HISTORY (in Millions of Dollars)

Year	Total Sales	Quarter 1	Quarter 2	Quarter 3	Quarter 4
1976	$494	$100	$204	$100	$ 90
1977	509	75	125	159	150
1978	564	264	100	110	90
1979	665	280	100	205	80
1980	600	174	176	100	150

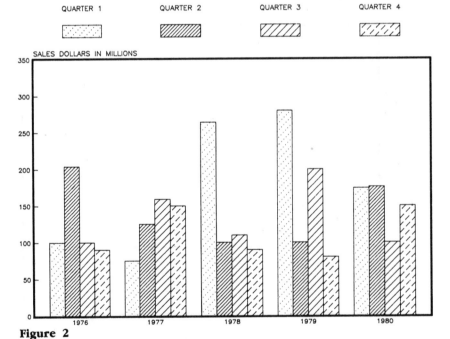

Figure 2

A grouped bar graph.

Line Graphs

Line graphs, like grouped, subdivided, or paired bar graphs, also show a time comparison. However, line graphs can be used to illustrate situations when you want to compare one or more items for a longer period of time.

For example, if you were to depict the quarterly sales history for D.T.D. Peripherals for a 10-year period using a grouped bar graph, you could imagine how cluttered the graph would be. But this is a situation where a line graph could be used more effectively to illustrate the quantities over a longer period of time.

For example, assume that HP Industries had the same 5-year quarterly sales history as D.T.D. Peripherals in the previous example. These 5 years, together with the following additional 5-year sales data, are illustrated in Figure 3:

HP INDUSTRIES
10-YEAR SALES HISTORY (in Millions of Dollars)

Year	Total Sales	Quarter 1	Quarter 2	Quarter 3	Quarter 4
1971	$301	$101	$ 60	$ 40	$100
1972	400	75	95	100	130
1973	401	80	71	150	100
1974	400	200	100	70	30
1975	511	105	20	306	80

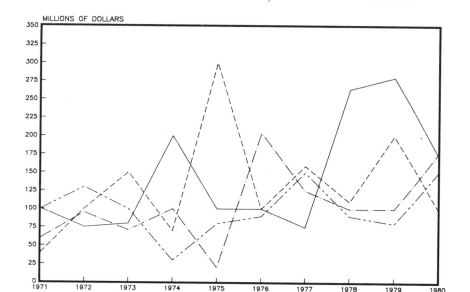

Figure 3

A line graph.

Pie or Circle Graphs

Pie or circle graphs are useful in situations when you want to show a comparison of components or parts in their relationship to a single total or whole. For example, you might want to show a comparison of how the sales from each division contributed to the total company sales. Whether you use percentages or absolute numbers (i.e., actual sales dollars), you should remember to show no more than seven or eight components or parts. Using the following divisional sales history, you can construct the pie graph shown in Figure 4.

HP MANUFACTURING COMPANY
1980 SALES BY DIVISION

Division	Percent of Sales
Computer systems	46.2
Analytical instruments	38.5
Medical instruments	15.4

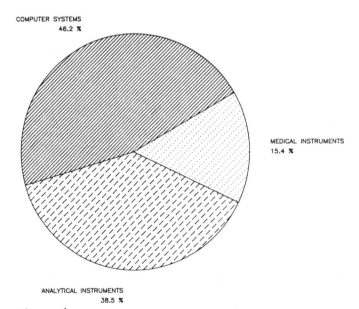

HP MANUFACTURING COMPANY
1980 SALES DOLLARS BY DIVISION

COMPUTER SYSTEMS
46.2 %

MEDICAL INSTRUMENTS
15.4 %

ANALYTICAL INSTRUMENTS
38.5 %

Figure 4
A pie or circle graph.

Although the pie graph shows an effective component comparison of a single total, what do you do when you want to show a component comparison of divisional sales by quarter? Obviously, you could prepare a pie graph for each quarter, but these four pie graphs would not be as effective as a 100 percent subdivided or component bar graph. This bar graph is more suited for multiple component comparisons because the bars representing each quarter can be placed adjacent to each other, while occupying less space.

Conclusion

The use of graphics, especially computer graphics, can provide a powerful tool for management decision making. Determining the type of comparison or relationship and selecting the proper graphic format to illustrate the comparison, requires careful thought and planning in the graphics design process. Poorly designed graphics that do not clearly convey the messages you want to make are not useful decision-making tools. When the graphics illustrate the points you want them to make, however, managers will be able to increase their productivity and become more effective decision makers.

Discussion Questions

1. What is the major purpose for using graphics in reports? Are there any other benefits? What are they?

2. Why is it important to understand the basic principles of graphic design?

3. Discuss the rationale behind using bar, line, and pie or circle graphs. Give an example of when each would be used.

Part IV

Cases

My-Sun Seeks Venture Capital

C. Glenn Pearce
Virginia Commonwealth University, Richmond, VA

Three years ago, you and your sister got into the solar energy business by forming My-Sun Systems, a partnership. You started making solar panels in a garage behind your sister's home in Chevy Chase, Maryland. You set up a distribution system and began selling your system to heat hot water tanks and for general heating and air conditioning in homes and businesses. This year, net profits were $375,000 on sales of $1.5 million. You have 20 employees and now rent a 20,000 square foot warehouse across town in addition to the 5,000 square feet in your sister's garage.

You have been successful during a period of general depression in the industry because you have a unique, patented conversion system. You can install your system in any home or business regardless of its location or the type of heating and air conditioning system in use. Your products are superior quality, priced low, and you guarantee a 30 percent reduction in energy costs the first year. The system will pay for itself within 4 years.

So far, you have reinvested most of your profits in the business. You have another $200,000 to invest but need $1.2 million more to centralize your operations, expand production, and strengthen your distribution system. You apply for loans with five local banks, but they turn you down. They know that the industry is depressed and are not convinced that your sales will continue to grow. You are unable to convince them that your conversion system is as good as it is.

You decide to seek venture capital through Venture Capital Associates in Bethlehem, Pennsylvania. VCA is an association that screens applications such as yours for prospective investors. Write a letter/report to the company about your plans and give them an overview of the history of your firm. Do not send any financial statements at this time, but do offer to send more information if they think your venture is worth pursuing further. You are willing to incorporate and offer stock for the capital you need or to offer a limited partnership.

To Build or Not to Build?

R. Jon Ackley
Virginia Commonwealth University, Richmond, VA

You have been asked by your employer, Chesterfield Home Builders (CHB), to conduct a survey of homeowners in one of the subdivisions built by CHB. Many of the residents of that subdivision have indicated a desire to have a recreation area developed by CHB. This recreation area would be on the flood plain behind the subdivision.

Your employer would like to know how all the residents of the subdivision feel about such a recreation area. Specifically, CHB wants to know how much each homeowner is willing to pay as the initial assessment for the construction costs, how much each family is willing to pay as annual fees for upkeep, and what facilities are desired.

To carry out the research, you design a questionnaire to solicit the opinions of the homeowners. After collecting and tabulating the questionnaires, you find that 56 percent want a recreation area, 37 percent oppose a recreation area, and the remaining homeowners have no opinion. For those homeowners who want the recreation area, the average (mean) amount they are willing to pay "up front" is $500. On the average, they would be willing to pay $150 per family as annual assessments. In order of preference (respondents could check more than one), the facilities preferred were swimming pool (92 percent), tennis courts (83 percent), all-purpose sports field (78 percent), and jogging trails (34 percent).

Several of the homeowners who did not desire a recreation area indicated on their questionnaires that they would go to court to block such a move if the recreation area were located behind their property. Other homeowners who did not want a recreation area said they would sell their homes and move if CHB attempted to assess them for the construction of such an area.

Questions

1. Write the "statement of the problem" for this study.
2. Construct a questionnaire that would have provided the information presented above.
3. Write a memo of transmittal that would accompany your report. Be sure to include major findings and conclusions.
4. Develop the outline around which the report would be written.

Automation and Telecommunications

One article in Part IV introduced the relationship between communications and technology. This part includes four articles that discuss this rapidly evolving relationship. In his article, "Business Communication in the Automated Office," Raymond W. Beswick describes how technology is affecting both oral and written communication. Among the technologies discussed are electronic mail, voice recognition, optical disk memory, voice-store-and forward, and videoconferencing. The article describes how each of these technologies affects communication.

Can we expect computers to write in the near future? Lee Dembart addresses this question in his article, "Computers as Writers: Bad Reviews." Communication is a complex, human process which computers may model; however, he concludes that only humans will be able to originate and adapt the language to accomplish the process of communcation.

Betsy Emish Stevens presents the results of a study on one of the oldest forms of technologically mediated communications—telephone conversations. In "Improving Telephone Communication," she states that most people do not understand or know how to use many of the telephone mechanisms to their best advantage. She suggests that most people need additional training on the use of the telephone.

In the article, "How to Overcome Mike Fright," H. Lon Addams states that many managers do not use dictation equipment because of the fear it creates. "Mike Fright" can be overcome by practicing the five-step plan of attack presented in this article.

Business Communication in the Automated Office

Raymond W. Beswick

Harwick Word Processing Consultants, Ltd., Edmonton, Alberta, Canada

This article examines office automation technologies to assess their impact on the traditional business communication techniques. Among those discussed are electronic mail, voice recognition, optical disk memory, voice store-and-forward, and videoconferencing.

Written Communication

Business Communication is a system that involves a seven-step process for written communications. The steps are:

1. Creation—the author does the thinking and research.
2. Capture—the ideas are transferred from the author's mind and put into a form which others can use.
3. Keyboarding—the document is transformed into "typewritten" form. At this point there is an editing "loop" in the system where the author reconsiders the draft and makes changes. This step ends with the final keyboarding of the document and its approval.
4. Expansion—multiple copies of the document are made for addressees and files.
5. Distribution—documents are delivered to addressees and files.
6. Storage—the document is filed for future retrieval.
7. Disposal—the final step, the document is destroyed.

This Business Communication System describes the life cycle of a written communication. Each of these seven steps has and will be affected by technological advances as described in the following discussion.

Source: Raymond W. Beswick. "Business Communication in the Automated Office." Reprinted by permission of the author.

123

Typewriter

The first modern advance in written business communication was the typewriter. By comparison to handwritten documents, typewritten documents allow for a consistently high-quality final product, reduced production time, and reduced storage requirements.

Dictation Equipment

The next advance was dictation equipment. Dictation speeded up the capture process and drove down the cost for this step. Voice dictation is faster—and, thereby, less expensive—than either handwriting or dictating to a secretary. The equipment has become progressively more sophisticated but the basic idea remains the same: to create a voice recording for transcription later.

Word Processing Equipment

The latest advance is word processing. Word processors are computer-based typewriters. By allowing manipulation of the text in electronic form, word processors facilitate error correction and such editing tasks as changing format, inserting, deleting, and moving text. Word processors make it easy to adapt major and minor changes in text, and (with judicious editing) most text becomes better with revision. There are already computer programs in existence which edit documents for spelling, grammar, clichés, readability, structure, and the like.

The word processor's ability to store blocks of text and recall them facilitates creation. This technique, often referred to as "boilerplating," allows authors to select and arrange text prepared in advance. Examples would be the standard paragraphs used by lawyers to create wills and the standard paragraphs used by airlines to answer customer complaints. The creation phase is shortened because someone has already done much of the audience analysis, content development, and writing style refinement.

Another use of stored text is the form letter. Rather than assembling boilerplate paragraphs to create a unique document, the author selects the text of an entire letter. Examples of such letters are the standard rejection letter sent to the unsuccessful job applicants and the letters about overdue accounts. The text of these can also be customized by inserting information to suit individual circumstances. Because the boilerplate and form letter text will be used again and again, it would be wise—and cost effective—for a business to spend a good deal of care in creating such text.

Electronic Mail

Another current technology is facsimile transmission or "Electronic Mail." This allows any kind of document—handwritten, typewritten, with graphics or with pictures—to be transmitted electronically from one place to another, usually over telephone lines.

Many very sophisticated electronic mail systems exist which, for example, read the address list of a document and automatically send copies to addressees by dialing up their "electronic mail boxes." These systems use computers to perform the tasks of electronic expansion and distribution.

Voice Recognition

Perhaps the most exciting advance will be in voice recognition where computers will recognize the spoken word and store it as typed text. Likely, authors will dictate to a machine which records their voice like a dictating machine and simultaneously stores the spoken words as typed text. Subsequently, a secretary would listen to the voice recording while checking the computer's typed version. The effect on the Business Communication System is to combine capture and keyboarding. This should reduce the need for shorthand dictation and increase the need for machine dictation skills in producing written communications.

Acceptance of machine dictation has been slow for a variety of reasons. It requires a change in the behavior of users who are often neither well trained in written communication nor in using dictation equipment. Future technology will likely force people to learn to dictate. While voice recognition is in use today for applications requiring limited vocabularies, large vocabulary systems will be widely available in the late 1980s.

Graphics

New technologies will allow graphics such as pie charts and engineering drawings to be created right along with the text, which will lead to their increased use. Indeed, many computer systems have software which takes data and turns them into graphic displays; consequently, rather than viewing the raw data, users view the graphic displays. Training is necessary for the effective use of graphics.

Printers/Videodisplays

New printer and videodisplay technologies will require communicators to have a knowledge of what are the current "phototypesetting" concerns. Output will no longer be confined to "typewriter" quality material. Rather, it will be produced the way books or newspapers are produced, in typeset quality. Video display terminals and printers are already in use which can produce the wide range of graphic and typesetting outputs described. While some of the output will be standardized within an organization, it will still be necessary to train communicators in layout, the best applications of various line lengths, point sizes, leading, and typefaces.

Electronic Retrieval

Electronic mail handles expansion and distribution, but what about storage and retrieval? Any document created on the computer will be filed and indexed by the computer. Virtually anyone in an organization could have access to all documents—unless prevented from doing so by some kind of security.

This suggests several possibilities for business. Examples of good writing could be flagged for reference by those creating similar documents. It is a common practice for employees to go to the files and search for a similar document before they create their own. Keeping a file of good examples would be an aid in improving written communication. Another possibility is to use computer-assisted instruction to teach the writing style, guidelines, and quality standards.

When a document is to be retrieved, the computer will be given a series of attributes and will find documents with those attributes. Typical attributes might be sender, addressees, date, file number(s), and keywords that delineate content. For example, the computer could be asked to find letters written to Bob Smith by Mary Jones in April of last year concerning networking. This high-speed, sophisticated retrieval is certainly better than searching through paper files. It is not perfect, however, and some studies indicate that only about 20 percent of required documents are found this way.

Such retrieval systems have been in use for at least a decade. They are becoming progressively faster, more flexible and less expensive. Currently, most midrange word processors are capable of automatically producing tables of contents and keyword indices to aid in retrieval from specific documents.

Optical Disk Memory

A problem exists with documents not created on the computer. A handwritten letter would have to be retyped for the computer to handle it. A typewritten letter could be "scanned" using optical character recognition devices. Most likely, however, a new storage technology called optical (video) disk memory would be used. The optical disk makes a photograph using a video (TV) camera and then stores it in a form which the computer can display on a video display terminal. Literally, it would be no problem to store a full-color advertisement from a magazine and then display it on a video display terminal. It is also possible to store moving images on the optical disk and to mix them with static images. You could record, in full sound, color and movement, an entire meeting and then view it on a video terminal.

Electronic Disposal

Disposal can be accomplished by computerization, too. If authors mark a disposal date on a document or if all documents in a certain file can be destroyed after a specific time has elapsed, then the computer can do the disposal automatically.

Thus, all phases of the Business Communication System are sped up by computerization; however, these technological advances do not change the basic process.

Telephone Communication

Telephones have been around for a long time, but most people still do not use them effectively. Most people fail to treat the telephone conversation as a formal communication, and so they do not prepare for it properly. Most frequently, the caller has some ill-defined objective in mind, with only a vague idea of how to accomplish that objective with the intended audience.

"Telephone Tag"

Only about one third of all business calls reach their intended audience on the first try. This problem leads to what is called "telephone tag." The first party calls and is forced to leave a message (usually "please call"), because the second party is not available to take the initial call. Often when the second party returns the call, the first party is not available so another message is left (usually "I returned the call"). This cycles continues until the tag is finally made.

Telephone Answering Devices

Existing technology can address the "telephone tag" problem by using telephone answering devices; however, a change in behavior is required. The caller should be prepared to leave a coherent message and not just a "please call." The technology, of course, should allow time for a variable-length message, not cut the caller off after 20 seconds.

Voice Store-and-Forward

A new technology called "voice store-and-forward" allows voice messages to be stored in a computer and then sent to or "picked up" by the intended recipient. The computer can switch messages to wherever the recipient happens to be, or the recipient can pick up messages using any touch-tone telephone. These messages can be permanently stored by the computer, if required.

Studies have shown that upwards of 60 percent of telephone communications are one way—typically a request for information which is not immediately available or the reply supplying such information. Rather than interrupting a person with a phone call, leave a message in a voice mailbox. The recipient can decide when to deal with messages which facilitate time management.

Face-to-Face Communication

The preferred method of transacting business is face-to-face. There may be two people involved or many—from two people meeting in a manager's office to one person making a presentation to a roomful of people. Both require planning and preparation, especially when dealing with large groups via teleconferencing.

Videoconferencing

All that advanced technologies offer is the ability to see and hear another person or persons without having to be in the same location. Videoconferencing makes use of audio and visual communication channels so that distant points can be linked into a conference situation using some form of television. Currently, national television newscasts are using videoconferencing to bring live reports from all over the world; witness the anchorman in New York discussing a situation live with a foreign correspondent in Lebanon.

Of course, conference telephone calls already exist. Many people can be connected via telephone so that all may hear and speak—but not see. Since there is no particular training afforded to conference call users, most calls are initially akin to chaos as everyone tries to talk at once.

Videoconferencing may save travel costs—both time and money—and increase managerial productivity. Very common uses for teleconferencing currently are manufacturers introducing new product lines and seminars featuring major speakers being given simultaneously in many locations.

All these electronic communication advances may lead to "telecommuting"—people remain at home and do their work using computer terminals. They do not need to go the their offices very often. Indeed, if videoconferencing becomes widespread, their visits to the office may become even less frequent. (Again, the amount of human contact required is not well researched—if you were truly "out of sight, out of mind" as a telecommuter, how much chance of promotion would you stand in comparison to someone who was actually working in the office?)

Summary

The skills necessary to participate effectively in videoconferencing will depend somewhat on the technology being used. However, basic presentation and perhaps television broadcast appearance skills will be required. In addition, further research is required to verify the types of communication suitable for videoconferencing.

Management and Organization

These new office automation technologies are not likely to swamp the traditional office overnight. Here are some of the major reasons delay is imminent.

- Cost justification is difficult. Office automation stresses the value of qualitative benefits, which are not currently widely accepted by management as a means of justifying massive capital expenditures.

- The target audience for office automation is the executive, managerial, and professional group. This group may not want to change its behavior very much. The resistance is often expressed like this, "I've been very successful doing things the way I do now. Are you sure your way is better? Can you guarantee better results?"

- Also, there is going to be a great deal of organizational resistance. Offices are social institutions, and since most office automation technologies will lessen social contacts, there is likely to be resistance. Then, too, there is the potential to monitor the work in progress—perhaps "Big Brother" will live. Also consider other practices, such as avoiding returning a phone call by saying that your secretary did not give you the message. With an electronic mail or voice store-and-forward system, this practice will become obsolete.

- And what about the "knowledge is power" axiom—will everyone truly be able to access all the information in an organization?

Conclusion

All forms of business communication will be affected by office automation and computerization. All phases of the Business Communication System for written communication will be facilitated by computerization. The computer will allow "voice mail" to augment normal telephone communications. Videoconferencing will allow face-to-face meetings to be held while the participants are separated by great distances.

The important point for business to note is that the product has not changed: one still gets an oral or written communication no matter how it might be packaged.

Regardless of the future technologies, the basic principles for creating effective business communications will apply. If people understand these principles, they will be able to adapt to whatever the future may bring. If they do not have a good grasp of the basics, then they will continue to produce ineffective business communications. The only difference will be in the speed with which all communications are created, distributed, and retrieved.

Discussion Questions

1. How does the comment, "There is no writing, only rewriting," relate to word processing equipment?

2. Do you believe that the increased technology in the office will increase or decrease the need for a level of proficiency in written communication? Why?

3. What are some of the reasons that office automation technologies may be accepted slowly in some offices?

Computers as Writers: Bad Reviews

Lee Dembart
Los Angeles Times, Los Angeles, CA

Ship sinks today.

That sentence might be a report of a naval disaster, or an order to the warehouse of a plumbing supply company.

They are biting dogs.

That sentence, standing alone, also is ambiguous. Is it a statement about ferocious canines, or about dogs under attack?

The English language abounds in such sentences. Human speakers make sense of them by inflection, by context and by applying their knowledge of the world.

Computers, on the other hand, have no knowledge of the world. As a result, except in limited cases, prodigious efforts by computer scientists to get machines to extract the meanings of ordinary written English sentences have been unsuccessful.

No Knowledge of World

The limited successes that have been achieved have all relied on severe restrictions in the subject matter under discussion in order to get around the problems first of amassing encyclopedic knowledge, and then of giving it to a machine in some usable form.

"We have not been able to build the universal understander," said Roger Schank of Yale University, one of the leading researchers in the field.

"Meaning is really in the mind of the reader and not on the paper," said Evon Greanias, who heads IBM's research in this area. The IBM program avoids the question of meaning for the time being and seeks only to analyze the syntax of the text.

Source: Lee Dembart. "Computers as Writers: Bad Reviews." Reprinted from *Los Angeles Times,* Jan 1, 1982, by permission. Copyright © 1982, *Los Angeles Times.* Lee Dembart is a *Times* Science Writer.

Language 'Too Vast'

"The language is simply too vast, there are too many meanings attributed to words, and with those meanings go varieties of syntactic properties," said Richard Kittredge of the University of Montreal, a specialist in machine translation.

Not that people aren't trying. Projects are under way across the country that seek to have machines do text analysis, write summaries, answer questions about stored information and translate from one language to another.

Many of the researchers share the belief that their successes will shed light on the workings of the language ability in humans.

But there is considerable disagreement about how the project should be carried out. Some researchers say they should determine how people do these things and then get computers to imitate them. Others say that is both unnecessary and wrong.

Some say that if they could at least have a complete knowledge of the rules of English, they would have the problem all but licked. Others say that there is no such complete description, that people don't use one and that it is chimerical to seek one.

Research continues nonetheless. As word processors replace typewriters for writing and editing, efforts are under way to harness the power of the computer as an aid in spelling, punctuation, grammar and style.

With spelling and punctuation, which follow clearly defined rules that can be applied mechanically, the efforts have succeeded. With grammar and style, the results are less impressive.

Ultimately, the goal is to get machines to do the writing themselves—once they have been told what the writer wants to say. That goal is far off.

Language translation, which has been an aim of computer scientists since the computer was invented, is still being worked on in some places. But it remains frustrated by the need to extract meaning, to understand what is being discussed.

Translation Fouled Up

In one experiment, a machine was asked to translate the sentence, "The spirit is willing, but the flesh is weak," into Russian. Its translation: "The vodka is good, but the meat is rotten."

The growth of computer data banks containing large amounts of stored information has fanned interest in so called question-answer systems. They allow users to ask a question in English and have the computer search through the information, draw inferences and come up with a reply.

At the very least, doing this requires the computer to extract what a particular passage or article or document is about.

The question is, "How can we capture the information that this paragraph contains?" said Donald E. Walker, a researcher at SRI International in Menlo Park.

"We don't really understand too well what that representation should look like," he said.

Another application of computer understanding would be in summarizing an article or document.

Schank, who is a professor of computer science and psychology at Yale, heads a team of researchers who have written programs that, for example, summarize wire service news stories about terrorism and earthquakes.

Limited Capability

The computer will read a story, tell you where the earthquake was, what it measured on the Richter scale and the extent of injuries. But if anything bizarre happened, such as a town being swallowed up, the computer skips over it.

"It doesn't know anything about towns being swallowed," Schank said.

Of the program that reads terrorism stories, Schank said, "It knows a lot about terrorism, but if you tell it about George Washington, it's not going to know what you're talking about."

All of the projects in machine understanding of language start off with grandiose plans, which have to be cut back as the complexity of the problem becomes clear.

"I had great expectations, and things have not proceeded as fast as I either expected or hoped," Walker of SRI said.

The machine translation project in Canada, which Kittredge headed for several years, was charged in 1965 with coming up with a computer to translate the proceedings of the Canadian House of Commons from English to French.

'Naively Optimistic Goal'

"This was just a naively optimistic goal," Kittredge said. "We find all sorts of encyclopedic knowledge, representation of people's feelings much, much too complicated. That sort of thing is still 30, 40, 50 years away."

Instead of translating the daily debate in the House of Commons, the Canadians have managed to translate short weather reports—believed to be the only machine translation system of any kind in use in the world.

At New York University, Naomi Sager and her colleagues have developed a machine that extracts information from patient health records at hospitals.

As in most technical fields, a special unambiguous sublanguage exists in hospital records that enables the machine to find and catalogue information about admissions, symptoms and treatment.

"We're struggling," Sager said. "But we can do it. We're testing it on a small number of documents. It's still an experimental research area."

There are so many overclaims in the computer field, she said, "that I hasten to say that there are no machines that are just taking documents in and cranking out whatever you want."

One area being investigated to help the computer is to supply it with information about what words can logically go with other words.

Consider the sentence: "I know a man with a car from France." It is a Frenchman or a Peugeot? The phrase "from France" could describe either the man or the car.

But consider these sentences: "I know a man with a car with a broken leg," and "I know a man with a car with a broken axle." There is no ambiguity. We know that cars do not have broken legs and men don't have broken axles.

"The problem is to get that information in without building in a whole encyclopedia to find out which words go with which other words," Sager said.

Limited To Specialized Subjects

"That's one of the reasons that so far we're all stuck with working in specialized subject areas," she said. "It's only there that you have pretty regular usage of what words go with what other words."

The biggest financial support for any of these projects is probably behind text analysis, which is being pursued with gusto at both IBM's Thomas J. Watson Research Center in Yorktown Heights, N. Y., and at the Bell Laboratories in Murray Hill, N. J.

IBM's approach is to do a grammatical parsing of each sentence, identifying the nouns, noun phrases, verbs, verb phrases and so on. When it cannot complete a grammatical analysis on the sentence, IBM's program, called EPISTLE, looks for one of 14 errors that it knows.

On a test of 8,400 sentences in ordinary prose, the program correctly parsed about 60% of the sentences.

Though its designers would eventually like to be able to ask the machine what a passage it has just read is about, they have had their hands full so far just trying to get the syntactic analysis to work.

"You really have to understand the whole thing to understand the sentence," said Lance Miller, an IBM psychologist who demonstrated the EPISTLE system for a visitor.

Analyzing each sentence requires several seconds. When the machine spots an error, it highlights the word or words involved. Then, on the author's request, it displays corrections or possible alternatives. The final choice is left to the author.

Then it looks for style errors, making suggestions about wordiness, questionable words, use of the passive voice and other rhetorical mistakes.

While there is general agreement among authorities about many areas of what constitutes good style, some rhetorical standards are elusive.

There is, for example, the standard of readability, which is usually measured by the average length of sentences, the average number of syllables per word and the familiarity of words.

The shorter the sentences, the smaller the number of syllables per word and the more usual the words, the greater the "readability."

However, a sentence like "He who has not has what he who has has not," which is short and consists of short, familiar words, scores high in readability, though its meaning is abstruse. (Read it as "He who has not/has/what he who has/has not.")

At the same time, a sentence like "The agricultural show featured exotic flavoring including Czechoslovakian horseradish and peppercorns" scores low in readability, though its meaning is clear.

Patricia Gingrich, a member of the technical staff at Bell Labs, said she was not particularly worried about trick sentences invented to show that a set of rules does not handle all possibilities.

"We're going on the assumption that our audience is not trying to trick us," she said. "We're not as concerned about trick sentences as people who love to stump the system might be. Yes, you can stump the system, but in real life we don't find that kind of thing very often."

Rather than trying to perfect a computer parser, which would pick up the grammatical relationships between parts of a sentence, Bell Lab's approach is to identify the part of speech of each word in a sentence.

Since many words can operate as several parts of speech, this is by no means easy, but it is much easier than a full grammatical analysis. It also means that the Bell Lab's programs, called Writer's Workbench, work very quickly but cannot spot grammatical errors.

The Bell Labs programs, which are being used by technical writers there but not yet by others, also try to spot stylistic defects and make suggestions for improving them.

But, like IBM's EPISTLE, the Bell Labs program stops short of meaning.

"We feel that meaning is a very human feature," Gingrich said. "We feel more comfortable right now with leaving the meaning and the organization up to the writer."

All of which leaves open the question of whether machines do these things the way people do and whether it makes sense to try to get them to.

"I haven't found it useful to appeal to a brain model," SRI's Walker said.

But Schank of Yale took the opposing view.

"We have some pretty good ideas about how people work at this point," he said. "The question is can we get computers to model them, and so far the answer seems yes."

Gingrich of Bell Labs took the middle ground.

"We really don't know enough about how people do these things to say that what we have done models people," she said.

Discussion Questions

1. Many people look forward to the day when computers will be able to write, translate, and even think. How realistic is this expectation in the light of what is presented in this article?

2. The humorous anecdote about "The spirit is willing, but the flesh is weak" is a good example of the inappropriate use of synonyms. Take a couple of old sayings and rework them in the same way. What does this tell us about the problems of relying on computers?

3. Will computers ever replace people as writers? Defend your opinion of why this will or will not happen in the near future.

Improving Telephone Communication

Betsy Emish Stevens
University of Michigan, Ann Arbor, MI

The telephone plays a crucial part in business communication, serving as a link-up between coworkers within an organization and frequently as the first contact outsiders have with the company. So much business is transacted via telephone that it would be almost impossible to speculate on the number of calls made per year. But in spite of this tremendous dependence on the telephone, it is often overlooked or forgotten when training employees to handle business transactions within and outside the office smoothly and efficiently. This is probably due to the fact that the telephone appears to be such a simple instrument, when, in fact, it amplifies any communication skills that may be lacking. Those who have examined the telephone as a medium of communication have found that telephone users tend to make the same mistakes over and over.

A study done in 1970 asked managers of one hundred and thirty-five companies which telephone habits irritated them the most when they were making or receiving calls. Those most frequently mentioned were:

- Excessive delay in answering the phone
- Failure of the responding person to identify him or herself
- Being transferred to another line without adequate explanation
- People who suddenly leave the phone without explaining why or for how long
- People who mumble or talk too loudly
- Lengthy silences on the other end of the line.[1]

Every respondent in the survey listed one of these bad habits at least once, showing that the above offenses are fairly commonplace.

The Telephone as Medium

One of the difficulties with the telephone as a communication medium is that not as much information is present as there is in a face-to-face situation. Speaking with an individual in person provides facial expressions, tone of voice and physical gestures, where the telephone offers only the voice as a clue to the more subtle aspects of the message.

Mehrabian includes the telephone in his list of seven communication mediums, which he has ranked according to what he calls "immediacy."[2] The term is used to describe the amount of personal closeness that each medium allows. Mehrabian classifies the telephone as less immediate than face-to-face speaking, or a picture-phone, but more immediate than telegrams, letters, messengers or a carefully leaked message.

Thinking of the telephone in this way allows us to realize both its advantages and limitations. As a system of communication, the telephone is unequaled in providing accurate information which can be immediately verified. It allows for instant interaction, i.e., two people can hear each other's voices, interrupt, and ask for clarification.

It should be remembered that in business we basically have three communication alternatives: to put the message in writing, to telephone, or to speak directly to the other person. In certain circumstances, choosing which medium to use can be a crucial decision. One fairly recent article on the subject points out that in a business situation, choosing a medium randomly or haphazardly can result in (1) ineffective communication, (2) discomfort to the sender, or (3) needless inconvenience or embarrassment to the receiver.[3] It concludes that the telephone is best used for simple-question quick-reply transactions where one does not need to talk to a particular person, or when one wants to pave the way for a difficult encounter.

An Updated Study

In an attempt to further study which telephone habits are considered most irritating, a survey was taken of 60 different office workers at the University of Michigan. Participants in the survey were selected at random: some were clerical workers and others held administrative positions. Although the randomness excluded an exact breakdown, an attempt was made to keep a fairly even balance between male and female workers. All 60 were given sheets of paper with instructions to write down any incidents they could recall where other people had annoyed them with certain telephone habits. Responses were hand-collected from participants about an hour later.

Results showed that of the 60 respondents, 56 were able to remember such incidents. Only four people said they were completely happy with the communication habits of others. This means that 94% mentioned at least one annoying telephone experience, while only 6% felt no dissatisfaction. The percentage of people who felt annoyed would indicate that there are significant problems with the way many people use the telephone and that further investigation into the causes of telephone habits would be beneficial.

Responses from this survey can be grouped under three different categories. The first deals primarily with general operating problems, the next with speech communication problems, and the final category with what we will call interpersonal problems, that is, ineffective communication styles. These statements are not intended to be in any order, nor do they encompass a complete listing of all responses obtained, but represent the most common complaints of the telephone users.

Group I

"I was put on hold for an inordinate amount of time . . . I would much rather have them take my number and call me back."

"People have put me on hold for ten minutes or more or transferred me all over."

"To call a number and immediately be put on hold without the courtesy of being told they will get right back to me."

"Some people leave you waiting and do not cut in to tell you the line is still busy."

"To be put on hold before they hear what I have to say—what if the call is coast-to-coast?"

"People that call, find they have the right office, then put me on hold."

"To be put on hold and then cut off."

"Chewing gum or food like a cow in my ear."

"People that eat while they speak."

"Having a radio blaring in the background."

"Slapping the phone down on the desk instead of putting it down gently or pressing the 'hold' button."

"Shuffling papers into the mouthpiece."

"Some people don't realize I can hear them while I'm waiting for a professor to answer and they're making smart remarks."

"Recorded music, followed by a recording, followed by a long pause—ten minutes later I get to talk to a real person."

"Very annoying to have someone talk to someone else while talking to you on the phone."

Group II

"Extremely loud or soft speakers."

"A patronizing tone of voice."

"Individuals who speak either too fast or too loud."

"A phone being hung up in my ear before the party says 'thanks' or 'good-by.'"

"Mumbling in a low voice."

"People who hem and haw over the phone—long periods of indecisiveness prolong a call."

Group III

"Being asked personal questions not pertinent to the topic being discussed."

"People who, when things don't go their way, scream and yell."

"People who get mad when you ask them to spell their name over."

"When people are unfriendly and don't offer any help."

"An angry complaint before the facts can be ascertained."

"People at the other end who cannot answer your inquiry, don't know who can, and don't seem to care very much whether you get any help or not."

"When a person does not identify himself or herself."

"Pulling rank—telephone mannerism that make me feel they have little regard for me as an individual."

"A person's unwillingness to say 'I don't know.' Also passing on misinformation."

"A hasty and curt response."

"Being passed from person to person, none of whom have any answers."

"People who sound like they're doing me a favor by answering the phone."

Results: Attentiveness Is the Key

The communication problems listed in the first group all have to do with operational aspects of the telephone. Probably almost everyone assumes he or she can operate a telephone effectively because picking up and dialing is so simple. The real problem is that most people do *not* understand or know how to use many of the telephone mechanisms to their best advantage. The "hold" button, for example, is an invaluable device for any busy office. It allows a secretary to answer more calls than he or she normally could handle at one time and to delegate them according to importance to the appropriate people.

Interestingly enough, abuse of the hold mechanism was the primary complaint in the survey. Forty-one percent of the respondents had a gripe regarding its use. This is not surprising when one considers that the nature of a hold button symbolizes power. It carries with it the implicit message, "You must wait to talk to me because I am more important." In certain corporations, one receives a hold button after achieving a particular rank. Thus, when people are kept waiting on hold, the message they receive is that they are not very important—at least, not important enough to warrant a quick response. The best way to solve this problem is to train employees on the use of the hold button and make certain they realize the importance of staying in communication with those who must be kept on hold for lengthy periods of time.

Other complaints in Group I are caused by the telephoner's apparent unawareness of the transmitting power of the telephone mouthpiece. Ten percent of the people surveyed complained of hearing eating and chewing noises. Since most people consider it bad manners to eat and carry on a conversation with someone who is not eating, it is interesting that many do it while on the telephone. They are either unaware that the microphone is transmitting the eating noises, or are rationalizing that it is all right to continue eating since the other person cannot see them.

Mehrabian's concept of immediacy probably applies to this situation. The person on the other end cannot be seen and is therefore less immediate, so the one party does not feel that he or she should stop eating. For the person on the other end, the chewing noises not only sound unpleasant, but often obscure the message, since only audio cues are being transmitted.

The last complaint in Group I is primarily due to the person's inattention to the other party. Suddenly breaking off a conversation to turn and talk to another is normally considered a rude gesture and would not be done, yet again, people often do things on the telephone which they would not do if the other person was physically present. Good telephone communications training would make the calling party more aware of the way he or she communicates with clients, and cognizant of the fact that attentiveness is the key to communication transactions.

Statements found in the second group reflect problems with the caller's speaking style. Again, not knowing enough about the strength of the speaker microphone seems to be a problem, along with the fact that many people need training in voice modulation. Also included in this group are statements reflecting a caller's improper sign-off techniques. Gumperz and Hymes studied conversation openings and closings on the telephone and observed that there are certain "rules" which are expected to be followed.[4] One of these is that the person initiating the call speaks first, and he or she is expected verbally to sign off at the end. Parties who do not say "good-by" violate this rule and leave the other person in a state of uncertainty.

Because recipients of the message receive only voice cues, a greater emphasis is placed on how the speaker sounds. Tone of voice, pitch, rate, and volume all add a dimension to the words being spoken. Training in speaking techniques, along with a better understanding of how the other person perceives the call, would undoubtedly help some office workers become better communicators.

Statements in the last group reflect interpersonal problems between the two parties. Some of these complaints would probably be perceived as offensive even if the two parties were face to face in conversation. People who raise their voices or lose their tempers will invariably offend the other person regardless of the medium. This reflects more of a personality problem than difficulty with the telephone.

Most people get offended when they ask for information and the other person does not seem helpful, but using the telephone compounds the problem. Because they cannot see the other person, there seems to be a tendency to be more suspicious and think of the other person in negative terms. Several people in this study, although speaking with just one person, referred to the other party as "they." In other words, the person mentally translated the other party into "The Company" or "The Organization." Because this mental transference frequently occurs, making the person answering the telephone the representative of the company, business and industry would profit by placing greater emphasis on training their employees to be effective telephone communicators.

Other complaints in this last group have to do with people who say the right words, but communicate a different message with the tone of voice. Because the other person has no way of picking up on nonverbal cues, he or she relies completely on sound. Consequently, a tired office worker may sound curt or disinterested when he or she is really trying to be helpful. There are several techniques that individuals can use to improve the sound of their voice. These include gesturing while speaking, sitting up straight, improving the voice range, and attempting to emphasize friendliness.[5]

This study was not so much an attempt to determine office personnel's ideas about offensive telephone communication practices, as to collect types of responses and draw observations from them. For the most part, it appears that these communication problems grow out of a lack of knowledge about the telephone, poor speaking habits and a lack of interpersonal sensitivity. All of these problems could be remedied through telephone communications training, and office managers would do well to make it a part of the standard training package for office workers.

References

1. Lester Marryshow, "Check Your Telephone Manners," *Supervisory Management,* Vol. 15 (May 1970): 22–24.

2. Albert Mehrabian, *Silent Messages* (Belmont, California: Wadsworth Publishing Co., Inc., 1971), p. 11.

3. Jane Bensahel, "Choosing the Right Medium for Your Message," *International Management,* Vol. 31 (May 1976): 40.

4. John Gumperz and Dell Hymes, eds., *Directions in Sociolinguistics* (New York: Holt, Rinehart & Winston, 1972), p. 346.

5. Cathy Handley, "Get Rid of Your Bad Telephone Habits," *Nation's Business,* Vol. 63 (May 1975): 82–84.

Discussion Questions

1. Describe the information which is not present when using the telephone that is available in a face-to-face conversation.

2. What did Mehrabian mean by immediacy? How does the telephone rate in terms of immediacy?

3. Summarize the results of the University of Michigan study that is discussed in this article.

How to Overcome "Mike Fright"

H. Lon Addams

Commerical Security Bank, Salt Lake City, UT

"I've been dictating to my secretary for years. Why should I dictate into an impersonal piece of machinery? My secretary knows how I want to say things, knows my jargon, and takes care of all the punctuation and grammar problems"

"Dictate? Never! I write out everything—every comma and period. I get it right the first time! Why should I waste my time by editing my secretary's mistakes? Besides, I've been doing it my way for years and the work gets out."

These are natural responses of many managers when faced with the introduction of dictation equipment. Yet even after they are told of the efficiencies this equipment will bring, why do such managers get so agitated when faced with the prospect of switching to machine or telephone dictation methods?

The answer is simple: *mike fright.*

"My voice hesitates and cracks when I try dictating into a microphone," admits one honest manager. Another exclaims, "I'm not about to let the company secretaries see that I don't know how to dictate!" Still another truthful soul admits the *most* prevalent reason for not dictating into a hand-held device: "I just *freeze* when I pick up the mike!"

If any of these responses sound familiar, be assured your reaction is only natural. After all, how often do you speak into a device that doesn't respond? How often do you indicate correct spelling and proper punctuation symbols in a face-to-face conversation?

However valid these arguments may seem, the time-saving benefits of machine or system dictation cannot be overlooked. An "average" manager communicates 10 words per minute by writing out his message and 20 words per minute by using a secretary and shorthand. However, 40 words a minute can be communicated by using dictating and transcribing machines, and 60

Source: H. Lon Addams. "How to Overcome 'Mike Fright.'" Reprinted from *Management World,* December 1980, by permission of the Administrative Management Society.

words per minute can be related by using a dictating device coupled with a sophisticated word processing/dictation system. Thus, by using some form of dictating equipment, a manager can double or quadruple his output, depending on whether he or she is presently using shorthand or longhand.

While many managers may be aware of such economics, they will rationalize that their way is better because they are familiar with it and it works just fine. But, the real reason why dictation is avoided is because of a lack of confidence in the ability to dictate effectively into a mechanical device.

How to Overcome Fear

To overcome "mike fright," try the following five-step plan of attack to build confidence in your dictating ability:

1. Decide your message *objective.*
2. Determine your *approach.*
3. *Outline* the content.
4. *Dictate* the message.
5. *Listen* to your dictation.

A short explanation and example will best illustrate how you can use these steps. Assume you need to send a letter to Lee Cannon, explaining that he was hired for a recent opening on your staff.

Decide your Objective   In this example, you want to express positive news and relate important hiring facts. You want Cannon to accept your offer.

Objective: Dictate a congratulatory letter to Cannon. Cultivate a "yes" response.

Determine Your Approach   Before dictating, consider reader reaction to your message and adjust the message accordingly. The tone of the message and the pattern of organization content cause reader reaction to be positive or negative.

If your message is to be in the form of a memo report to your boss, consider his or her situation and preferences. Ask yourself: does he or she expect conclusions and recommendations at the beginning of my report (direct order) or at the end (indirect order)?

If you are writing a letter, decide whether your message is good news or bad news. Good-news letters begin with the favorable message (direct order), whereas bad-news letters typically play down the unfavorable message by putting it in the middle or toward the end of the letter (indirect order).

Applying these principles to the Cannon letter, be sure to express immediately the favorable news to Cannon; consequently, begin your letter with a positive word, such as "congratulations."

Approach: Direct order.

Outline the Content   Organize your thoughts by jotting down three or four *key* words for each paragraph.

Outline:
Para. 1: Congrats/ /Asst. Admin. Mrg.
Para. 2: $14000//January 1//Joel Muir
Para. 3: Call and confirm

Dictate the Message   Look at your key words—visualize Lee sitting across from your desk and talk to him (using your predetermined approach). Try speaking a bit slower than normal, however.

Inject the unnatural element—indicate all punctuation and unusual spelling. But don't let this throw you. Actually, stopping to spell a word gives you additional time to think ahead to your next sentence.

As you dictate, utilize the assistance of the stop button or the machine's capacity to pause and wait for you (depending on the type of dictation equipment). Use this button to collect your thoughts, and replay the last few words if needed.

Here's how this sample letter would be dictated, using the AMS Simplified Letter format. Follow along with the example illustrated.

"This is Jan Jones in the Operations Department. This is a top priority, one-page letter to Lee Cannon. Please put the letter on our company letterhead; send a copy to Hal Wight (*W-i-g-h-t*) in Personnel and make a copy for my files. The address for Lee Cannon (*C-a-n-n-o-n*) is 15 Park Avenue, Chicago, Illinois, 60000. (*Subject heading*) Assistant Administrative Manager Position.

"(*Paragraph*) Congratulations! (*exclamation point*) You have been selected for the assistant administrative manager position. (*period*)

"(*New paragraph*) As we discussed, (*comma*) the starting salary is $14,000 per year. (*typist, please use figures*) (*period*) You mentioned you could start January 1, (*comma*) which is the day I would like you to report. (*period*) Please see Joel (*J-o-e-l*) Muir (*M-u-i-r*) when you arrive. (*period*)

"(*New paragraph*) Please call me to confirm your acceptance; (*semi-colon*) at that time we can discuss any questions you might have. (*period*) I look forward to working with you. (*period*)

"(*Closing*) Jan Jones . . . Chief of Operations Department . . . (*Thank you*)

Listen to Your Dictation   Before allowing your communication to be transcribed, replay your message so that you feel comfortable with your delivery and content. If you want to change a word or phrase, simply push a button on your hand device (or dial if using a telephone) and "talk over" your original words. Having dictated a bit slower than normal, you can easily inject needed punctuation or spell an unusual word. Also, if you do not like your entire message, erase it. This will save the transcriptionist much time in correcting your letter.

One final note—*practice!* Build your dictation skill by starting with short, relatively unimportant messages. By doing so, the content of the message will be neither a hindrance nor a worry, and your confidence will increase with each piece of correspondence.

Before long, you will find that you will want to dictate longer messages irrespective of length or difficulty of content. And in realizing the efficiencies gained in your correspondence work, you'll finally be able to kick the "my secretary is better" habit!

Discussion Questions

1. What is involved in the five-step plan to build confidence in dictating ability?
2. What is the purpose in giving each message a specific designation when it is dictated?
3. When should a word be spelled out by the dictator?

PART V

Cases

Dictating to the Old WP

Judie Cochran
Management Consultant, Scottsdale, AZ

Doris is a supervisor of a sales department for a major office furniture manufacturing company in the Midwest. Every six months, Doris is responsible for dictating confidential information about her subordinates' work habits so that the information can be typed and placed in the respective employees' personnel files for their review interviews.

Doris has outlined the main points she will need when dictating via her word processing dictation equipment to a transcriber in the central word processing department. The two outlines follow:

CHERRIE MARLAR Chief administrative assistant for U. S. Sales:

A. Has performed well in newly created position as of March 1.

B. Supervisory skills excellent; typing/transcription skills excellent.

C. Works well with employees and customers.

D. Punctual, willing to stay after 5 P.M. if needed to finish a project; does not complain.

E. Recommend maximum raise as sanctioned by budget limitations.

BETTE KICKE Sales clerk for western U. S. region:

A. Excessive errors in performance in order taking functions, especially via phone orders.

B. Excessive breaks; late for work habitually; not willing to stay after 5 P.M. if needed to finish a project.

C. Chain-smoking habits have caused two small fires to paper on desk when she leaves desk unattended and cigarette burning.

D. On several occasions has spilled coffee onto papers on desk in last few weeks.

E. Responsiveness to work load and peers seems very low.

F. Recommend 90-day probationary status; no raise.

151

Questions

1. What are the first instructions Doris will give the transcriber?
2. What instructions must be given about typing format and personnel folder layout?
3. What special words need to be spelled out carefully?
4. How does the information in the outline influence the "tone" of the evaluation?

Boiler Plate Persuasion

R. Jon Ackley

Virginia Commonwealth University, Richmond, VA

As head of Accounts Receivables for Ratchet, Inc., you find that many companies take unearned discounts on invoices which you have sent them. The terms of your discounts are 2/10, n/30. Some companies take the 2 percent discount even though they haven't paid their bill within the allotted time. Although the amount of the discount on a particular invoice may be only a few dollars, over a period of time these unwarranted discounts add up to thousands of dollars of lost income. Consequently, you frequently have to write letters to companies asking them to send you a check for the amount of the discount. In fact, you sometimes have to write two or three letters and even become a little nasty.

Because you find this a time-consuming and distasteful task, you decide to develop a series of three form letters to collect unearned discounts. In the first letter, you will remind the customer of the terms of the discount and ask for a check for the amount of the discount taken. Of course, complete details concerning the transaction—order number, date, amount of invoice, amount of discount, etc.—will need to be included.

The second letter, which will take a somewhat more forceful approach to the problem, will once again remind the customer of the terms of the discount as well as the necessary details of the original order. You, of course, want to maintain the goodwill of the customer but also feel a need to obtain the discount at this time.

The third letter in the series will indicate to the customer that further credit privileges will be suspended unless the discount is paid within 10 days. Although this is an extreme action on your part, you certainly feel justified because the customer has been so inconsiderate of your requests for payment.

Write the series of letters. But, as you compose them keep in mind that they will be stored in your new word processor, so underline all information that will have to be changed each time the letter is processed. In other words, what will be different in each letter in the series and what will be what is known as "boiler plate"?

Interpersonal Communications

The first article in this part mentions that no manager or supervisor ever believed his or her organization had an excess of interpersonal skills. To help in this area, five articles are included which discuss this critical aspect of communication. In the first article, "Learning How to Influence Others," Marvin Weisbord and C. James Maselko suggest a do-it-yourself approach to interpersonal skill development. The two basic skills discussed are supporting and confronting, both of which are necessary to be successful.

Natasha Josefowitz presents five different methods of getting through to a "difficult" person in her article, "Getting Through to the Unreachable Person." A key point made in this article is that one can reach most people, but it is important to know when to stop putting effort, time, and energy into a hopeless situation.

Empathy is an important concept in interpersonal communication. People use language and labels to demonstrate empathy in Thomas E. Harris's article, "Empathy—An Essential Ingredient of Communication."

Nonverbal communication is the topic of Stanley B. Cater's article "Actions Speak Louder than Words." Some 55 percent of communication is delivered through nonverbal behavior. This article presents six different ways in which verbal and nonverbal messages work together.

The final article in this part, "Nonverbal Communication Can Be a Motivational Tool" by John E. Baird and Gretchen K. Wieting, differs from the previous articles in that it reviews specific nonverbal cues. The reading discusses the meanings that one can attribute to the environment, proxemics, postures, and head/face/eye behaviors.

Learning How to Influence Others

Marvin R. Weisbord
C. James Maselko
Block Petrella Weisbord—Training Consultants, Ardmore, PA

While it is possible for organizations to have too many levels of management, or too many goals and objectives, we have never met a manager or supervisor who believed their organization suffered an excess of interpersonal skills. Indeed, the number-one frustration reported by managers is finding ways to influence the behavior of people they work with or for.

Those who do this easily or naturally are said to have "good interpersonal skills." Those who don't are frequently packed off to workshops and seminars.

In this article we want to suggest a do-it-yourself approach to interpersonal skill development that any manager can experiment with on the job without announcing to the world that some changes are about to be made. Over many years and dozens of workshops we have reduced the basic skills required to just two—"supporting" and "confronting."

Supporting is something you do for the *other person*. To do it well requires that you separate your judgments about what somebody else is saying from the feelings that that person is expressing. Confronting, on the other hand, is something you do for *yourself.* It requires that you accept others' wants as legitimate *and* speak up directly for you own.

Support—the ability to hear, understand, and act upon what others are saying—shows up prominently on the list of characteristics of high-performing managers studied by Rensis Likert. At the same time, P. R. Lawrence and J. W. Lorsch in their widely-quoted differentiation-integration research show that confronting differences openly is the preferred method for conflict resolution in productive organizations.

In his classic case for managerial teamwork, the late Douglas McGregor graphically described what "a really good top management team" does in meetings. "The members listen to each other!" he wrote. "Every idea is given a hearing . . . even if it seems fairly extreme." At the same time, "there

157

is disagreement. The group is comfortable with this and shows no signs of having to avoid conflict . . ." In short, the members support and confront one another.

Self-Diagnosis

Improving supporting and confronting skills requires a bit of self-diagnosis. Some people are better at one skill than the other, and some have trouble with both. Take a minute to rate yourself on the accompanying scale. Which skill do you use least now? That is the one to start practicing immediately, and learn to use *together with* the skill that's better developed.

You don't need to go to workshops to practice. Instead, try the behavior we will recommend with bosses, subordinates, and peers. We're talking about using the innate abilities most people are born with: the ability to hear and be heard. Unfortunately, many of us lost these abilities on the education treadmill and must relearn them later in life as "interpersonal skills."

Think about a relationship you want to improve, a task you want to accomplish, an unsolved problem you want solved. Think about the person you must speak with, what you want him or her to do, and what your discussions with that person have been like until now. Then, consider the relationship in light of your own ability to support and confront.

SELF-DIAGNOSIS

(Circle the number that fits best for you right now.)

Receiving support from others for me is:
Embarrassing/difficult   Pleasant/easy
                   1   2   3   4   5   6   7

Offering support to others for me is:
Unnatural/rare event   Easy/frequent event
                   1   2   3   4   5   6   7

Confronting others for me is:
Clumsy/awkward/usually avoided   Natural/smooth/useful
                   1   2   3   4   5   6   7

Being confronted by others for me is:
Uncomfortable/scary/avoided   Welcome chance for dialog
                   1   2   3   4   5   6   7

What have you concluded about yourself? Check below:

_____ I'm satisfied with my skills as they are.
_____ I need to support more.
_____ I need to confront more.
_____ I need more of both skills.

An Emphasis on Resolution

In working with mangers we often ask what word "support" conjures up in their minds. Responses are surprisingly consistent: trust, help, assistance, back-up, aid, and agreement. This list is notable in two ways. First, the words are loaded with positive feelings. Second, the words always imply that the supporter *agrees* with the person being supported.

At first, it seems contradictory to managers that it is possible (and productive) to support people they don't see eye to eye with. It seems somehow dishonest to support someone with whom we disagree. But that would be to hear only the *facts* in another's statements and to miss the *feelings* behind the facts.

Consider this recent situation, for example, where the parties could not hear the feelings for the facts. The scene was a meeting among physicians and administrators of a hospital to work out a new practice plan.

Administrator #1: "The plan we want you to accept is fair, reasonable, and essential to the survival of this hospital."

Physician #1: "I think it's a threat to our practice. We won't have control over the management of our patients."

Administrator #1: "No, it's not a threat. That's ridiculous. It's hardly any change at all from . . ."

Physician #2: "There's no way we can buy this plan."

Administrator #2: "Well, if that's an example of your cooperativeness, we're in serious trouble. The government is insisting . . ."

Trustee: "We *have* to have this issue resolved. I want you all to sit down together and work out a plan for the survival of this hospital."

Physician #1: "We're sitting down now!"

Trustee: "Yes, but we're not getting anywhere."

Administrator #1: "Well, if the physicians would just cooperate and try to see this thing in its true perspective . . ."

Physician #1: "Who's uncooperative? We didn't dream up this plan."

Both physicians and administrators are blaming each other and digging in their heels for a long battle. Neither side had been heard by the other. Each fuels the disagreement by treating the other's feelings as unreal or irrelevant.

So long as the antagonists hear only the facts, they are stuck with judging whether the facts are "true" and whether, therefore, they can agree and still hold on to their own integrity. This confusion between the words (facts) and the music (feelings) is the single biggest stumbling block to supporting others. Supporting can happen only if agreement is treated as a secondary matter, one to be held in abeyance, while we try to hear and understand what the other person is saying. In short, what's required is the skill of *supporting* the feelings of people with whom we disagree.

Consider this "instant replay" of the physician-administrator meeting—an event incidentally that actually took place after the group had been introduced to the concepts of supporting and confronting. The dialog, based on mutual supporting, takes a turn for the better.

The problem is unresolved. The substantive disagreements have still to be confronted. Yet the mood of the parties to work it out has changed dramatically.

Physician #1:	"We still see the plan as a threat to our practices."
Administrator #1:	"Well, that isn't what we intended. I recognize that it's a threat from your point of view, and that all of you are opposed to it. I think it *could* be a threat in the long run unless we work together to minimize the impact. Given the heat from government, I don't see many choices."
Physician #1:	"Well, we know that you need to go in this direction and that you're doing the best you can with a bad situation. However, we want a voice in this. If you're willing to take our problems into account, I think we can work out a plan to achieve what you want."

Really Listening

Sometimes the *intention* to support is evident from the start, yet people still end up behaving in ways exactly the opposite of what was intended. Consider this vignette, overheard in a factory:

Supervisor:	"I'm running late. If we don't finish this job by 5, we'll blow the contract. What'll I do?"
Office manager (who is also his friend):	"Don't sweat it. Look at the job you did last time. With a record like yours they can't fire you for one mistake."
Supervisor:	"Well that's easy for you to say. I *am* sweating it, and with a boss like mine you never know what he'll do."

| **Office manager:** | "Ah, why don't you have a cup of coffee and calm down? It'll be all right." |

The supervisor has asked his friend for help. *Intending* support, she fails him by denying his feelings ("Don't sweat it") and providing a rationalization for *not* solving his problems ("a record like yours"). In short he is advised, as a solution, to stop feeling what he feels.

In fact, the foreman *does* have a good record and won't lose his job. In fact, even if the job isn't finished by five, the contract will not be blown. It is also a fact, though, that he's running late and believes catastrophe will ensue. Those are the facts that *he* considers important. He will not feel supported unless his friend validates *his* priorities by demonstrating that he is being taken seriously. A better response would have been:

| **Supervisor:** | "I'm running late. If we don't finish this job by 5, we'll blow the contract. What'll I do?" |
| **Office Manager:** | "Yeah, I can see you're running late, and if the contract's blown that could be serious. What's the best way I can help you?" |

The office manager shows that she accepts the supervisor's feelings. Instead of providing a nonsolution, she asks how to help. If the supervisor feels supported, he will be more open to influence, on the one hand, and more capable of discovering his own solution, on the other.

There are four things people often do, *intending* to support, that are not at all supportive:

1. Give unsolicited advice. "If *I* were you, I would . . ."
2. Tell people they "*shouldn't* feel that way." Who says so? They *do* feel that way.
3. Minimize the problem. "Oh, that's not so bad. You should be glad you don't have *real* troubles. Let me tell you about *my* boss."
4. Accept the obligation to solve the problem—without being asked. "Well, the first thing you should do is get on the phone and . . ."

There are also four actions that most people will see as supportive:

1. Repeat what you've heard. "Let's see if I understand you. You're saying that . . ."
2. Put *both* facts and feelings into a statement about what has been said. "You're annoyed (feeling) with me because (fact) I haven't made the phone call yet."

3. Empathize. "I can see why you're angry in this situation. I would be too."

4. Ask the other person what, if anything, they want from you. "How can I help you with this?"

The last point is especially important. Frequently, people just want somebody to *hear* them. Simply listening often solves the problem. Offering advice, denying feelings, or proposing courses of action without being asked tells others that they have *not* been heard.

Suppose You Don't Agree?

What happens when the other person is wrong in what he or she has said or indirectly contradicts a belief or course of action important to us?

Here we need a second skill that requires us to recognize differences. This was the stage toward which the physicians and administrators in our earlier example were moving, the point at which they would confront their disagreement.

When we ask managers what the word "confront" means to them, we consistently get back words loaded with negative feelings: challenge, fight, argue, defend, battle, force. These words are consistent with only *one* of several dictionary definitions, the one that means "to face in hostility and defiance." Rarely do managers provide another, equally valid connotation—to "face squarely." This is not the same thing as challenging, arguing, or fighting.

Learning to face a difference squarely is not always easy to do. Most people find they must give up the attitude ingrained since childhood that disagreement is "bad" and avoiding conflict is "good." Paradoxically, this attitude directly contradicts an equally powerful feeling that solving problems is "good" and indecisiveness is "bad." This leads to two traps—avoiding conflict on the one hand and moving towards premature resolution on the other.

It might be helpful here to note that nonconfronters often fear the risks of genuine interaction—anger, rejection, tension, and so forth. They have a strong need to be "nice" all the time. Yet the risks of not confronting seem equally unappetizing—less power, reduced influence, lower performance, less likelihood of achieving goals.

The issue is not *whether* to confront, but rather *when* and *how* to confront skillfully. Conflict is inevitable, legitimate, and potentially useful in all important relationships.

To exploit fully the potential of conflict, however, we must also avoid rushing toward premature resolution. Conflict often starts innocently, with relatively simple differences, yet the drive to premature resolution can quickly escalate the conflict.

We now have an escalated misunderstanding—each party actively opposing the other's stand and refusing to accept the other's solution. One or the other party may hate conflict. In that case a guerilla action—delay or denial—will probably ensue.

TIPS ON CONFRONTING

1. Accept *whatever* feelings the differences generate—helplessness, anger, disappointment, elation, anticipation. Treat them as real and important for both parties.
2. Really listen to what the other person is saying, and make sure you have been heard. Call time out if you're not sure.
3. Be responsible for your own feelings. Others don't *put* feelings into us. It's unreasonable and unhelpful to blame them for what's going on inside of us.
4. Treat confronting as an exercise in rationality. It requires clarity, calmness, and patience in the presence of often strong feelings.
5. Go for a resolution both parties can live with. Don't try to *change* the other person. Let others do what they want.
6. If the issue seems unresolvable, experiment—try it one way or the other and evaluate together after a short time.

Exploring the Differences

What's called for early on is an exploration of the differences that lie between disagreement and misunderstanding. Confronting means making explicit the differences that exist between two individuals, and its success depends entirely on the ability of both parties to express their differences as strongly as possible.

There is a verbal clue that a conflict is about to escalate without sufficient exploration of differences. That clue is "but." It has no place in successful confronting.

Sales manager: "I'm a little behind on first-quarter results, maybe 8 percent short of forecast. I know you said we need to be ahead of forecast at this point. I'm not sure how much. Anyway, that's the story."

Vice-president—sales: "Well, I don't like it. You may be 8 percent behind, *but* you said eight weeks ago things were looking good. I'll never be able to explain this to my boss—he expects us to be ahead of forecast every quarter, and I expect you to be too."

Sales manager: "I didn't realize then that the new promotional displays would fall flat. Besides, marketing really let us down in sending out samples. *But* I wouldn't worry. We'll make it up in the second quarter."

Vice-president-sales:	"I want you to be ahead of forecast, no ands, ifs, or buts."
Sales manager:	"But I'm not ahead."
Vice-president—sales:	"Well, you better get ahead."

Here each party moves to cancel the other's feelings. The vice-president seeks to deny the reality of the worrisome 8 percent with a "but you said." The sales manager, in turn, has a "but" of his own. *He* wouldn't worry, even though the boss is obviously worried. Neither confronts the issues—the difference between goal and performance, the consequences for each party, the potential for resolution. It never develops that the sales manager sees the issue as a temporary slump easily overcome, nor that the vice-president may be in serious trouble with *his* boss unless he can make a convincing explanation. The parties have no resolution. The implied threat, "You better get ahead," suggests that warfare, open or underground, is where they're heading.

Imagine that each knew how important supporting the other person's position was to a productive resolution. The conversation might go something like this:

Sales manager:	"I'm a little behind on first-quarter results, maybe 8 percent short of forecast. I know you said we need to be ahead at this point."
Vice-president—sales:	"Well, I'm disappointed, and I guess you are too. I'm glad you let me know. How did it happen?"
Sales manager:	"The new promotional displays bombed out; and we were slow to get the samples out. I think we can make it up in the second quarter."
Vice-president—sales:	"Well, my boss isn't going to like it either. At the same time he has a right to know that's where we stand. I'm counting on you to catch up. Can you do it? Do you need any help?"
Sales manager:	"I think we can do it. I realize your boss keeps the heat on. I'll do my best to avoid this the next time."

Here, both parties treat the differences—in this case, of expectations—as real. The slack sales are real, so is the vice-president's disappointment, so is the pressure from above. By acknowledging all this, the parties clarify the potential misunderstanding from the beginning. Instead of escalation, they move towards resolution.

Some of us confront more naturally than we support. For others it's just the reverse. To always confront and never support is to deny the needs of others. To always support and never confront is to deny your own needs. Without both skills, working with others will be much less successful than any of us would like. As we improve these skills we will put more energy into solving the problem and less into fighting to be heard.

Discussion Questions

1. Describe an example of supporting. Also give an example of confronting.

2. The authors state that most people are born with the ability to hear and to be heard, but many of us lose these abilities on the education treadmill. Would you agree or disagree with this statement? Why?

3. In your own words, explain how differences between two people can escalate.

Getting Through to the Unreachable Person

Natasha Josefowitz

San Diego University, San Diego, CA

Do you always reach your boss, your colleagues, your friends at the level you want to communicate with them? Can you be reached satisfactorily by employees, the boss, your spouse? Do you give, or receive, unthinkable responses—an automatic "unhuhh"..."umm"..."yes, dear?" Have you ever felt you really weren't getting through?

Some people work much of the time on automatic pilot, habitually giving programmed responses. Children tend to go through an early period of saying "No" to parents' suggestions; later on, youngsters who have misbehaved often respond almost on cue that "I didn't do it." There are adults who can be counted on to react to almost any suggestions with an explanation of why "it can't be done." Many adults automatically go on the defensive when they believe they are being criticized.

We all know people who are jokesters, others who are pessimists, those who question endlessly and can never decide, and those who have all the answers—or who never say anything until directly asked for an opinion.

The problem with stereotypical reactions is that they may be appropriate to some situations but not to all. The person who relieves tension with humor renders an important service to a group. But if he or she jokes when there is nothing funny, the humor may needlessly divert fellow workers from their tasks. That people tend to react predictably is not unusual; as a matter of fact, it's the unpredictable people who are often seen as unreliable and threatening, since you never know what they will do next—or how you will react to it.

But there are patterns of responses; however, that people tend to react in certain ways does not necessarily preclude the ability to change this pattern in specific instances. Such people can be reached; they will see the logic of an argument they previously did not understand; they will agree in situations in which they disagreed before; they can accept the position of another person even if it is different from their own.

Source: Natasha Josefowitz. "Getting Through to the Unreachable Person." Reprinted from *Management Review,* March 1982, by permission of the publisher. Copyright © 1982 by AMACOM, a division of American Management Associations. All rights reserved.

Then there are the unreachables, the stubborn, impossible-to-convince persons with whom it is difficult to maintain a dialog. These are persons who switch to automatic and become immune to input from the outside, who are unwilling or unable to see the possibility of another way of looking at an issue. Because they do not see the merit of a different side, they cannot accept another's feelings as legitimate; they do not attempt to understand the world except through their own filters. People like this who hold influential positions are feared and humored; if they have no power, they are avoided and discounted. Either way, they elicit a vague feeling of discomfort—we wonder what's wrong with him or her? Their abnormality is felt but not identified.

Some people go on automatic pilot only rarely; others are on it most of the time. Most of us have known the feeling, particularly when we want protection from having to think or to feel.

It is reasonable to assume that the persons who cloak themselves in a protective device need that protection. The unreachables so fear their own over-reactions—having been hurt by some past relationship or event—that their potential vulnerability must be locked up at all costs. Hence their unavailability, their inability to react appropriately to another person's attempt to communicate.

The impact of the programmed response varies, of course, with the relationships of the persons involved—does it come from a boss, a subordinate, a spouse? If it's the boss, the people who have the most at stake are subordinates trying to reach their superior. If they are not seen or heard, they may be blocked in their careers; those who attempt to force a way through to the boss are taking a risky course.

On the other hand, managers may want to reach employees to train them, delegate responsibility, or otherwise involve them in decision making. An employee on automatic pilot will miss a manager's signals, perhaps losing opportunities for development and moving up the hierarchy—unless he or she has a needed expertise. These people often show up at training programs, to which they have usually been sent because, after a promotion, they have demonstrated little managerial ability and are seen as rigid, with little understanding of human problems.

Similar problems develop at the personal level. One of the more frequent causes of divorce is the unreachability of one spouse. "He won't listen to me" or "she doesn't understand me" are often-heard complaints. Good morale at work and at home generally depends on working and living in congenial surroundings with people who can communicate and who support and maintain dialogs with each other. Those who go on automatic pilot to protect their private space from intrusion may pay a high price for such privacy. The cost is measured in terms of unproductive work relationships, lack of collegiality, and other interpersonal benefits.

When queried about their unreachability, many persons deny that they set themselves apart. Some employees have told me they care little about others' perceptions. One boss said he had no time to pay attention to everyone;

another said he preferred to be selective in his reachability—that is, usually available to colleagues but not to subordinates.

Some people are aware of their unreachability, others are not. I, who think of myself as always "right there," have had students tell me that they were put off when I shuffled papers while they were visiting me in my office. Obviously I was transmitting a message that I did not intend to give.

Symptoms of Unreachability

There are many symptoms of unreachability. When the observer can detect a pattern in their frequent use, we can say that person is on automatic pilot. Eyes are particularly revealing—the person may avoid eye contact; the eyes may keep shifting rapidly; there may be a vacant stare. Fidgeting or rigid body posture are also signals. The person may appear to be absorbed in other activities or allow phone calls and other interruptions to disrupt the conversation. Other symptoms include repeated yawning, frequent looking at one's watch, giving "Yes, but . . ." responses, or not responding to the topic under discussion or to the questions posed. Repeating the same phrase or comment over and over, or seeming to be in a hurry to go on to the same topic also are signals.

Getting Through

Five basic methods of getting through to the unreachable person can be used. They include:

1. *The direct approach,* which requires you to
    - Confront the issue—for example, "I do not feel you hear me, and I don't know what else to do."
    - Express a feeling—try saying, "It upsets me when you don't pay attention to me."
2. *The preventive approach,* which takes this format—"I know you have had trouble listening to me in the past, but would you try this once to hear a different point of view?"
3. *The therapeutic approach,* which requires you to say something like this—"You seem to have difficulty focusing on the discussion and often retreat behind a wall. This makes you unreachable—are you aware of it?"
4. *The punitive approach,* which requires posing an ultimatum: "If you can't discuss the issue without interruptions (or without changing topics, or whatever the person is doing), I will have to decide or to act without your input."

5. *The indirect approach,* which can takes these routes:

   • Writing a letter—some people communicate better through the written word than through face-to-face exchange.

   • Using a third party who has the confidence of the person.

   • Humoring and discounting.

When to Give Up

It is important to know when to stop putting effort, time, and energy into a hopeless situation. Some people are not reachable or educable because they cannot be otherwise or will not be otherwise. The only times I have seen extremely distant people become suddenly open to input from others is when tragedy has struck. In their pain, their vulnerability is exposed at last. This reaction lasts only briefly, however, and the old defenses take over again quickly.

Most of us can recognize when we ourselves are on automatic pilot. When we realize what's happening, we should switch to manual. When we see the syndrome in others, then at least we will be able to identify the problem and attempt a breakthrough—or know when to give up. Awareness of unconscious processes provides alternatives that we don't have otherwise. The more we know and can understand about our own behavior and the behavior of others, the more control we can assume over the effect of our communications, and the greater our efficiency will be in both personal and professional pursuits.

Discussion Questions

1. Give an example of "automatic pilot" that you have observed in yourself and others.

2. What are some of the symptoms of unreachability that are presented in this article?

3. Explain the five basic methods for getting through to others.

4. When should a person give up in the attempt to reach the unreachable person?

Empathy—An Essential Ingredient of Communication

Thomas E. Harris
University of Evansville, Evansville, IN

To be effective, a manager must be able to relate to the members of an organization in a way that maximizes each person's ability to contribute to the functioning of the organization. In doing so, this serves to increase productivity and satisfaction. No great body of research is necessary to indicate that people work more effectively for an organization that shows concern for the welfare of its employees.

A key concept from a management communication perspective is *empathy*. This is the process whereby we try to see the perspective of another person, which includes their feelings and views about situations. Literally, we are placing ourselves "in the other person's shoes"—we try to see the world as they see it. In any interaction or conflict, we try to look at the various viewpoints of those involved.

In dealing with others in an organization, the manager must make judgments regarding the underlying feelings of the other person, which can range from fatigue, fear, joy, happiness, etc. To a great extent, we draw these inferences from the rules that govern social situations, and from the relationships that exist between people.

Learning to empathize with people we work with and interact with is beneficial to management/employee relations and, ultimately, productivity. Thus it can be helpful to see that someone "marches to the tune of a different drummer" before we reject their entire point of view about a critical management decision. Practically all innovations come from an openness to alternative ideas. An attempt to "see it another way" often is the first step to a more comfortable, relaxing, and profitable work climate.

Two specific areas—language and labels—provide interesting examples of the significance of empathy. Consider first the restrictions that exist in the language structure itself. The words and terms we use can keep us from

Source: Thomas E. Harris. "Empathy—An Essential Ingredient of Communication." Reprinted from *Management World,* January 1981, by permission of the Administrative Management Society.

empathizing with another. For example, try to find a parallel word that means the same thing as "little old lady," "spinster," or "broad," *when describing a man.* Can you find a male counterpart for these words that carries the assumptions of the three mentioned, including status, degree, and implications? Does it carry the same implications as the one used to describe a female?

Most people have little success in finding equivalent words for both sexes. Words that can be applied to men often cannot be similarly applied to women. For example, in writing a job description or progress report, to say a man is a professional is fine, but to say a woman is a professional is questionable.

The tendency to accidently or unconsciously restrict our interactions with members of the opposite sex because of language assumptions is further demonstrated by the story about a boy who was involved in a serious automobile accident. His father was driving the car and was killed instantly. The boy was rushed to the hospital in critical condition. The doctor in the emergency room took one look at the boy and screamed, "My God! It's my son!" Many would wonder how the boy could be the doctor's son when his father had been killed in the same accident. The answer, of course, is that the doctor was the boy's *mother.*

Due to language expectations, we can unintentionally discriminate. If we are to enhance our empathy levels, we must be aware of the limitations created by common language usages.

Another language example lies in the prejudice against the color black and for the color white. For example, *blackhearted, Black Death* and other similar terms indicate negative aspects that center around the use of the word *black.* The *white knight, White Christmas* and *Snow White* indicate a positive feeling generated by the color white.

Now to test the language bias, try to list words or phrases which use the color black in a positive way or the color white in a negative way. As a start, we could refer to *in the black* (positive for any corporation or company) or *white as a ghost* (negative). Try to think of others. If you can come up with ten for each color, you have done much better than most people. Although not as dramatic as the sex role example, finding the open or nonbiased use of the colors is more difficult than is usually expected. The important point is that language structure can easily limit our perception and block empathy.

The two examples of sex and race are chosen because they are easily demonstrated. There are many other built-in biases in the language structure that tend to restrict our ability to empathize effectively in the management situation. Increased awareness which leads to increased sensitivity helps any manager becomes a more effective communicator.

Labels provide a second example of the difficulty of overcoming barriers to effective empathy. As an illustration of this, rank the following five professions in terms of their "right to strike." Do the ranking with the anticipation that you will be asked to defend your choices. The occupations are: fireman, farm labor, retail sales clerk, bus driver, and doctor. You will need to decide how you wish to define the right to strike. As seems to be the case in any strike, the issues are rarely clear. To test this premise, ask someone else to also rank the occupations and compare your conclusions. In the process of trying to reach some type of agreement, the need for empathy to be able to communicate should become evident.

After trying to reach some type of legitimate ranking, most of us realize the need to try and see it from someone else's viewpoint. It is a small wonder that we tend to "call it as we see it" first and consider the other person's perspective second. To be truly effective, we need to try and reverse the process to open up our communication abilities. To enhance empathy, we must be open to information.

Probably the first dictum for giving a good speech is that we must analyze our audience. Few speeches succeed that do not follow this simple rule. Audience analysis is merely empathy at a very superficial level. At the interpersonal level, we need to consider the reasons for other people believing and feeling the way they do if we want to be effective in our communication.

This is not a naive appeal for management to "go along with everyone else."Rather it is a call for understanding the other person's perspective to enhance the decision-making process. Early application of empathy will often prevent the type of spiraling conflicts that lead to confrontations. Understanding the subtle influences of language and labels will pay off for any manager.

Learning to better understand people will always lead to better relationships in any situation. Empathy is an essential aspect of management communication and learning to increase this will pay off in many ways for all concerned.

Discussion Questions

1. Harris states that due to language expectations, we can unintentionally discriminate. Give an example of how this may occur.
2. Explain the statement that audience analysis is merely empathy at a very superficial level.
3. What is the difference between empathy and sympathy?

Actions Speak Louder Than Words

Stanley B. Cater
State Farm Auto Insurance Co., Scarborough, Ontario, Canada

You're in the middle of explaining to your boss why your unit's production has been down over the past three months. Suddenly, your boss pushes away from the desk, crosses her legs, and assumes a blank stare past your shoulder. Is the boss believing your explanation? How should you react?

Suppose you're conducting a performance review on your lead worker. You notice that during the conversation, he moves up toward the edge of the chair, places his hands on his knees, and leans towards the desk. How does your worker feel about your evaluation?

The answers to those questions lies in the non-verbal clues. Unfortunately, many of us are not trained to know what certain non-verbal signals mean, and how they fit into the entire process of communication.

Communications experts tell us that only about seven percent of all our messages are sent with words. Of the remaining 93 percent, 38 percent are communicated through tone of voice or delivery. This leaves the majority of communication—some 55 percent—to be communicated through non-verbal behavior.

Although non-verbals supply the majority of messages, we cannot interpret a gesture alone without considering how an accompanying verbal message relates to it. We can't effectively evaluate either without taking a look at the context from which both were extracted. Non-verbal and verbal messages work together in six ways, as follows.

Repeating

The most visible connection between verbal and non-verbal messages is that one simply repeats the other. A classic example would be rejecting a request by saying "no" and unconsciously shaking your head at the same time. In this case, your head shaking would be repeating your verbal denial.

Source: Stanley B. Cater. "Actions Speak Louder Than Words." Reprinted from *Management World,* Vol. 10, No. 6, June 1981, by permission of the Administrative Management Society.

Contradicting

Often, non-verbal behavior and verbal behavior communicate two different, and conflicting, messages. When this happens, we instinctively accept the non-verbal cues and discount the words. The reason for this rather automatic decision is that non-verbal behavior is more difficult to fake. An example of conflicting verbal and non-verbal messages might occur when an employee slams a phone, kicks a file drawer, or shows other signs of anger. However, when you ask the person what's wrong, you get the reply, "nothing."

Substituting

A non-verbal message can substitute for a verbal message that may be socially unacceptable, or that you might feel uncomfortable expressing. For instance, you probably won't actually tell your employees when you're having a bad day and when to avoid you, but your knitted brows, frowning mouth, and withdrawn posture will convey your message loud and clear.

Complementing

Non-verbal behavior can elaborate on, or complement, verbal messages. These complementary cues may be signals of changes in attitudes or intentions toward another person. Jane may display signs of discomfort when you reprimand her for tardiness: downcast eyes, shuffling feet, and a red face. If her non-verbal behaviors continue throughout the rest of the week, chances are your reprimand has affected your working relationship with her. Unless you perceive this change in attitude and confront it, Jane may be uncomfortable in your presence for some time to come.

Accenting

Just as you might underline a written word to emphasize it, you can use body language to give a particular idea a special "punch." When you find yourself pointing or gesturing during your presentation at the unit meeting, for example, chances are you're trying to emphasize a concept that's especially important to you. Of course, don't overdo it, but, in moderation, it's a good technique for making listeners aware of your priorities.

Relating and Regulating

Whether you're talking to your boss, your co-workers, or your employees, you use non-verbal feedback to relate and regulate your verbal messages.

Non-verbal feedback acts as a controlling device to alert you to your listener's measure of understanding. Often unconsciously, you watch for nodding heads, forward positions, and direct eye contact to verify comprehension. The slightest changes in your listener's position might cause you to repeat, restate, or ask a question.

Getting work done through others requires an understanding of both types of communication—verbal and non-verbal—and how they relate. As a supervisor or manager, you can't avoid the situation by not communicating—for that in itself sends a message. And you can't reverse communication that's already taken place in your office, you can't turn it back or stop it. What you can do is be aware of and use both verbal and non-verbal messages to more effectively plan, organize, direct and control—in short, to manage.

Discussion Questions

1. According to this article, what is the difference between complementing and accenting?

2. Give an example of repeating as explained in this article.

3. What are the most common accenting techniques you have observed?

Nonverbal Communication Can Be a Motivational Tool

John E. Baird, Jr.
Corporate Manager, Baxter Travenol Laboratories, Deerfield, IL
Gretchen K. Wieting
Merrill, Lynch, Pierce, Fenner and Smith, Ann Arbor, MI

Of the issues which have haunted managers ever since people began form-ing organizations, none has been more persistent than the question, "How do I motivate my employees?" For years, motivation was thought to be a trait possessed in varying degrees by everyone. Recently, however, theorists have come to the realization that much of motivation is external to the individual. As Hill concludes, motivation "is not so much a personal characteristic as it is a product of the interaction between an executive and an individual staff member."[1] Still, such interaction is closely related to employee characteris-tics. Hill points out that "nothing is as important in individual productive functioning as self-esteem," and adds that "no influence is as great in the development of a person's self-esteem as the feeling that someone whom he respects believes in him."[2] Superior-subordinate communication therefore serves both to influence a subordinate's personal characteristics and to es-tablish his or her level of motivation.

The impact of communication is dramatically illustrated by the "Pygma-lion effect," whereby the expectations of a manager influence the perform-ance of subordinates. Berlew and Hall, for example, found that the relative success of 49 AT&T employees depended largely on the company's expecta-tions of them.[3] Rosenthal and Jacobsen observed the same effect in educa-tional settings, and since the 1968 publication of their *Pygmalion in the Classroom,* nearly 100 studies have obtained findings supporting their con-clusions.[4] All of these studies underscore the importance of communica-tion—particularly nonverbal communication. Livingston, for example, claims that "what seems to be critical in the communication of expectations is not what the boss says, so much as the way he behaves."[5] "The nonverbal communication which accompanies your verbal communication,"

Source: John E. Baird, Jr. and Gretchen K. Wieting. "Nonverbal Communication Can Be a Motivational Tool." Reprinted from *Personal Journal,* Vol. 58, No. 9, Sep-tember 1979.

McSweeney adds, "will very likely project the message that you are expecting the workers to live up to their potential."[6] Similarly, Hill argues that "expectations are communicated in a variety of ways besides verbal messages."[7] Through their nonverbal behavior, then, managers motivate—or demotivate—their employees.

Despite recent interest in nonverbal communication, the relationship between managers' nonverbal cues and employees' motivation has not been explored. Many authors have discussed the interpretation of nonverbal cues, and a few have considered the effective use of nonverbal communication, but none have examined specifically the use of cues to transmit high expectations.[8] Indeed, Livingston implies that such an examination would be fruitless: "If a manager believes the subordinate will perform poorly, it is virtually impossible for him to mask his expectations, because the message is communicated unintentionally, without conscious action on his part."[9] We contend, however, that managers can "mask" their expectations—that if they understand the role of nonverbal cues in transmitting expectations, they can consciously use those cues to motivate their employees.

Content and Relationship

According to Watzlawick, Beavin and Jackson, communication has two levels: "content," or the words one person transmits to another, and "relationship," or the nonverbal cues which accompany those words.[10] They use the term "relationship" because nonverbal behaviors serve chiefly to define the relationship between the interactants by indicating how the spoken words are to be interpreted. Argyle provides more specific information, claiming that nonverbal communication serves to express one's emotions, convey interpersonal attitudes, present one's personality and regulate the interaction.[11] To determine which nonverbal behaviors ought to be displayed by managers, then, we must determine the sorts of superior-subordinate relationships which seem most desirable and then identify the cues which, by conveying certain emotions and attitudes, contribute to the development of such relationships.

Livingston supplies several characteristics of good superior-subordinate relationships.[12] In his opinion, subordinates are more likely to be productive if they feel that the supervisor views them with confidence, respect and concern. McSweeney adds yet another factor: "Having the worker perceive you as a capable authority in your work is valuable, but your projections to the workers that you share a commonness with them is even more important."[13] Hill similarly argues that managers should reward initiative, correct mistakes, ask for input, share feelings and be open-minded in their relations with subordinates.[14] Therefore, desirable nonverbal cues are those which express warmth, respect, concern, equality and a willingness to listen; while undesirable behaviors are those which show coolness, superiority, disinterest and disrespect. With this knowledge, we can begin to isolate the specific nonverbal behaviors which managers should strive to exhibit or avoid.

Effects of Nonverbal Cues

In his summary of research in nonverbal communication, Knapp discusses several categories of nonverbal cues, including the environment, proxemics, postures, gestures, facial expressions, eye behavior and vocalics.[15] Each of these categories plays an important role in superior-subordinate communication; consequently, we will examine each category in turn.

The Environment

This first category considers the setting in which communication occurs, including time elements, room color, temperature, lighting, attractiveness of the surroundings, furniture arrangement and so on. Three environmental factors particularly relevant here are time, arrangement and attractiveness, for all three communicate subtle messages to the people present in the setting.

Expectations and attitudes toward a specific employee are shown in three temporally related issues: how long he or she must wait to see the supervisor, how much time the supervisor devotes to the conference, and how frequently the supervisor communicates with the employee. If a supervisor keeps an employee waiting a long time (probably more than ten minutes), devotes only a short time to the meeting when a longer conference is appropriate, and meets only occasionally with the employee, then the supervisor is communicating a negative, disrespectful attitude toward that individual. Conversely, if the supervisor sees the employee immediately, devotes adequate time to the meeting, and confers with the employee frequently, he or she demonstrates esteem for that person.

Furniture arrangement also has an impact on superior-subordinate relationships, serving to establish a cold, formal, authoritative environment or a warmer, informal, cooperative setting. Michael Korda, publishing house executive and author, describes how placement of a desk and chairs in an office can influence the atmosphere of a meeting.[16] Korda cites three specific basic office arrangements, each creating a different sort of climate. In the first, dominance is minimized and warmth maximized. The visitor sits next to the desk, making him or her virtually equal to the occupant and forcing the latter to assume a relatively uncomfortable position in order to talk face to face. Arrangement number two is more powerful and less warm; the occupant sits regally behind the desk, which serves as a barrier. But the third arrangement is the least warm of all. The visitor is sitting back to the wall, occupying minimal space, while the occupant has the remainder of the office in which to move about. This, coupled with the interposed desk, makes the situation the most domineering possible. But Korda points out one final extreme instance of furniture and power. One executive not only arranged his desk as in the third example, but also placed it on a platform so that he could look down at his visitors, and gave the visitors an extremely soft chair so that they sank up to their chins when they sat down. Peering over one's knees at an executive sitting behind a desk on a platform would almost certainly make anyone feel rather submissive.

Finally, there is some evidence that environmental attractiveness has an influence on interaction. Maslow and Mintz[17] and Mintz[18] asked subjects to evaluate a series of photographs while working in three different settings: an ugly room, an average room and a beautiful room. Comparisons of the ratings given in these settings showed that people felt more positively toward the faces in the photographs when working in the beautiful room than when in the ugly room. In addition, the subjects reported changes in their emotional states. In the ugly room, they describe their experience as irritating, tiring, dull and generally unpleasant, while in the beautiful room they reported feeling comfortable, pleasant and eager to continue the activity. Apparently, then, one's feelings about an environment extend to the people encountered there.

Consideration of environmental factors is thus important to establishing desirable superior-subordinate relationships. Employees should not be kept waiting, should be given adequate time and should be met with relatively frequently. Employers should seek to establish an informal, cooperative atmosphere by interposing little or no furniture between themselves and their employees. The surroundings of the conversation, finally, should be as pleasant and attractive as possible to promote positive interaction.

Proxemics

Proxemics involves the placement of one's body relative to the placement of someone else—their physical proximity. A number of studies have noted a relationship between people's physical distance and the sorts of attitudes each infers the other to hold. Patterson cites research indicating that people located in relatively close proximity are seen as warmer, friendlier and more understanding than people located further away.[19] Moreover, Mehrabian found that status differences are emphasized by physical distance and minimized by greater closeness.[20] Indeed, after reviewing research on proximity, Mehrabian concluded that "the findings of a large number of studies collaborate one another and indicate that communicator-addressee distance is correlated with the degree of negative attitude communicated to and inferred by the addressee."[21] Thus, assuming a position close to the employee seems to convey a variety of positive attitudes.

Postures

General bodily movements also have a message value. In studies of bodily posture, Mehrabian found a close relationship between posture and liking for the other person.[22] When confronting someone they intensely dislike, women particularly tend to be very indirect in their direction of face, looking away from the other person as much as possible. If they like the other person, they vary their direction of face, sometimes looking squarely at that person and sometimes looking away, while when dealing with a total stranger, they tend to look directly at that person. Similar although less consistent results were obtained for males. Mehrabian also found that openness of the arms or legs serves as an indicator of liking, as people maintain open positions when meeting those they like, but establish closed postures (arms folded and legs crossed) when speaking with people they dislike. Lastly, a forward lean seems to indicate liking for the other, while a backward lean seems to convey negative feelings. A manager's postures thus tell much about his or her feelings toward the others.

Gestures

Studies of gestures or specific bodily movements have found those behaviors to convey rather specific information. Research summarized by Bonoma and Felder indicates that positive attitudes toward another person are shown by frequent gesticulation, while dislike or disinterest usually produces few gestures.[23] However, the types of gestures displayed are also important. Random fidgeting, such as drumming the fingers or twiddling the thumbs, is a set of gestural activities which convey extremely negative attitudes. Similarly, aggressive gestures with clenched fists and menacing postures convey hostile feelings, while frequent use of relaxed, open-palm gestures toward the other person typically conveys positive attitudes.

A specific sort of gesture is touch, something used rather infrequently in American society. Yet there are indications that this element of communication may be extremely important. Bardeen compared reactions to three situations: communication by words only, communication by sight only and communication by touch.[24] He found that reactions to the first two were largely negative. The talk-only setting was rated distant, artificial, formal, insensitive and noncommunicative, while the visual-only situation was termed artificial, childish, comical, cold and arrogant. But the touch-only situation was rated trustful, sensitive, natural, mature, serious and warm. It would seem, then, that this element of nonverbal interaction, important in other cultures but neglected in our own, could do much to improve relations with other people.

Head/Face/Eye Behaviors

Perhaps the clearest indication of interpersonal attitudes comes from the combined actions of the communicator's head, face and eyes. Head nods are signs of positive feelings, and as Matarazzo, et al., demonstrated, they have a significant impact on the recipients' behavior.[25] Similarly, head shakes indicate negative attitudes. But head behaviors can be even more subtle. Lowering the head and peering, perhaps over glasses, at the other person is, according to Levy, the nonverbal equivalent of "you're putting me on."[26] Sheridan observes that cocking the head slightly to one side may indicate rejection or suspicion.[27] Indeed, progressively lifting the head backward while the other person speaks also indicates doubt or disbelief. Thus, a variety of head cues convey information to the recipient.

Facial expressions also indicate communicator attitudes. Rosenfeld noted that people seeking approval seem to smile more frequently, and Mehrabian and Williams observed that people trying to persuade others also show an increase in facial activity.[28] In research of another sort, Ekman divided the face into three regions and attempted to determine which regions best express certain emotions.[29] He found that happiness is shown most by the lower face and eyes; sadness is seen primarily in the eyes; surprise is indicated by the eyes and lower face; anger is shown in the lower face, brows, and forehead; and fear is shown most clearly in the eyes. While facial expressions are relatively difficult to control, they nevertheless clearly mirror a manager's intentions and emotional state.

Studies of eye contact in human communication have identified the situations in which one seeks or avoids eye contact with others. Generally, one will seek eye contact with others when wanting to communicate with them, when physically distant from them, when friendly toward them, when feeling extremely hostile toward them (as when two bitter enemies try to stare each other down), or when wanting feedback from them. Conversely, a person will avoid eye contact if he or she wishes to avoid communication, is physically close to the other person, dislikes the other, is trying to deceive or is disinterested. Given the positiveness of eye contact, one should find that it improves communication—and indeed it does. Exline and Eldridge found that messages accompanied by eye contact are more favorably interpreted by observers than are messages sent without eye contact.[30] Therefore, if a manager maintains eye contact with subordinates, communication with them probably will be significantly improved.

Vocalics

The aspects of the voice, such as pitch, volume, quality and rate, which accompany the spoken words comprise this final category. Apparently, people make two sorts of judgments about others on the basis of vocal cues. First, as Addington discovered, one judges personality characteristics on the basis of voice.[31] Second, and perhaps more important, Davitz discovered that judgments of emotion are also perceived in vocal cues.[32] Affection, for instance, seems to be indicated by low pitch, softness, slow rate, regular rhythm and slurred enunciation. Anger is best perceived when the source speaks loudly, at a fast rate, in a high pitch, with irregular inflection and clipped enunciation. Boredom is indicated by moderate volume, pitch, and rate, and a monotone inflection; joy by loud volume, high pitch, fast rate, upward inflection and regular rhythm; and sadness by soft volume, slow rate, low pitch, downward inflections and slurred enunciation. While specific individuals may differ in the ways in which they express these emotions, for the most part these patterns seem to reflect the vocalic behaviors typifying particular emotions. Through the careful use of vocal cues, supervisors can convey positive attitudes and, if necessary, mask negative ones toward their subordinates.

At this juncture, three conclusions seem abundantly clear:

1. Supervisors motivate or demotivate subordinates by communicating high or low expectations to them.

2. Much of that communication is accomplished nonverbally, so that environmental, physical and vocal cues convey information to the employee.

3. By carefully using these nonverbal factors, supervisors can deliberately eliminate low-expectation cues and substitute behavior indicating high expectation.

One question remains: Can managers actually learn to control something as subtle as nonverbal communication? We believe they can, both alone and with training. On their own, they can make a conscious effort to observe the nonverbal behaviors of others and note their own responses to those cues. Moreover, they can engage in some "role playing," trying to convey the positive attitudes discussed above and observing the recipients' responses as a gauge of their success. Role playing according to prestructured exercises with feedback provided by a qualified trainer may speed learning, as might the opportunity to view one's efforts with video-tape playbacks. Still other methods have been used successfully by Argyle, Ekman and Friesen, and others.[33] Certainly, managers can learn skills in communicating nonverbally.

Granting the desirability and practicality of using these nonverbal behaviors, one still might ask, "Is it ethical to convey cues which are contrary to one's true feelings?" That is, should a manager feign high expecations when, in fact, they are low? Our response is two-fold. First, there are situations in which the "polite lie" benefits everyone. The person who, upon leaving an incredibly dull party, thanks the host for a "wonderful evening" illustrates the point. Typically, the supervisor who transmits high expectations, whether true or not, will have a more productive, happy employee as a consequence. Second, by changing behaviors, a supervisor may also change his or her own attitudes. Evidence exists that people infer their attitudes from their personal behaviors.[34] Thus, a manager who exhibits high-expectation cues may actually develop higher expectations of employees. The self-fulling prophecy will then become doubly effective.

Discussion Questions

1. Explain the "Pygmalion Effect." What kind of evidence indicates that such a phenomenon exists?

2. What is the difference between proxemics and postures? Give an example of each.

3. What component of nonverbal communication provides the clearest indication of interpersonal attitudes? What indicates a negative attitude? A positive attitude?

References

1. Norman Hill, "Staff Members Do Better When You Set High Standards," *Association Management,* Vol. 9, No. 2 (February, 1977): 75–77.

2. Ibid.

3. David E. Berlew and Douglas T. Hall, "Some Determinants of Early Managerial Success," Alfred P. Sloan School of Management Organization Research Program #81-64 (Cambridge, Massachusetts Institute of Technology, 1964), pp. 13–14.

4. Robert Rosenthal and Lenore Jacobsen, *Pygmalion in the Classroom* (New York: Holt, Rinehart and Winston, 1968).

5. J. Sterling Livingston, "Pygmalion in Management," *Harvard Business Review,* January–February, 1969, p. 84.

6. John P. McSweeney, "Pygmalion in the Plant," *Personnel Journal,* Vol. 56, No. 8 (August 1977): 380–381.

7. Hill, p. 75.

8. See, for example, Ed Roseman, "People Reading: The Art of Recognizing Hidden Messages," *Product Marketing,* Vol. 6, No. 6 (June 1977): 36–39; Richard W. Brunson, Sr., "Perceptual Skills in the Corporate Jungle," *Personnel Journal,* Vol. 51, No. 1 (January 1972): 50–53; D. M. Ehat and M. Schnapper, "What Your Employees' Non-Verbal Clues Are Telling You," *Administrative Management,* Vol. 35, No. 8 (August 1974): 64–66; "Listen With Your Eyes," *Industry Week,* Vol. 178, No. 3 (July 16, 1973): 37–39; Julius Fast, *Body Language* (New York: M. Evans, 1970).

9. Livingston, pp. 81–84.

10. Paul Watzlawick, J. H. Beavin, and Don Jackson, *Pragmatism of Human Communication* (New York: W. W. Norton, 1967).

11. Michael Argyle, *Bodily Communication* (New York: International Universities Press, 1975).

12. Livingston, pp. 81–84.

13. McSweeney, p. 380.

14. Hill, p. 76.

15. Mark Knapp, *Nonverbal Communication in Human Interaction,* 2nd ed. (New York: Holt, Rinehart and Winston, 1978).

16. Michael Korda, *Power: How To Get It, How to Use It* (New York: Random House, 1975), pp. 194–197.

17. A. H. Maslow and N. L. Mintz, "Effects of Esthetic Surroundings: I. Initial Effects of Three Esthetic Conditions Upon Perceiving 'Energy' and 'Wellbeing' in Faces," *Journal of Psychology,* Vol. 41, No. 3 (1956): 247–254.

18. N. L. Mintz, "Effects of Esthetic Surroundings: II. Prolonged and Repeated Experience in a 'Beautiful' and 'Ugly' Room," *Journal of Psychology,* Vol. 41, No. 4, (1956): 459–466.

19. M. Patterson, "Spatial Factors in Social Interaction," *Human Factors,* Vol. 2, No. 3 (1968): 351–361.

20. Albert Mehrabian, "Significance of Posture and Position in the Communication of Attitude and Status Relationships," *Psychological Bulletin,* Vol. 71 (1969): 363.

21. Ibid.

22. Albert Mehrabian, "Inference of Attitude from the Posture, Orientation and Distance of a Communicator," *Journal of Consulting Clinical Psychology,* Vol. 32, No. 2 (1968): 296–308.

23. Thomas V. Bonoma and Leonard C. Felder, "Nonverbal Communication in Marketing: Toward a Communicational Analysis," *Journal of Marketing Research,* Vol. 14 (May 1977): 169–180.

24. J. P. Bardeen, "Interpersonal Perception Through the Tactile, Verbal, and Visual Modes," paper presented at the convention of the International Communication Association, Phoenix, 1971.

25. John Matarazzo, et al., "Interviewer Influence on Durations of Interviewee Speech," *Journal of Verbal Learning and Verbal Behavior,* Vol. 1, No. 4 (1963): 451–458.

26. Robert Levy, "Through a Glass, Darkly," *Dun's Review,* Vol. 107, No. 2 (February 1976): 77–78.

27. John H. Sheridan, "Are You A Victim of Nonverbal 'Vibes'?" *Industry Week,* Vol. 198, No. 1 (July 10, 1978): 36–42.

28. H. Rosenfeld, "Instrumental Affiliative Functions of Facial and Gestural Expression," *Journal of Personality and Social Psychology,* Vol. 13, No. 1 (1969): 37–58.

29. Paul Ekman, "Differential Communication of Affect by Head and Body Cues," *Journal of Personality and Social Psychology,* Vol. 2, No. 4 (1965): 726–735.

30. Robert V. Exline and Carl Eldridge, "Effects of Two Patterns of a Speaker's Visual Behavior Upon the Perception of the Authenticity of His Verbal Message," paper presented to the Eastern Psychological Association, Boston, 1967.

31. David W. Addington, "The Effect of Vocal Variations on Ratings of Source Credibility," *Speech Monographs,* Vol. 38, No. 2 (1971): 242–247.

32. J. R. Davitz and L. Davitz, "Nonverbal Vocal Communication of Feeling," *Journal of Communication,* Vol. 11, No. 1 (1961): 81–86.

33. Michael Argyle, *Social Interaction* (New York: Atherton, 1969); Paul Ekman and William Friesen, *Unmasking the Face* (Englewood Cliffs, N. J.: Prentice-Hall, 1975); also see J. W. Pfeiffer and J. E. Jones, *A Handbook of Structured Experiences for Human Relations Training* (Iowa City, Iowa: University Associates, 1969–1970), Vol. 1, pp. 109–111, Vol. 2, pp. 102–104; M. Wiemann and M. Knapp, *Instructor's Guide to Nonverbal Communication in Human Interaction* (New York: Holt, Rinehart and Winston, 1978).

34. Joseph DeVito, *The Psychology of Speech and Language* (New York: Random House, 1970), pp. 238–252.

Part VI

Cases

The Monday Morning Bubble Burster

William J. Buchholz
Bentley College, Waltham, MA

Every Monday morning you can look forward to meeting clients who have spent the weekend dreaming. In the banking business this dreaming is known as the "Monday Morning Bubble" syndrome. Here is how it works. On Saturday and Sunday small business owners (and nonowners who want to start a business) meet with people who tell the most fantastic success stories. Always they're the same: A small outlay invested in a risky venture is parlayed into huge gain. For example, one man who sold second-hand furniture assumed a small business loan a few years back and bought up all the old oak furniture he could find in every farmhouse around. Today, he owns the biggest antique dealership in the country and is estimated to be worth over $100 million. Another fellow took a second mortgage on his home, invested in pig bladder futures, and got rich overnight when the ruling junta in the Republic of San Lucar toppled. Stories like these abound on weekends in every country club, locker room, tennis court, and nightclub in the country. By Sunday morning, enterprising risk-takers have earnestly begun to formulate their own schemes for capturing millions of homeless dollars. On Monday morning, they come to see you.

As a new commercial loan Vice-president for the Guaranty Mercantile, you've heard the officers of the bank discuss the Bubble syndrome, but you've never had to deal with it yet. Today is your day. Here comes Percy Fraphjord, owner of Fraphjord's Plucked Pullets. Percy has spent the weekend dreaming up a way to expand his operation and to corner the plucked pullet market in your state. What he needs is a loan of about $150 thousand to buy out the stiffest competition, Parker's Pullets. As you listen to Percy, you discover that his scheme is very interesting, but you don't feel it would be responsible for you to pass his request along to the loan review board (the board must okay all substantial loans). In your judgment, Percy Fraphjord is simply spread too thin right now. His farm is mortgaged for $80,000; his business has been operating at a profit, but not a large one; and his debts for the coming year will be significant because of the high cost of pullet food and pullet processing (electricity, fuel, water, and the like). His plant is old, and a good deal of new equipment will have to be replaced soon if he is to continue to operate in the black. Besides, you're not so sure that Parker's

189

Pullets is a wise investment; lately, Parker has lost a good share of the market to Fraphjord himself. Furthermore, people are buying fewer pullets than they did last year because of the increased cost; in short, pullet demand has dropped steadily.

Now here's the problem. Percy Fraphjord is a good customer of the bank. He has a sizable mortgage with you, holds all accounts with you, and has always come to you for small business loans. You don't want to offend Percy and yet you see too much risk here for him to assume right now. You've got to decline his request.

Questions

1. How can you burst his bubble in such a way that you will not insult him and not hurt his pride?

2. What communication barriers can you identify in this situation?

3. How will you overcome these barriers?

4. How do you propose to listen actively to Percy? Remember, in your discussion with Percy, there will be a great deal of opportunity for him to misunderstand your points; in effect, you will be confronting him on an issue about which he is very sensitive.

5. How will you keep your differences of opinion from escalating into open hostility?

6. How will you handle Percy's needs for self-esteem while protecting your own needs to make a sound financial decision and to appear as an effective loan officer?

If your instructor permits, role play this scene, paying special attention to the interpersonal skills necessary to burst Percy's bubble without inflicting undue pain. Can you engineer this situation in such a way that you don't' even have to refuse Percy? See if you can get Percy to refuse himself.

Southern Kisses

William J. Buchholz
Bentley College, Waltham, MA

Every morning when you arrive at work, Mr. Fosdick, your boss at Southern Kisses (a quality chocolate retail store in an exclusive shopping mall), greets you with a hearty "good morning" and instructs you on the plan of the day. You know that Mr. Fosdick likes your work because he has told many of the customers, right in front of you, how efficient you are. The customers tell him too how kind you are and what a pleasure it is to buy chocolates from you. You embody the best that Southern Kisses represents to the public.

Lately, though, Mr. Fosdick has demonstrated some very annoying behavior. In fact, things have gotten so bad that you are contemplating leaving Southern Kisses unless something can be done to change things immediately. Mr. Fosdick has been having some trouble at home: His wife has left him, and his older boy has been picked up on a drug charge. His younger boy got hold of some firecrackers and blew off his little finger. A homemade chocolate specialty shop has just opened on the other end of the mall and has drained nearly half of Southern Kisses' business. To top it off, you've heard via the grapevine that Mr. Fosdick's mother has been seen dating the local numbers man. You can understand Mr. Fosdick's short temper lately.

But what you cannot understand is the way Mr. Fosdick has been treating you, especially in front of customers. The other day Mrs. Halliwell, a loyal and honored customer, witnessed your public humiliation when Mr. Fosdick hollered at you for leaving the cash register drawer open while you stepped in the back for Mrs. Halliwell's gift box. Is Mrs. Halliwell, philanthropist and society matron, going to reach over the counter and dip into the till? Mr. Fosdick positively insulted both of you by even implying such a thing. And two days ago he furiously thumped your hands because you put the white almond bark too near the chocolate almond bark in the display case. He likes a distance of 1½ inches between display items; you had set them 1 inch apart. But today was the last straw.

At about 10 A.M. Robert Anthony III came in to buy a box of his favorite chocolate mints. Even with all his millions, R. A. III (as he is affectionately known) is something of a pig. He will buy a half-pound box of the chocolate mints and eat them right in the store. Another bad habit of his is to taste the display items. Occasionally, he will just reach out and grab an almond cluster or a small handful of chocolate-covered raisins and pop them into his mouth. Invariably he buys a pound or two of whatever he tastes, so all the

191

employees of Southern Kisses indulge R. A. III his eccentricities. Today, though, Mr. Fosdick saw R. A. III grab a handful of chocolate spearmint clusters. He called you over and hissed, loudly enough for R. A. III to hear, "If I *ever* catch one of your customers stealing from us again, you lose your job, do you hear?"

R. A. III wasn't really very upset; he has an exceedingly thick skin. But you are upset. After all, Mr. Fosdick has known for years about R. A.'s light fingers; in fact, he's the one who told you and the other employees to allow it because R. A.'s patronage is so valued. And now here he is blaming *you* for R. A.'s indiscretion. Well, you've had it. You simply have to confront Mr. Fosdick, or else you'll have to quit. There is no way you can continue to work under these conditions.

Questions

1. How will you go about discussing this matter with Mr. Fosdick?
2. Where will you speak with him? When?
3. What mood will you try to catch him in?
4. Will you threaten to quit?
5. How many of the past embarrassing instances will you bring up? Need you mention any of them?
6. What kind of tone will you adopt? Self-righteous? Hurt? Indignant? Understanding?
7. Will you offer an ultimatum?
8. Should you make reference to Mr. Fosdick's personal troubles?

See if you can set Mr. Fosdick straight, make yourself look very good, and come out of this intolerable situation with a raise.

Meeting With People in Business Situations

Business people meet in many different formats which require them to be able to manage meetings, make formal presentations, conduct intelligent dialogue, and listen effectively. Five articles in this part address these topics.

Glen M. Morgan discusses four basic problematical aspects of meetings in his article, "Meeting the Meeting Challenge." He discusses how a critical and objective evaluation of meeting analysis and renovation can produce visible improvement in these four problematic areas.

"How to Conduct a Productive Meeting" by Laverne Kindred Brown presents 11 simple guidelines to follow in order to produce an effective meeting. These guidelines serve as a valuable aid prior to a meeting by ensuring coverage of all the details.

Sometimes a formal presentation is necessary. Eugene Raudsepp explains how to make a persuasive, convincing speech in his article, "When It's Your Turn to Speak At the Podium." The importance of preparation is a central theme throughout this article.

To reach sound decisions, one must conduct a systematic dialogue. Jack E. Hulbert presents a series of necessary steps in his article, "Conducting Intelligent Business Dialogue." When one follows this series of steps, intelligent, purposeful business dialogue will result.

Any time two people meet, listening is required for successful communication. Barriers to listening and techniques for overcoming these barriers are presented by Larry R. Smeltzer and Kittie W. Watson in their article, "Effective Listening Improves Success." The four techniques presented will help business people develop a more accurate exchange of information.

Meeting the Meeting Challenge

Glen M. Morgan
Free-lance Writer

Ever wondered why the last conference you went to failed miserably in its attempt to solve the problem at hand?

Ever wondered why your group normally spends more of its time off the problem than on the problem?

Ever wondered why there are times that you never seem to get your point across to the other members of the group?

Well, the answer is quite simple: Whenever two or more people get together to solve a problem, it becomes increasingly difficult for them to complete their objective. Groups are more complex than they themselves believe. Most group arrangements tend to only "surface act" rather than follow a definite plan of action in order to save money, man hours, and group sanity.

In fully understanding that next meeting you are going to take part in, you need to first come to realistic grips with four problematic areas which have a tendency to plague groups and group members.

First of all, you should realize that "Problems Are Man-made" and, furthermore, that only "man" can solve them. Reliance cannot be on a computer or outside mechanical source because it seems that someone is directly responsible for initiating the final solution anyway. Some group members can lose proper perspective on simple problems and get those problems presented as complexities at weekly conference settings. Most groups end up spending valuable company time trying to solve a problem that wasn't theirs to begin with. The problem should have stopped with the foreman or third shift rather than spawning its way up the organizational stream to a group of people who do nothing but send it back with a memo stating, "We're looking into it."

The second area concerns that of the "Unclarified Group Purpose." For some reason, there are a number of called meetings that should have never

Source: Glen M. Morgan. "Meeting the Meeting Challenge." Reprinted from *Industrial Management* Magazine, May–June 1981, with permission of *Industrial Management* Magazine. Copyright © Institute of Industrial Engineers, Inc., 25 Technology Park/Atlanta, Norcross, GA 30092.

met to begin with. Sometimes they meet because "We always meet at 2:30 on Friday afternoons"; sometimes they meet because "It's in our job description"; sometimes they meet because "We were all called into the supervisor's office ASAP and that's all we know!" That last reason, by the way, is probably the "Devil" of all conference agendas. The members have no reason why they are being called—to be rewarded or to be reprimanded! So rather than coming to the meeting with a clear mind ready to do business, they come defensed with a storehouse of excuses and ready to "get the business."

Third, "Personnel Conflict is Heightened by Personal Conflict." That old authority level concept is usually the culprit in this group ill. People tend to be aware of administrative levels whether they say that it doesn't bother them or not. It comes down to being in the presence of your boss or other leader that seems to hold back that imaginative and creative thought until you get home; and for some people, all that takes place is "persnaky flowering."

Problematic area four is that of "Total Group Organization." Some people don't know how to lead because they have never learned the skills necessary for adequate leadership; and some individuals don't know how to participate because they never learned the rudimentary skills needed for group cohesiveness. The mainstream of misunderstanding in this area comes from being thrown into a group situation which we only theorize that we can conduct and participate in to a legitimate degree. The only group involvement most of us have had has been in an educational arena where in a human relations class we debated whether abortion was legal or not, or whether Saddie Slapsaddle, down in Quality Control, should be told about her deodorant problem.

Another way of finding out about how that complicated group operates is a method called the "Up the Ladder Approach." In this method, you ascend in the company structure on a seniority and/or productive scale with on-the-job training guiding your way. The only problem with this approach is that you may learn that the only way to hold discussions and conferences is by the way they have been held in the past—not always effective nor efficient.

Now that the four basic problematic areas have been assessed, let's look at what can be done to alleviate them in our business and industrial settings.

For that man-made problem area, first note that you must realize that people are problems in themselves. Their illogical thinking at various time periods should be part of your awareness in how they perform in interaction. Try to analyze each group participant before, during, and after the discussion-conference meeting. Be sure to analyze objectively and not subjectively as you have done in the past. A member's performance at the last meeting gives you no right to ascertain that the next performance will equal or surpass previous involvement or lack of it. You should, however, note ways in which you could deter a person's tangential sayings by asking him/her to stay with the problem at hand, to support the claim with factual data, and to realize that discussion takes a group effort, affording group results.

The unclarified group purpose can best be rectified by alerting all group members as to why the meeting is to take place. This solution does not mean that you have to go into a lengthy exposition on the meeting rationale. All that is needed is enough to warrant clear-headed participation during the meeting. If meetings are held with a direct purpose and for that purpose only, affirmative results will accrue and noteworthy meeting conduct will take place.

Personnel conflict and personal conflict are quite unique in that they both deal with the psychology of people. The personnel situation can never be eliminated, but it can be understood and controlled to the degree of having people want to get the job done satisfactorily. Understanding human nature and organizational inhabitants takes time and patience. Enrolling in a basic psychology or organizational psychology course will increase your perception of this "people" difficulty and in turn curb the personal conflict because you have learned more about yourself. In this context then, you'll be better able to understand the group in which you may spend much of your time.

Total group organization can take on a new air if you allow yourself the discipline that is needed to conduct or participate in a well-developed meeting. Some groups believe that because a chairperson is at the head of the table, the meeting will be organized, controlled, and well led. However, because the chair is occupied does not necessarily indicate that the individual can lead.

Some leaders in groups are those silent majority who speak with quality rather than quantity because they understand particular positions in the group situation. Also, it's the understanding that a participant not only participates but many times leads group thought and process indirectly. He/she never gets "outward" credit but feels accomplishment. The task may be completed by merely reestablishing the group purpose when it seems to get off the track, by asking a silent member his/her thoughts on the issue in focus, or by indicating to a talkative member that although he/she has conversed with importance on the issue, it may be a noteworthy idea to get information from some of the other passive members of the group.

Discussion and conference skills, both leadership and participatory, are those which must be learned and occasionally reviewed so that effective meeting conduct can take place. Business and industries can only secure themselves with meeting relationships that are worthwhile if they themselves review their own meeting skills. A critical and objective evaluation of meeting analysis and renovation can visibly show improvement in those four problematic areas; and with a continuous analysis of yourself as a leader and participant, you will also feel worthwhile after meeting your next meeting challenge.

Discussion Questions

1. Briefly review the four problematic areas that plague groups and group members.

2. What is meant by the comment that some group members speak with quality rather than quantity?

3. If a person is to be effective in a meeting, it is suggested that he/she analyze each group participant before, during, and after meeting. Why is this so important?

How to Conduct a Productive Meeting

Laverne Kindred Brown

You are attending a management meeting, a group conference, or a workshop. The women are doing needlepoint, writing their grocery lists, or making mental plans for a weekend dinner party. The men are dozing, doodling, or rattling the change in their pockets. Feelings range from sleepy boredom to outright antagonism. Everyone yearns for the final moment of adjournment.

Sound familiar? Then someone is doing something wrong! *Every* meeting can be stimulating, informative, fun, or challenging. Every group gathering will be *all* of these if the group leader will follow these simple guidelines.

Plan and Prepare Carefully

This may be the most important step of all. Decide the purpose(s) of the meeting and make an orderly list of the pertinent topics or points to be covered. Plan ahead as far as possible and post the agenda on a bulletin board or send a copy to group members prior to the meeting whenever possible.

Plan specific activities which will best achieve your purposes. The methods you choose depend upon whether you wish to inform, discuss and seek input, educate, entertain, change attitudes, etc. If you do not have a clear-cut purpose and adequate time to prepare, don't meet! Delay the meeting until you are prepared to offer an approach that will better assure your desired results.

Choose an Appropriate Meeting Place

Be certain it has adequate space to meet your needs. Arrange seating that will promote your goals. For instance, if you want to tell or instruct (but want

Source   Laverne Kindred Brown. "How to Conduct a Productive Meeting." Reprinted from *Supervision*, Vol. XLIV, No. 3, March 1982 by permission of *Supervision* magazine. Copyright © 1982, The National Research Bureau, 424 N. Third St., Burlington, Iowa 52601.

199

discussion kept to a minimum) don't use roundtable or conference type seating. If you desire eye contact and want to foster group interaction, don't line people up in theater or "classroom" seating arrangements.

If the gathering is to be held outside your own institution, consider additional factors such as rental costs, convenience of location, parking space, food service, adequacy of restrooms, audio-visual outlets and equipment, etc.

Pay special attention to selecting a place that will provide privacy and absence of distractions such as ringing telephones and paging systems. Leave instructions with the operator or secretary that the meeting is not to be interrupted and to take messages carefully of any calls that need to be returned by group members.

Have All Materials Ready

Be certain materials are within easy reach and are arranged in the order they are to be used. Any written materials should be clearly copied and free of distracting typographical errors. If you are meeting with 20 or more persons, it will save a great deal of time if you prepare "packets" of materials in advance of the meeting.

Start and End Promptly

Don't worry about or wait "just a little longer" for late comers. If they are late and embarrass themselves, perhaps they will be on time for the next meeting! Stop when you said you would. Participants will have made other plans based on the timetable you established for the meeting. If you have planned properly, you will have allowed adequate time to meet your purposes.

Open the Meeting
in a Suitable Manner

Briefly review the purpose of the meeting as this will draw all participants toward the same train of thought and purposes.

If group members know one another, and you are here to problem solve or give information, take a friendly but firm "let's get the meeting started" approach. If the meeting is to be educational or is best handled with informality, take a little time to break the ice with introductions, an anecdote, a non-threatening pretest, or a brain teaser. Try to establish a climate of mutual respect and openness as this will promote success in achieving your goals.

Define Roles Clearly

If you have special experience or credentials for leading the group, state these briefly and confidently. Lengthy credentials can be in written form on the program or meeting outline. Tell the group what you will be doing and what is expected of them.

If you expect to achieve positive results, you must approach any group with patience, confidence and enthusiasm. You must also accept responsibility for maintaining control and direction of the meeting so it will progress as you planned.

Do not refer constantly to your own opinions and thoughts. Avoid talking too fast, too softly, or too loudly. Speak clearly and alternate the tone of your voice to prevent it from sounding monotonous. Change your facial expressions often. Keep your attention on the group and what is being communicated verbally and non-verbally.

Hold Steadfastly to the Basic Meeting Goals

Discuss only one point at a time and bring its discussion to a conclusion before moving to the next topic. Don't allow participants to get you off the track. Bring the discussion tactfully but firmly back to the point. This doesn't mean you must follow the agenda exactly as written. You may choose to allow the group to move from point one to point four if they choose, but assure that they stick with the original agenda.

Use Appropriate Audio-Visual Aids

Whenever possible, put it in writing, draw a diagram or picture, or use other visual aids. This will better assure that all group members leave with the same understanding of the information shared.

If films, slides, transparencies, etc., are utilized, be certain they can be seen clearly from all areas of the room. Speaker systems must provide adequate amplification and clarity. Intersperse humorous pictures, cartoons, etc., periodically to better assure maintaining group attention.

Encourage Active and Equal Participation

Ask for ideas, opinions and suggestions by using open, leading questions such as: "Does anyone have a suggestion for . . . ?" or "Has anyone had any personal experience with . . . ?'' If individuals seem to be shy or apart from the group, draw them in with direct questions such as, "Kathryn, what do you think would be the best way to handle the problem?" Never embarrass or belittle participants who make poor contributions.

Don't allow any person to dominate the meeting. Avoid looking toward the overbearing person when asking questions. Practice selective deafness if she and another participant begin to speak simultaneously. Encourage the other person's comments with questions such as, "Ann, you were saying . . .?" If the monopolizer doesn't take your hints, take a break and tactfully tell her she is dominating the discussion and preventing others from sharing their ideas. Voice your appreciation of the positive contributions made.

Don't Feel Threatened or Intimidated

Use disagreement or open criticism of ideas to stimulate further discussion. Stating simply and calmly, "It seems we've encountered differing opinions. Is a compromise possible or do we need further discussion?" may ease tensions and stimulate positive interaction again.

Periodically Sum Up or State Decisions

Before going on to a new topic, be certain to state majority points of view or group decisions. This better assures that each member of the group leaves with the same information or understanding.

Be diplomatic in restating opposing views in order to avoid implying partiality to either view. If the final decision rests with you as the group leader, make the decision and then state it briefly, clearly and in a manner that does not embarrass or belittle those who supported another view.

End Every Meeting on a Positive Note

Summarize information, decisions, or group accomplishments. Thank those present for their attention, contributions and willingness to work together through the sharing of ideas and information.

After the meeting adjourns, individually thank those participants who were particularly contributive during the meeting. If the contributions were especially good, you might drop them a short personal note or commend them to their superiors.

Evaluate the Meeting

Review the original agenda and written purposes of the meeting. Were the goals met? Was the group climate what you hoped it would be? What were the verbal and non-verbal reactions of the group? Were they consistent, or did the non-verbal actions seem to imply underlying problems or disagreement that was not voiced?

How could your presentation, selection of audio-visuals or general management of the group have been improved? What would you do differently next time?

Any person can develop the skills necessary to conduct a productive, interesting, stimulating meeting. Patience and persistence are required, and you must be willing to evaluate your abilities in a direct, objective manner. As a personal aid, you might make a numbered list of the guidelines listed within this article and use it as a guide for the next meetings you conduct. With practice, your skills may amaze you!

Discussion Questions

1. The author states that the most important step may be to plan and prepare carefully. What should be included in this step?

2. What are some techniques that can be used to encourage equal participation?

3. What is your reaction to this comment: "As the leader of the meeting, I should be able to express my opinion and suppress any opposition"?

When It's Your Turn to Speak at the Podium

Eugene Raudsepp

Princeton Creative Research, Inc., Princeton, NJ

Many speeches die on the vine. The topic may be a good one. The presenter's delivery may be good. But if there is inadequate preparation, the presentation itself may fail. Ideally, after a speech the audience should feel that all of the details necessary for the integrity and unity of the topic have been covered.

The best way to present a talk is *extemporaneously*. Of course, all points are thought out and planned in detail beforehand. However, the exact wording and phrasing are not memorized. You may want an outline, or you may prefer to write out your text in full, to memorize salient points but don't take the complete speech to the lectern. In addition, you will want to spend a good deal of time making your introduction and closing remarks as clear and concise as possible. A strong beginning and ending are absolutely critical to an effective presentation.

It is best to prepare speaking notes and use them in a rehearsal before taking them to the podium. There are essentially five methods you can use:

- An outline of the speech on a single 8½-inch by 11-inch sheet of paper that has been divided into the required number of sections.
- Manuscript notes where the points at which your memory may fail are marked with a red pencil.
- The 3-inch by 5-inch stack of cards technique. This is the most frequently used and the most flexible. Each major point is placed on a single card in large, clear letters, enabling the speaker to grasp the points on each card quickly.
- A single 3-by-5 card, which contains the key words expressing the main thought in each major section of the speech. This technique is often used by experienced speakers. If the rehearsal is adequate and the speaker

---

doesn't have to glance down at the notes too often, it frequently creates the impression that he or she is speaking without notes.

- A properly designed set of visual aids—flip charts, overhead projection transparencies, or 35mm slides. These enable a speaker to make a presentation without the use of any sort of notes.

The extemporaneous presentation provides a more natural, closer contact with the audience; it also enhances credibility. Finally, it enables you to "play" to the moods and reactions of your audience. You can thus adapt your delivery for maximum impact. The following checklist will help you in sizing up your preparedness for making a presentation.

1. Have I completely examined and thought through my topic? Have I subjected it to stringent and objective self-criticism?
2. Is my presentation organized into logically sequential units?
3. Does it attempt to cover too many points? (Due to prevailing time-limitations, even some good items will occasionally have to be discarded.)
4. Is the organization of my material easy to follow?
5. Have I determined which points need special emphasis and highlighting? Are some of the minor points overemphasized?
6. Have I checked all supporting facts and evidence for accuracy?
7. Am I planning to use a sufficient number of examples, illustrations, visuals, and analogies to support and reinforce the presentation? Which of them can best help to clarify, intensify, prolong, and deepen the participants' awareness of my topic's merits, attributes, and qualities?
8. Have I orchestrated the rhythm and pace of my delivery so that it is varied, interesting, and attention-sustaining?

Practice Thoroughly

Even the most meticulous research, writing, and planning will not guarantee an effective presentation without the three "P's": practice, practice, practice! Practice will build that all-important ingredient of self-confidence. Even Winston Churchill recognized the importance of rehearsing. One day while Churchill was bathing, his valet heard his voice over the splashing water. Entering the bathroom, the valet inquired, "Did you call, sir?" "No," shouted an angry Churchill, "I was just giving a speech to the House of Commons. And next time knock on the door, before you come barging in."

Rehearse your speech several times using a tape recorder or a sympathetic listener. Speakers who appear cool, calm, and collected arrived at their public composure through many hours of studying their topics and then even more time practicing and rehearsing how they were going to present them.

Steve Bevens, a well-respected teacher of presentation skills to executives, suggests that the following key techniques and skills should be mastered:

- Speak informally and conversationally. Consider your talk an "enlarged conversation."
- Be enthusiastic and sincere. If you're not convinced and comfortable with what you're saying, nobody listening will be either.
- Vary the pace and volume of your voice.
- Look at the audience; make eye contact.
- Glance at—don't read—your notes.
- Maintain good posture. Don't slump or sway with the breeze.
- Use gestures that help to emphasize a point, not draw attention away from what you're saying.
- Speak loudly enough so that every member of the audience, regardless of where seated, can hear.
- Avoid fillers such as "ah" and "um." If you need a second to collect your thoughts, take it. The sound of silence is not that painful.
- If using visual aids, make sure everything is in shape before you approach the podium.
- Be friendly—like begets like.

Know Your Audience

Learning about the audience in advance is another important component in presentations. As one administrator and accomplished speaker put it: "Ask yourself these important questions: Who will be in the audience? Why? How much do they know about the subject? What are their attitudes toward the subject? Today, audiences are more sophisticated and demanding. We should do all we can to understand their needs before we take up their time. Communication is a two-way street and we can't *connect* with our listeners if we don't know who they are."

The more you have empathy for your audience, the more easily you will be able to handle the subjective and objective requirements of the situation. At the same time, there is no place for manipulation in a genuine presentation. When people sense that someone is appealing to their emotions and feelings at the expense of their reason, they become suspicious and resentful. They may ignore your talk on that basis alone. You cannot demand your audience's attention—you must deserve it. And frequently the duration of your presentation is restricted.

A lecturer may ask, "How much time does this subject need?" But a presenter's question is "How much time can the audience spare?" Remember that you have a "captive audience." Do your best to make their captivity as pleasant—or as painless—as possible.

Suppose that, in making your presentation, you will be introduced to the audience by someone else. You can use this to advantage. Get together with the person who is to make the introduction, beforehand. Go through your achievements and credentials that will help strengthen your credibility in terms of the topic you are going to present. If your audience sees you as a "winner," they will be in your corner when the bell rings. Even so, an introduction should not be too long or gushy. And it should be as relevant as possible to content presentation.

Beginning and Concluding

A good introduction will provide you with an audience that intends to listen. Your conclusion is your opportunity to reinforce the ideas you've just presented. Both should be carefully planned. If your topic is fairly complex, it should probably even be memorized. Presentation authority Antony Jay says that a presenter's introduction is his opportunity to "harness the horse of the argument to the wagon of the audience's interest and understanding." He adds that if you "gallop straight off, you may hurtle along without realizing you left everyone behind at the starting gate. You have to start in the area they know. You have to identify correctly the assumption and questions in their minds before you can take them with you into unknown territory."

Organize your presentation into (1) a broad, overall consideration of your topic, and (2) a detailed discussion of the main points of your talk.

A long presentation should be interspersed with visual aids, demonstrations, and chalkboard use. This furnishes variety and helps your audience stay alert and attentive. Try not to keep people pinned to their seats for long periods of time. For the longer presentation, take a break—then reconvene.

Get to the Point

Be concise. Avoid longwindedness. Some people introduce their topics with so many preliminaries that the main idea itself gets buried. At the same time, sidestep no main points. Use simple language. Clarity is a must. Avoid jargon or highly technical language, unless necessary. People tend to distrust what they do not understand.

At the same time, you may have to translate a difficult technical concept into one that a nontechnical audience will understand. Try to use analogy, allegory, and alliteration to illustrate these technical points.

Studies of tape recordings in which engineers tried to present nonengineering management with new products ideas have been helpful. Most of the verbal impasses and communication gaps were due to the use of highly technical terminology by presenters. Little attempt was made to translate this into what management would be comfortable with. So if you have a specialized vocabulary, and it ties into your idea, be careful. Try to make your message as particular, precise, and articulate as you can. Relate it to your audience's experience and frame of reference.

Maintain Audience Contact

Pay attention to feedback from your audience. If facial expressions, restlessness, or other reactions indicate you are not getting across, slow down, or ask questions to see if you have been understood. Various types of "body language" such as shuffling feet, yawns, glances at watches, talking among audience participants, and so on, may signal that it's time to call for a break, or to sum up your presentation quickly. It is better to leave them a little ignorant than sound asleep, frustrated, or irritable.

Use Visuals

Illustrations, pictures, drawings, photographs, slides, film strips, motion pictures, models, sketches, diagrams, charts . . . all can be appropriate to your presentation. As a minimum, use a chalkboard or an easel pad to illustrate your points.

Visuals Aid Comprehension

Few managers use good visuals. Ignorance is one reason. Another is the cost and time required to prepare some types of good visuals. On the other hand, we have the individual who uses visuals that are far too elaborate for the kind of topic he or she is presenting. This creates a "showman" image and can actually hurt the presentation. At the same time, it is probably better to commit this sin, than to avoid visuals, thus robbing your audience of the opportunity to picture your main points and thus understand them better.

People remember about 10 percent of what they *read,* 20 percent of what they *hear,* 30 percent of what they *see,* 50 percent of what they *hear and see,* 70 percent of what they *say,* and 90 percent of what they *say as they do a thing.*

CHECKLIST FOR USING VISUALS

- What are the key points of my talk? Which of these should be underscored by visuals? Will they achieve my objectives?
- Will my visuals clarify my ideas? Or will they merely support them? If they only support them, should I consider them?
- Are my visuals appropriate and concrete? Are they informative?
- What visuals should I plan to use? Transparencies to be used with the over-the-shoulder projector? Slides? Filmstrips? Motion pictures? Opaque materials? Flannel board materials? Models? Drawings? Diagrams?
- Have I considered the cost, time, and thought any of these visuals will take? Does the particular presentation of my topic justify these? Can I manage just as well without them, or without some of them?
- Is each visual I plan to use consistent with my objectives? Do they add up to a consistent basic structure and unity? Are they free from complicating type faces, art techniques, and symbols?
- Can my audience easily grasp what they see, or is an added explanation necessary? Are my visuals direct and to the point?
- Should my visuals be representational, pictorial, or symbolic? Which treatment is best for my topic? Which treatment is best from the standpoint of the audience?
- Is the sequence with which I plan to use the visuals logical? Are they so organized that they add strength and cogent relevance to one another and to my overall topic? Is my purpose sequential disclosure, or build-up?
- Are my visuals as effective as they can be made? Did I put enough thought and effort into the planning of the visuals? Did I consider all the ways in which the topic could be reinforced and clarified by the visuals?
- Are my visuals believable in terms of the overall topic? Will my audience appreciate and understand them? Will they be completely readable and will my audience have an unobstructed view of them?

Helping Management "See"

Consider another example from the corporate world. The vice-president in charge of personnel wanted a new policy that would save the company a lot of money. In spite of several meetings with management, he could not make them see how the new policy would work in practice. Frustrated, he finally wrote it up as it would appear in the new policy manual and had it typeset, sending proofs to the top management team, requesting their approval or suggestions for revision. In a week, all proofs were cleared without any changes. Why? Top management had now been able to "see" how the abstract policy would work in practice.

For a presentation to be effective, it has to activate participants' minds. It must transform a passive ingestion of information into a persuasive, convincing experience.

Handling Questions

Your presentation should include most of the answers to anticipated questions. If you fail to anticipate these questions and answer them, your audience is apt to feel frustrated and impatient. Depending on the format of your presentation, unanswered questions may even burst forth during the presentation. This can disrupt the continuity of your delivery.

Consider writing down all of the questions that you would anticipate, with respect to your topic, if you were in the audience yourself.

The Question of Humor

Ideally, a talk should not only be informative, but entertaining and engaging as well. It pays to let your listeners have fun, and that is where humor comes in. Humor is as essential to a talk as seasoning is to a good meal. But the humor you introduce should never be forced or unrelated to your message.

Using humor that is irrelevant to your message is as appropriate as offering a drunk in the gutter a bottle of whiskey. Using humor doesn't mean that you should try to become a stand-up comic telling jokes. The only exception to this is to attempt a few jokes on yourself. This makes you look less superior and more human, permitting audience's identification with you.

Discussion Questions

1. What is meant by the term *extemporaneous?*
2. How is it possible to make a formal speech an "enlarged conversation"?
3. The author states that few managers use good visuals. Why is this true? What can be done to overcome this problem?

Conducting Intelligent Business Dialogue

Jack E. Hulbert

North Carolina A&T State University, Greensboro, NC

In numerous surveys, business executives have ranked "ability to communicate" first among factors necessary for promotion to and within management. They have chosen business communication as one of the most useful college courses in accomplishing their work. They readily attest that sound communication skills facilitated their promotion to executive positions. In fact, many top members of management spend as much as 90 percent of their working day communicating—reading, writing, speaking, and listening.

However, education for management rarely provides balanced emphasis in these four communication skills. Although research indicates that managers use oral communication more frequently than written communication in performing their duties, reading and writing—as components of the three R's—are emphasized in most business curricula. Speaking and listening—skills indispensable to intelligent business *dialogue*—are frequently slighted.

Dialogue is conversation with a purpose. It is the medium through which the enlightened reason. True dialogue expands our minds so that they can grasp new ideas and intelligently reconcile new concepts with old beliefs.

Through dialogue, participants seek natural understanding, enlightenment, and expansion of their knowledge. All participants contribute to the dialogue; no one dominates the conversation; and no one is denied an opportunity to speak. True dialogue is based upon the assumption that participants will speak openly and honestly with good will for the purpose of aiding understanding.

Democratic business institutions cannot survive without rational dialogue—the sharing of ideas and information through deliberation, discussion, and criticism. To reach sound decisions upon which to base productive action, managers must seek the understanding provided by continual consideration of alternatives. The path of successful management does not lie in pursuing *final* decisions but in continuing dialogue to exchange and create the new ideas necessary for progress. If sound decisions for productive ac-

Source: Jack E. Hulbert. "Conducting Intelligent Business Dialogue." Reprinted from *The ABCA Bulletin,* June 1980 by permission of the author.

211

tion are to be reached, managers must possess sound oral communication skills and understand the process of conducting effective dialogue.

Conducting Dialogue

The purpose of intelligent business dialogue is to discuss problems and their potential solutions. If conducted systematically, dialogue involves (1) defining the problem, (2) gathering facts, (3) interpreting evidence, (4) considering alternatives, and (5) reaching decisions. In practice, managers may not always be able to follow this plan step by step; but if they keep this framework in mind, they are less likely to produce clouds of hot air and more likely to accomplish their objectives—a decision for action.

Defining the Problem

Accurate definition of the problem is imperative for mutual understanding. The perceptive manager makes certain that the *real* problem is brought out into the open. Sometimes—intentionally or unintentionally—the problem voiced is only a symptom of the actual problem. Or, it may be a subterfuge to call attention to or test management's reaction to the real problem. Accurate definition of the problem is vital; for there can be no solutions to undefined problems.

Smart managers do not hesitate to ask questions until the problem is clearly delineated. Some participants are reluctant to ask questions for fear of appearing foolish; but no man really becomes a fool until he stops asking questions. In seeking clarification and definition, one should follow Kipling's example: "I had six honest serving men who taught me all they knew; their names were Where and What and When, and Why and How and Who." Also many a problem ceases to exist once it is openly discussed and clearly defined.

Gathering Facts

It is a great disappointment to realize that accurate knowledge can only be acquired by hard work. Fact seeking can be an arduous task because although most men are eager to learn, they do not usually like to be taught by others. However, we must be willing to share facts because only rarely does any one of us possess sufficient facts to solve all our problems. Our problems exist primarily because we lack adequate information to solve them.

In fact finding, we always learn more by letting the other fellow tell us what he knows than by telling him what we know. Actually, the wise man can often acquire knowledge even from those who do not realize they possess it. By asking the right questions, one frequently can learn from someone things that he himself didn't know he knew.

Intelligent business dialogue should provide ample opportunity to share facts among all participants. Everyone knows more than somebody, but nobody knows more than everybody. Therefore, the goal of each participant should be to encourage those who possess the facts and experience to reveal their knowledge in order to shed light on the problem at hand.

While engaged in dialogue, one should be aware that participants usually can be classified in two categories: those who always know more than they tell, and those who always tell more than they know. The key is to encourage the former *to* participate and to discourage the latter *from* participating.

Reputable experts rarely know their subject as thoroughly as they would like to know it; but they should know where to find out the things they don't know. Research and fact finding are what the intelligent do when they become aware that they don't know what they are doing. The truly creative problem solver attempts to learn what everybody else knows and—after analyzing this information—to think what nobody else has thought. Frequently, the more thorough we are in our search for facts, the more clear our perception of our own ignorance and the necessity for further fact finding.

Interpreting the Evidence

Facts are like pieces of evidence to a detective—they must be logically arranged and correctly interpreted to be useful. The ability to interpret facts insightfully makes the difference between possessing knowledge and possessing wisdom. One can know a lot about something and not really understand it.

Accumulating facts without interpreting them is like piling a load of books on a donkey's back. They just lie there—useless! Many people are loaded with factual information, but they don't let it go to their heads— where it could be profitably processed. To paraphrase a familiar adage, the person who has the facts will usually have a job; but the one who knows how to interpret them will always be boss.

One should not confuse facts with opinions or evidence with beliefs. Facts are different from opinions. Opinions are formed by interpreting facts, and much confusion can result because individuals often arrive at different opinions based upon the same facts. Generally, there is more fuss about interpreting the facts than about deciding upon them. Truly, it is not facts but peoples' interpretations of facts that trouble mankind.

One of the primary objectives of dialogue is the free exchange of information among participants; therefore, it is to be expected that many irrelevant facts will be presented. It is the responsibility of the wise decision-maker to sort the wheat from the chaff so that essential information can be correctly interpreted. If this step is overlooked, a manager's success in decision-making is doomed to be smothered beneath a crushing load of irrelevant information. Knowledge is power, but only if one knows what facts to ignore.

Considering Alternatives

After facts are presented and various opinions voiced about a complicated problem, several alternatives usually emerge. This is fortunate, not unfortunate; for we only increase our odds of finding the best possible solution by considering various alternatives. Competent managers give all alternatives a fair chance to be examined *thoroughly;* for they know that in the long run, the hardest way to solve a problem is to seek the easy way out. There *is* usually an easy solution to every problem—neat, plausible, and wrong. Fortunately, the person who knows how to solve all the world's problems ordinarily lacks the authority to do so.

It is only through comparison of logical alternatives that we reason our way toward the truth. It is often helpful to contrast clearly conflicting alternatives to identify their similarities and differences so that participants' minds are freed of trivia and focused on critical differences. What is usually missing from a hot disagreement about alternatives is a clear understanding of the cold facts.

A cooperative, democratic atmosphere must prevail if all alternatives are to be analyzed fairly. Ideal participants in intelligent dialogue are those who are candid and fair, who do not pretend to have knowledge they do not possess, who confess uncertainty when they are uncertain, and who tell the truth as they see it and do their best to learn it from others. Phrases such as "Well, if my alternative is not acceptable, perhaps you could make another proposal" should be frequently heard and said. When weighing alternatives, participants should feel unthreatened and cooperative and free to modify their viewpoints if given convincing evidence.

Reaching Decisions

If productive action is to occur after thoroughly considering all viewpoints, a decision must be reached about which alternative to pursue. In most cases, there is as much danger in delaying decisions past their point of usefulness as there is in making decisions prematurely.

Obviously, problems should be considered thoroughly before a decision for action is made. Some managers, however, appear to practice perpetual suspended judgment while irons cool in the fire. The only time they seem willing to make a decision is when they can't find volunteers for a committee to investigate the situation further. Others appear to be waiting for Judgment Day before exercising any. Procrastination is a serious threat because decisions can be delayed until an idea's time has come—and gone.

On the other hand, there is real danger in making premature decisions. Wise managers do not undertake vast projects with half-vast ideas. They are leery of those who solve problems by charging blindly for the finish line, for they know that people frequently lose sight of the hurdles when they jump to conclusions. And, jumping to quick conclusions seldom leads to happy landings.

The secret to successful decision-making lies in striking an intelligent balance between jumping to premature conclusions and procrastinating until productive action is no longer feasible. If managers expedite dialogue by clearly defining the problem at hand, obtaining the necessary facts, interpreting accurately the evidence presented, and considering thoroughly the alternatives, they are on the right road to reaching timely, efficacious decisions.

Agreeing (or Disagreeing) in Dialogue

Ideally, after thoughtful dialogue, all participants agree with the decision reached; but total agreement is not always achieved. In fact, the possible range of agreement varies from total agreement to total disagreement and includes all kinds of partial agreement as well as "agreement in name only"—when participants believe the action to be taken is correct but not the reasons for taking it. If all participants have been given ample opportunity to provide input, however, they generally are willing to accept—if not agree with—a democratically discussed decision.

If, after defining the problem and discussing and interpreting the facts, total agreement exists, the problem has solved itself; and time should not be wasted on further dialogue. Obviously, for worthwhile dialogue to occur, there must be at least two sides to each problem discussed because when there are no longer two sides, it ceases to be a problem. Nothing is more boring and wasteful than dialogue in which everyone agrees. However, if the problem is worthy of discussion, such rapid, total agreement is indeed rare. Solutions so readily accepted are either those of an extremely brilliant individual—or the boss's.

Sometimes we are pleasantly surprised by reaching unexpected agreement. In an effort to share information openly, participants at times rightly present ideas with which they do not fully agree themselves or which they have not had opportunity to consider thoroughly. After exchanging ideas and opinions with others, however, they become convinced that their solution is plausible. On these occasions, it appears that the best way to convert oneself to an idea is by talking others into believing it.

Normally, however, agreement is reached by exchanging ideas and opinions and selecting the best from each argument until an amalgamated solution is agreed upon. Theoretically, this coalescence of resolutions will be more durable than any one solution alone. Most of us believe that agreement is achieved by changing peoples' opinions—other peoples'—but in the process of rational dialogue, we must be willing to change our own. In dialogue, it is always a good idea to exchange ideas and, many times, even a better idea to change ours. Generally, the best way to prove that we have good judgment is by not relying upon it alone.

A certain amount of disagreement is healthy because we rarely learn anything new from those who totally agree with us. In the long run, the person who agrees with everybody is not worth agreeing with. On the other hand, excessive disagreement can be nonproductive. Some problems seem to be good for nothing except to be argued about. The only time agreement about problems of this nature can be reached is when participants become so tired of arguing that they will agree to anything. If dialogue becomes deadlocked because of total disagreement, perhaps the problem is presently insoluble and should be abandoned or reconsidered later from a fresh perspective.

Disagreement can be caused by the personalities or moods of the participants. At times, there seems to be only one major problem—how to deal with the people who are trying to solve it. These individuals come in wide variety; for example: The Antiquated—the man whose head you can't get a new idea into; he's usually the same man whose head you can't get an old idea out of. The Obdurate—when his mind is made up, he's always willing to listen to reason because it can then do him no harm. The Dull—in his head, ideas die quickly because they can't stand solitary confinement.

Other individuals really only agree with themselves. They don't agree with the opinions of others; they merely agree with their own opinions expressed by others. These individuals can always tell a well-informed person—his views are identical with theirs. They like a person to come right out and say what he thinks—as long as he agrees with them. Dialogue with individuals of this nature is futile and frustrating, and perhaps the only feasible solution is to change the cast of characters.

In seeking agreement, as in all human endeavors, we catch more flies with honey than with vinegar. Reasonable managers refrain from arm twisting because they know that most people are much more agreeable when asked their opinion than when told it. They don't attempt to push opinions down the throats of others because they realize that people will usually react negatively in self-defense. Dialogue should be more an occasion to seek light than to generate heat.

Total agreement is not always possible nor necessary, but tolerance of the ideas and opinions of others is. Ideas are like children—there are none so wonderful as one's own. One should always be tolerant of the opinions of others; after all, they have a right to their own stupid opinions. Participants should not feel they have failed because total agreement has not been achieved. In dialogue, the right to be heard does not automatically include the right to be taken seriously. The right to be taken seriously depends entirely upon what one says. The art of effective dialogue lies in the ability to disagree without being disagreeable.

After thorough dialogue—no matter what the degree of agreement achieved—it is management's responsibility to make the decision for action. Wise managers know that all final decisions are made in a state of mind that is not going to last. They realize that they will not always make the best decision, because good judgment comes from experience—and experience often comes from bad judgment.

In practice, the process of dialogue sometimes seems simply a matter of progressing from cocksure ignorance to thoughtful uncertainty—but decisions have to be made. After all the dialogue, it is ultimately the managers' responsibility to take the action they deem most advantageous to their organization, their employees, and themselves. To do otherwise would be shirking their duty and disloyal to all concerned.

Discussion Questions

1. Give a definition of dialogue. What five factors are involved in dialogue?
2. What is the difference between possessing knowledge and possessing wisdom in the context of this article?
3. Why is it healthy to have a certain amount of disagreement?

Effective Listening Improves Success

Larry R. Smeltzer
Louisiana State University, Baton Rouge, LA

Kittie W. Watson
Tulane University, New Orleans, LA

Business professionals are responsible for retaining a tremendous amount of information while talking on the phone, attending meetings, and conversing with employees and customers. In each of their interactions, listening is the key to ensuring accurate exchanges of information. Comments such as, "Bill just doesn't listen," "Betty is easy to work with because she always takes time to listen," or "Somebody wasn't listening!" are common. It is important to be good listeners, but sometimes during pressure-filled schedules we fail to listen effectively.

When we fail to listen well, problems occur which may affect our performance on and off the job. It is estimated that listening errors cost businesses over $10 billion annually. Mistakes cause order cancellations, employee conflict, and even personal injury. A few years ago a group of new employees attended a training session in which they were instructed in the use of grappling irons. The new employees were told to place the hot irons to the right of the hot oil and the cool irons to the left. The system had worked well until one of the new men placed his hot iron on the left instead of on the right of the oil. The next man that came along grabbed the hot iron with his bare hand and the metal stuck to his hand. The excruciating pain caused him to faint and his hand was injured permanently. Even though all employees were given instructions on the proper use of grappling irons, one person failed to listen. Most people can think of numerous examples of the costs of poor listening, yet the benefits are what we should remember.

Benefits of Effective Listening

A quick review of a few of the benefits of effective listening emphasizes why business people need to listen effectively. First, decision making is made

Source: This is an original essay prepared for *Readings and Cases In Business Communication.*

much easier and is more accurate when we listen effectively. If we fail to listen well, we are likely to miss information that is critical to making good decisions. Second, listening also saves time. Jobs have to be redone, letters have to be retyped, and orders have to be reshipped because certain information was missed during conversations. Third, listening carefully to other's verbal as well as nonverbal cues helps us detect when a person has not understood what has been said. When we listen carefully to someone explaining an unfamiliar or complicated operating procedure, we may find that we need additional information or need to ask questions. Fourth, listening also helps develop trust and cooperation between individuals when problems in communication do occur. People are not as likely to hide their mistakes if they know you will listen to their side of the story. People are more cooperative when their ideas are "listened out."

Although listening is important, it is not easy. If it were, we would remember a person's name the first time, rarely get lost when following directions in an unfamiliar city, or infrequently fail exams. Unfortunately, internal and external barriers create a "listening maze." Listening mazes make it difficult for messages to get through accurately. The remainder of this article will discuss the major barriers contributing to the listening mazes. Then in an effort to improve listening success, we will examine techniques that can be used to overcome listening barriers.

Barriers to Listening

Listening barriers can be external or internal. A natural tendency exists to make excuses for poor listening. These excuses usually revolve around external distraction barriers, such as boring speakers, the noise of typewriters and telephones, or too many people talking at the same time. Obviously, external barriers can be and are a problem, but effective listeners have learned techniques to help overcome these obstacles.

Internal barriers are those we can learn to modify and control. We have both physical and psychological internal barriers. Our greatest physical barrier is *ourselves:* We think faster than we listen. Most Americans speak at a rate of about 125 words per minute but are able to think at rates four times that fast. Impatient with the plodding rate of the spoken word, the mind tends to wander onto other things while checking in only periodically to what is being said. Because in most cases our daydreams or fantasies seem to be more interesting than what we are listening to, we let them overpower the spoken message. Physical barriers such as headaches, growling stomachs, or sore feet also are often difficult to ignore.

Psychological barriers must be taken into consideration together with the physical barriers. One of the greatest psychological barriers is motivation. Unfortunately, because the physical barriers discussed earlier present obstacles to listening, we must continually concentrate on listening. This concentration requires motivation, and motivation problems are compounded by our emotions. Having an argument with a friend, receiving bad news, or flunking an exam make it difficult to put energy into listening. Our emotions are also affected by a speaker's mannerisms or ideas that are presented. This can cause us to react emotionally and filter the messages we should be hearing.

Another psychological barrier is the "debate" or "rehearsing a response" barrier. When listeners find themselves disagreeing with the speaker, they begin planning the great comeback, blocking out the speaker, and missing the meanings in messages. Perhaps the greatest psychological barrier is a personal willingness to listen. We may unconsciously not want to listen. This can happen when we believe that what the other person has to say has no novelty or value, or when we think we know what the person will say before he or she says it. Without a willingness to listen no real communication can take place.

Techniques for Overcoming Listening Barriers

With an understanding of the benefits and barriers to effective listening, we need to learn how to improve listening skills. Research suggests that listening improves dramatically when using the following simple techniques.

Set an Objective

Why are you listening? What are you attempting to determine? What information are you seeking? These questions may seem obvious, but too often we don't stop to determine the goal of listening; consequently, without a purpose, our attention wanders.

Prepare to Listen

Right now the logical question may be, "How am I supposed to get prepared to listen when I don't know when someone is going to talk to me?" This is a valid question, yet it is always possible to prepare to listen. The key to remember is that listening preparation will vary with the situation. Regardless of the situation, however, try to check off the following list:

Could you pick a better place to listen?
Is it possible to listen at a better time?
Should you take notes?
What are your biases in this situation?
What specific information do you need?

Even though this list is basic, you should go back and review this list period-ically because it serves as an important guide for all interactions.

Organize the Message

Once you have prepared to listen, you want to organize and remember the message. Five techniques that will help you organize the message and im-prove your listening effectiveness are:

1. Identify the main and supporting points.
2. Mentally outline the message.
3. Summarize the message.
4. Visualize the message.
5. Fit the message to personal experiences (personalize).

The first three techniques should be self-explanatory, but a few words on the last two may help. Visualizing a message, putting it into pictures, re-duces the chance of letting your mind wander. This technique challenges you to concentrate on the topic. If you do this, you are less likely to miss critical information.

To personalize, to select those aspects of the message that are the most important or affect you, is to personalize the message. As you do this, you will become more interested in the ideas being presented and it will be easier for you to concentrate on the message.

Ask Questions

As you develop your mental outline and summarize the key points, you may find that the message is either unclear or incomplete. The ability to ask questions is probably the easiest but most neglected technique for effective listening.

Use questions to request additional information on a topic that is not clear and to verify the accuracy of what is heard. Some people are afraid to ask questions because it may show they were not listening, it may show a lack of understanding, they may appear demanding, or because they think that questions or answers will not really help. We shouldn't be afraid to ask questions to make this critical listening process more meaningful. Remem-ber, listening is the key to communication, which in turn is the key to ex-changing information.

Summary

We rarely evaluate our ability to listen. When we do, we usually conclude that we are good listeners! After all, one would think that after having a lifetime to practice everyone would listen well. Regrettably, research highlights two important aspects about the process of listening. First, we tend to "slip" and listen poorly at times; but we can quickly improve listening skills by reminding ourselves of the potential barriers to listening and the techniques to overcome them. Second, listening is a key to the successful exchange of information. Companies operate on the exchange of information, and people play a key role in this process. Applying the techniques presented in this article should improve your listening ability, which will improve accurate information exchanges.

Discussion Questions

1. List and describe at least three barriers to listening.
2. Give examples of personalizing and visualizing the message.
3. What do you consider the main reasons that people do not ask more questions?

Part VII

Cases

The Five Forks Fiasco

William J. Buchholz

Bentley College, Waltham, MA

As sole proprietor of Snopes's Hardware and Variety Store in a small, elegant New England town, you have decided that if your business is to prosper and if you are to serve the greater community better, you will have to relocate.

About a year ago you purchased a choice piece of property nearly a half mile from your present site. An unsightly tumbledown barn occupied part of the 40,000 square foot lot, for which you paid $100,000. To prepare the site for your new location, you first had the barn demolished; then you had graders excavate the land; and finally, you had a beautiful 6-foot pine stockade fence erected to separate your lot from the adjacent residential properties. All in all, your expenditure for site preparation totaled approximately $15,000. Thus, to date you have invested $115,000 in the site and its preparation. The building you hope to construct, plus the landscaping and paving for the parking lot, will cost you in the neighborhood of $235,000. Your total outlay, then, is estimated to be about $350,000 to $400,000, a sizable commitment, to say the least. But you feel the increased business in the new location should recoup your investment within 10 years. All financing is arranged, and your backers are eager for you to begin construction.

On the next page is a map of your new location, known as "Five Forks" (so called because five roads actually intersect here—a very dangerous area).

You can see from this map that the site is a good business location, because traffic converges from so many directions. You intend to have two traffic feeds into your parking area, one from Washington Road and the other from Barrett Street. Further, your plan calls for disposition of the lot footage in this way:

Retail space: 12,000 sq ft

Office space: 8,000 sq ft

Parking/Grounds: 20,000 sq ft

The architects have designed a beautiful two story New England brick and clapboard colonial that will harmonize perfectly with the residential flavor of the area. You certainly are proud of the improvement your building will make over the ramshackle barn that stood there for 100 years.

You are sensitive to the fact that your business, if it is to be as prosperous

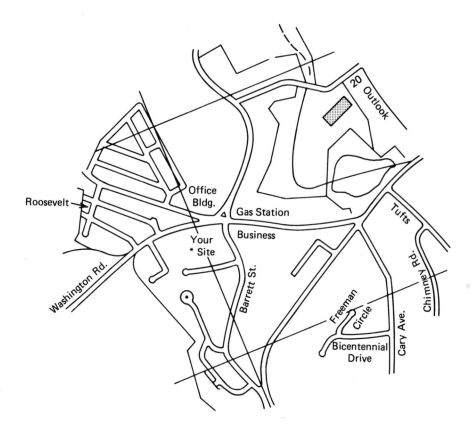

as you hope, will draw a good deal more traffic into the area. Therefore, you hired a traffic engineering firm to perform an impact study of the intersection. The engineers have indicated in their final report that with minor traffic flow adjustments and the addition of two traffic islands, the intersection can sustain optimum traffic levels for minimal cost (a cost you have volunteered to underwrite). All in all, with these improvements, the traffic situation at Five Forks would appear to become even safer than at present.

As far as you're concerned, the whole plan is perfect: a beautiful new building on a gorgeously landscaped lot will replace the eyesore that had blighted the area for decades. And, you'll be able to set up a larger hardware store to serve both the neighborhood and the town more efficiently. Also with the larger building you will be able to lease some retail space and a number of offices for professionals (lawyers, doctors, etc.).

But even the best laid plans often go awry. In the last four months or so the neighbors in the area have grown positively rabid in their opposition to this venture. The main problem seems to be that they simply do not want another business in the neighborhood. This doesn't make a lot of sense to you, though, because already three commercial enterprises occupy the other corners of the intersection. Some of these people, especially those who abut your site, are almost hysterical in their cries of "creeping commercialism." They'll do anything to keep another business out of the neighborhood. It's downright dangerous, they say, to erect another business here, because of increased traffic; as it is, the area is saturated. What about the little children going to school? It's frightening enough now for them to cross these busy streets. Besides, there's no real need for the new store, since the old store is only a half mile down the road—just another example of a self-serving businessman out for more bucks.

And what about the residential development encroachment? Two beautiful homes could be erected here instead. Or even a little playground/park area. No matter what else, one more business here will erode housing valuation. Opposition is so strong that certain members of the neighborhood have conducted a campaign to oust you from the site. They have circulated petitions against the proposal, conducted a letter blitz to the local paper, contacted town officials, and promised you that they will stop at nothing to defeat your plan to relocate.

You recognize that these people, your future neighbors, have some powerful arguments against your proposal, and they pose a serious threat, indeed. But the biggest weapon they have is the zoning law. Years ago, after the other businesses at the intersection had been established, the town rezoned the whole Five Forks area as residential; in other words, no more businesses could locate here. You were well aware of this problem, but were convinced that you could easily get the area rezoned from single-family residential to what is called "controlled commercial," especially because this is a unique site, and you are not proposing a rezoning precedent. Besides, you were assured by a very important town official that the rezoning would be a mere formality, because the other corners are commercial anyway.

To achieve the rezoning, you have to convince two bodies of your venture's worthiness: the five-member Board of Selectmen and the Town Meeting Assembly. The selectmen conduct all initial hearings on the matter and then submit a report and recommendation to the Town Meeting members. It is this assembly of 125 elected members who will ultimately accept or reject your proposal to rezone. To pass Town Meeting, your bid to rezone will have to receive a two-thirds favorable vote.

You've got approximately three months before the town meeting. In this time, you have to convince three constituents of the worth of your project: the neighbors, the Board of Selectmen, and the Town Meeting members. To do so you must counter a vocal and growing opposition which, in your opinion, is largely emotional and unfounded. You will have to show good faith and adopt a reasonable stance.

Questions

1. How will you go about winning over the formidable opposition?
2. What role will problem definition play in your initial strategy formulation?
3. What kind of research will be necessary?
4. How important is open and honest dialogue in this situation?
5. What is the most important constituent?
6. What method will you use to conduct your dialogue with the opposition?
7. What alternatives can you present to the opposition?
8. How can you "package" yourself (i.e., what image is desirable for you to project)?
9. What facts do you want to emphasize?
10. What facts should you deemphasize?
11. Is it possible for you to reach an "amalgamated solution" here?
12. Can you bring the opposition into the discussion in such a way that together you forge a solution both sides can accept?

Develop a strategy that you feel will ensure the acceptance of your proposal to rezone. Remember, you've invested a great deal of money already, and your future business growth depends on the success of relocating to this spot. If your instructor permits, write letters to the three constituents, trying to persuade them of the benefits of your relocation. You might also write some ads for the local paper and outline the speech you hope to present to the voters at the crucial town meeting.

The Zane Automobile Parts Company Audit

Steven Golen
Louisiana State University, Baton Rouge, LA

John Bimmert has just graduated from State College with a degree in accounting and has accepted a staff position with a local CPA firm. John found his accounting courses at State College to be both challenging and intellectually stimulating. Therefore, John was excited about his new job and very eager to start applying what he had learned in school to actual accounting situations.

After a week of job orientation, John was assigned to assist Jim Thompson, a senior staff accountant, on an audit of Zane Automobile Parts Company. Because John was a new accountant joining the firm, and obviously because of his lack of auditing experience, Jim asked John to verify some inventory items once they arrived at the automobile parts company.

When John began to verify the inventory items, he ran into difficulty in interpreting the inventory records. So, John went to see Bill Jones, the company controller, to get some help in understanding the inventory system used at this company. Much to John's surprise, however, Bill seemed very rude. Bill told John that the records have been maintained accurately and carefully for many years, and he didn't understand why someone with a degree in accounting had trouble interpreting inventory records. Bill said that he was very busy, and that he didn't have the time to go through the entire inventory system with John. Bill said he would respond only to specific questions.

John, feeling awkward because of the way Bill reacted to his inquiry, decided to review the system further before approaching Bill. John couldn't understand why the controller seemed to be annoyed at his presence at the audit. John also couldn't understand why the controller was not cooperative in helping him interpret the inventory records.

John has yet to use any of his accounting skills. He suddenly realized that working as an accountant isn't just "cranking out" numbers, but it involves an ability to communicate as well.

Questions

1. How would you approach this situation differently?
2. What should John remember when dealing with future clients?
3. How important are communication skills for accountants?
4. Are there any implications of this case study to other professions? If so, what are they?

Improving Employment Searches

The résumé, cover letter, and interview are the main components of an employment search. Each of these elements of the employment process is discussed in this part.

A person must first write a well-organized résumé that relates qualifications and interests. This is the topic of Jerrold Simon's article, "How to Write a Resume."

The second article, "Reading Between the Lines of Employment Correspondence," emphasizes that the letter of application creates an impression when it is received. Jack D. Eure and T. J. Halatin state that the appearance, thought, attitude, and style conveyed "between the lines" of the letter create this impression.

Suzanne Seixas presents a comprehensive discussion of the interview process in her article, "How to Handle a Job Interview." She directs the article toward the various situations that may develop and suggests how to manage them. The article also presents a quick quiz for the job candidate to use as a self-evaluation tool.

How to Write a Resume

Jerrold G. Simon
Harvard University, Cambridge, MA

If you are about to launch a search for a job, the suggestions I offer here can help you whether or not you have a high school or college diploma, whether you are just starting out or changing your job or career in midstream.

"What Do I Want to Do?"

Before you try to find a job opening, you have to answer the hardest question of your working life: "What do I want to do?" Here's a good way.

Sit down with a piece of paper and don't get up till you've listed all the things you're proud to have accomplished. Your list might include being head of a fund-raising campaign, or acting a juicy role in the senior play.

Study the list. You'll see a pattern emerge of the things you do best and like to do best. You might discover that you're happiest working with people, or maybe with numbers, or words, or well, you'll see it.

Once you've decided what job area to go after, read more about it in the reference section of your library. "Talk shop" with any people you know in that field. Then start to get your resume together.

There are many good books that offer sample resumes and describe widely used formats. The one that is still most popular, the *reverse chronological*, emphasizes where you worked and when, and the jobs and titles you held.

How to Organize It

Your name and address go at the top. Also phone number.

What job do you want? That's what a prospective employer looks for first. If you know exactly, list the next under *Job Objective*. Otherwise, save it for your cover letter (I describe that later), when you're writing for a specific person. In any case, make sure your resume focuses on the kind of work you can do and want to do.

Now comes *Work Experience*. Here's where you list your qualifications. *Lead with your most important credentials.* If you've had a distinguished

Source: Jerrold G. Simon. "How to Write a Resume." Reprinted by permission of International Paper Company, 1981.

233

work history in an area related to the job you're seeking, lead off with that. If your education will impress the prospective employer more, start with that.

Begin with your most recent experience first and work backwards. Include your titles or positions held. And list the years.

Figures Don't Brag

The most qualified people don't always get the job. It goes to the person who presents himself most persuasively in person and on paper.

So don't just list where you were and what you did. This is your chance to tell *how well you did.* Were you the best salesman? Did you cut operating costs? Give numbers, statistics, percentages, increases in sales or profits.

No Job Experience?

In that case, list your summer jobs, extracurricular school activities, honors, awards. Choose the activities that will enhance your qualifications for the job.

Next list your *Education*—unless you chose to start with that. This should also be in reverse chronological order. List your high school only if you didn't go on to college. Include college degree, postgraduate degrees, dates conferred, major and minor courses you took that help qualify you for the job you want.

Also, did you pay your own way? Earn scholarships or fellowships? Those are impressive accomplishments.

No Diplomas or Degrees?

Then tell about your education: special training programs or courses that can qualify you. Describe outside activities that reveal your talents and abilities. Did you sell the most tickets to the annual charity musical? Did you take your motorcycle engine apart and put it back together so it works? These can help you.

Next, list any *Military Service.* This could lead off your resume if it is your only work experience. Stress skills learned, promotions earned, leadership shown.

Now comes *Personal Data.* This is your chance to let the reader get a glimpse of the personal you, and to further the image you've worked to project in the preceding sections. For example, if you're after a job in computer programming, and you enjoy playing chess, mention it. Chess playing requires the ability to think through a problem.

Include foreign languages spoken, extensive travel, particular interests or professional memberships, *if* they advance your cause.

Keep your writing style simple. Be brief. Start with sentences with impressive actions verbs: "Created," "Designed," "Achieved," "Caused."

No Typos Please

Make sure your grammar and spelling are correct. And no typos!

Use 8½" by 11" bond paper—white or off-white for easy reading. Don't cram things together.

Make sure your original is clean and readable. *Then* have it professionally duplicated. No carbons.

Get It Into the Right Hands

Now that your resume is ready, start to track down job openings. How? Look up business friends, personal friends, neighbors, your minister, your college alumni association, professional services. Keep up with trade publications, and read help-wanted ads.

And start your own "direct mail" campaign. First, find out about the companies you are interested in—their size, location, what they make, their competition, their advertising, their prospects. Get their annual report—and read it.

No "Dear Sir" Letters

Send your resume, along with a cover letter, to a specific person in the company, not to "Gentlemen" or "Dear Sir." The person should be the top person in the area where you want to work. Spell his name properly! The cover letter should appeal to your reader's own needs. What's in it for him? Quickly explain why you are approaching *his* company (their product line, their superior training program) and what you can bring to the party. Back up your claims with facts. Then refer him to your enclosed resume and ask for an interview.

Oh, Boy! An Interview!

And now you've got an interview! Be sure to call the day before to confirm it. Meantime, *prepare yourself.* Research the company and the job by reading books and business journals in the library.

On the big day, arrive 15 minutes early. Act calm, even though, if you're normal, you're trembling inside at 6.5 on the Richter scale. At every chance, let your interviewer see that your personal skills and qualifications relate to the job at hand. If it's a sales position, for example, go all out to show how articulate and persuasive you are.

Afterwards, follow through with a brief thank-you note. This is a fine opportunity to restate your qualifications and add any important points you didn't get a chance to bring up during the interview.

Keep Good Records

Keep a list of prospects. List the dates you contacted them, when they replied, what was said.

And remember, someone out there is looking for someone *just like you.* It takes hard work and sometimes luck to find that person. Keep at it and you'll succeed.

Discussion Questions

1. According to the author, what is the most difficult question that must be faced when writing a resume? Describe a strategy that can be used to answer the question.

2. What is meant by the comment, "Figures don't brag"?

3. Why is the information presented in the Personal Data section important?

Reading Between the Lines of Employment Correspondence

Jack D. Eure
T. J. Halatin
Southwest Texas State University, San Marcos, TX

When searching for employment, job applicants need to be aware that employers often attach as much significance to the way in which job credentials are presented as to the actual experience, education, and factual information contained in those credentials. Indeed, employers often "read between the lines" when examining letters of application and other employment correspondence. Thus, any negative nonverbal indicators in employment correspondence can cause the applicant's real message to be overshadowed, distorted, or misunderstood.

One assumption that is vital to the understanding of nonverbal communication and its role in employment correspondence is that it is impossible *not* to communicate. Each thing said (or left unsaid) and its presentation communicate something to perspective employers, creating an impression and signalling the reader to make employment decisions. While the factors involved in such an impression cannot be reduced to a mathematical formula, the nonverbal aspects of appearance, thought, attitude, style, and tone exert considerable impact on the outcome of job-seeking effort.

Creating Impressions

Appearance

Does the letter's appearance make a good first impression? Consider the type of stationery used; is it bond paper with a 16 to 20 pound weight or high-grade tissue paper? Bond paper has rag content, as opposed to the wood pulp used in newspaper, and it looks and feels good to the person holding it. Good stationery makes the writer appear successful and results in a non-verbal plus.

Does the letter style comply with correct usage? Two basic letter styles are used for employment correspondence: block and semi-block. When an employer receives an application letter that is not set up in a consistent, recognized, accepted style, a negative impression is formed about the prospective employee.

The "mechanics" of employment correspondence also should be carefully checked. Obvious concerns include spelling, grammar, punctuation, syllabication, and page balance. An application letter containing mechanical errors may cause the reader to conclude that the writer is sloppy, of marginal intelligence, or lacking an eye for detail. If the letter has erasures, strike-overs, or was typed with a worn-out ribbon, employers may conclude that they are not considered very important because the applicant did not take the time to correct these errors. In addition, the letter should be well-balanced on the page—much like a picture in a frame. In short, poor handling of mechanics is an insult to a prospective employer.

Are the paragraphs short enough to invite easy reading? If all pertinent qualifications are lumped into one or two extra-long paragraphs, an applicant may communicate an inability or refusal to organize the material into logical components. In effect the message is, "Here it all is, you figure it out if you don't get tired of reading." One- or two-sentence paragraphs are permissible, particularly in the opening of a letter. After that, it is best to vary the paragraph length with none exceeding five or six sentences.

Thought

Does the application letter reveal careful thought about its fundamental purpose? In most cases the objective of a letter is not to get the job, but to persuade the reader to schedule an interview with the applicant. To do this, applicants should employ a basic psychological organization plan such as follows:

1. Use an attention start. Ask a pertinent question or express an interest in the company. (This is easiest to do after having done research on the company.)

2. Develop the reader's interest by revealing a desire to be considered for a job.

3. Combine in an interesting way an understanding of the job requirements and a well-developed section on qualifications. (This part may be several paragraphs long and is the heart of the letter.)

4. Use an action close. Ask the reader to grant an interview. Do not be bashful or just hint at the possibility of an interview; come right out and ask.

The goal is to persuade without pushing and to show by selection of fact, interpretation of fact, and writing personality an ability to perform the work the reader needs done.

Material should be presented in a logical order. In answering a job advertisement in which four qualifications are detailed, applicants should arrange their material so that it speaks to each of the major points. Ignoring major points may nonverbally communicate an attempt to cover up a weakness. All information needed by the reader should be included. In presenting the facts, it is desirable for applicants to include their strongest selling points early in the letter while saving one strong point for the close.

Attitude

The key idea here is to communicate the benefits an employer will derive from the action suggested in the letter. The basic thrust of the letter should be "work the reader needs done." Applicants shouldn't emphasize their own egos; instead, they should show how their qualifications will benefit the company. This amounts to using what is called the "you attitude," or stressing how the reader will benefit from hiring them. Admittedly, it is difficult to do this when writing about oneself, but it is a "must" in doing a good selling job.

Anyone who sees many application letters knows how sadly they lack this "you attitude." Actually landing a job is a difficult task in many cases, but the process could be simplified greatly if applicants would constantly keep in mind the prospective employer's point of view. Compare the following opening paragraphs?

> *I happened to see your advertisement for section manager in this morning's paper, and would like to be considered for the position. I am very much interested in working for your company because I have heard of its liberal vacation allowances and attitude toward employees.*

> *My four years' education in management at Southwest Texas State University and two summers working as assistant manager for Southern Lumber Company should prove to be valuable training for the section manager's job which you advertised in this morning's* RECORD NEWS.

The major difference in these paragraphs is the point of view of the writer. It is possible that the first applicant is better qualified than the second, but the first letter gives no thought to the reader's interests. From the nonverbal standpoint, the first letter suggests the writer may be immature and self-centered, while the second appears to be the work of a well-rounded, caring individual who relates well to others.

Style

Employment correspondence should be clear, concise, and readable. It should avoid business jargon and trite, meaningless, or wordy expressions. Words selected to denote meaning also connote or offer nonverbal cues to the reader. Formal language, such as that used in writing a scholarly dissertation or report, is out of place in employment correspondence. Short, well-known, conversational words are more appropriate. Compare the following lists:

Formal	**Informal**
utilize	use
anticipate	expect
deem	think (believe)
endeaver	try
terminate	end

Phrases and sentences should likewise be expressed in conversational, informal language. The following closing paragraphs for an application letter provide a stark contrast:

By interrogation in an interview you can ascertain more about my capabilities. Please do not hesitate to contact me if you desire a list of references or further information for investigation.

Through an interview, you can learn more about me and my abilities. Please let me know if you need additional information or a list of references, and I'll gladly furnish it.

In short, the use of long, heavy, formal words nonverbally convinces the reader of an intention to "impress" rather than "express."

It is also important to demonstrate conviction with words. This is best achieved through concrete writing—writing which vividly brings an applicant's accomplishments to life in terms of the reader's interests and understanding. For example, it is better to write, " I *earned* a degree in management from Louisiana State University," than to write, "I spent four years at Louisiana State University and got my degree in management."

Likewise, variations in the concreteness of describing the course work that prepared the applicant for the job may vary the nonverbal picture of accomplishment communicated. Compare "I took a course in motion and time study" with "In a college course I learned the fundamentals of motion and time study. Thus, I could assist in your time study work with only a minimum of specific instruction." The first statement is dull on contrast to the conviction wording in the second. The secret of concrete presentation lies in selecting words that emphasize accomplishments and the desire to do work the reader needs done.

Tone

Employment correspondence must sound sincere, as though one human had written it to another. Unfortunately, many writers of application letters take one of two approaches: Either the letter they produce sounds like the work of a raving egomaniac or else it has a tone of "Poor little me, I need any job you have." Obviously, neither approach is good.

An ideal approach involves walking a tightrope between exaggeration and restraint. On the one hand, it is desirable to be enthusiastic and full of self-confidence; on the other hand, it is best not to appear conceited. The tone should convey the idea that the writer has much to offer the company, yet still has plenty to learn by becoming a part of the company and growing with it.

The close of an application letter offers a final opportunity to make non-verbal communication work for the writer. The objective of most application letters is to get an interview. Although wording must be natural, applicants should avoid three objectionable types of interview requests: the weak, hinting type, which lacks conviction and courage; the take-it-or-leave it type, which may be either passive or arrogant; and the high-pressure type, which is discourteous.

The first type says, "An interview would be appreciated," but it does not ask for it directly. The second type says, "An interview will show my ability to meet the job requirements. Between eight and five you can telephone me at ————." This may suggest the writer is too proud to request this action. Although the high-pressure type may take many forms, a common one says, "When may I have an interview?" This apparently takes the prerogative of refusing the interview away from employers and allows them only to choose the meeting time.

By walking the tightrope between high-pressure and restraint, skillful writers may conclude their letters with friendly, tactful, courteous, direct action words such as the following: "As my interests do lie in the realm of useful and satisfying work in the field of industrial management, may I meet you personally and talk with you? I can make myself available at any date convenient to you." This approach sets a tone of modest confidence while avoiding the extremes of timid deprecation and egotistical boasting.

The High Cost of Ignoring Nonverbal Factors

Of all the business letters written, only a small portion concern employment. But few will place more responsibility on writers than will these letters, for they directly concern the course of human lives. The success or failure of these efforts can affect career outcomes. With the high level of unemployment and recent recessions, job applicants literally cannot afford to ignore the nonverbal factors of appearance, thought, attitude, style, and tone in their job-seeking efforts. Wise job applicants will make nonverbal communication work for them instead of unconsciously letting it work against them.

Discussion Questions

1. Why is it impossible not to communicate? Give several examples of how a person may be communicating even though he or she is not aware of it.

2. In your own words briefly review the basic psychological organization plan presented in this article.

3. What do the authors mean when they say that it is important to demonstrate conviction with words? Give an example other than the one presented in this article.

How to Handle a Job Interview

Suzanne Seixas

Money Magazine, New York, NY

Like the first meeting with the person you're going to marry, a job interview is one of life's important and usually awkward encounters. To make matters worse, if you are looking for a middle-level position in a large organization, you'll probably have to endure not one but a minimum of three interviews: one with a personnel manager, a second with the boss you would work for and a third with *his* boss.

Of the three, the personnel interviewer is the one most apt to screen you out; part of his job is gate-keeping. The second interviewer, the department head with a job to fill, usually makes the actual hiring decision. To avoid being eliminated at any point, both entry- and middle-level candidates should learn how to handle themselves while they're being sized up—though the middle-level applicant's experience makes his situation trickier and more complicated than the beginner's.

Any applicant should start by boning up on the company. Write for the annual report and, for a more candid view of the company's future, ask a stockbroker to get you a brokerage-house report. For recent business-press coverage of the company, consult a public library's copy of the *F&S Index of Corporations and Industries,* or the *Business Periodicals Index.* It also helps to know something about the executives you're likely to meet. Try *Standard & Poor's Register: Directors and Executives* or *Who's Who in Finance and Industry.*

Leisurely But Manly

First impressions are important, and what you wear to an interview can affect your chances. John T. Molloy, author of *Dress for Success* (1975), says, for instance, that an applicant to Texas Instruments, a Dallas-based maker of

---

A QUICK QUIZ FOR THE JOB CANDIDATE

1. If you can wear blue jeans on the job, you can wear blue jeans to the interview.   TRUE____FALSE____
2. Most interviewers lose interest on learning a candidate has been fired from his last job.   TRUE____FALSE____
3. When an interviewer says, "Tell me all about yourself," he wants a thorough review of your background.   TRUE____FALSE____
4. If you're asked why you left your last job, it's perfectly okay to say, "So I could make more money."   TRUE____FALSE____
5. An interviewer risks charges of sex discrimination if he asks a woman applicant her height and weight.   TRUE____FALSE____
6. It's best to talk salary early on, before you and the interviewer have wasted too much of each other's time.   TRUE____FALSE____
7. If you think the job being described isn't right for you, you should move to end the interview quickly.   TRUE____FALSE____

Answers reflecting the majority opinion of personnel specialists and others interviewed by Money *are on page 249.*

---

electronic equipment, should know that the company has "leisurely" dress code. Jack Troster, TI's manager of corporate staffing, agrees—to a point. "Yes, we're a shirtsleeve outfit," he says, "and like other southwestern companies, we don't mind a candidate in a sport coat. But he should have a tie. And a leisure suit on an engineer may look effeminate to an older manager "

Aversion to blue-jeaned applicants is nationwide, and it applies to industries from banking to offshore construction. Typical is the comment of Sam Whitehead, personnel assistant for Colonial Pipeline, an Atlanta firm that operates pipelines for petroleum products: "Even if you're going to wear them on the job, we don't like to see blue jeans in an interview."

If you don't know exactly how to dress, err on the side of conservatism. Women are safe in tailored shirtwaists or separates, and pantsuits are widely acceptable. As for men, Robert Marin, a Washington, D.C. "wardrobe consultant," says, "The flippant, foppish business dress of the '60s is gone, and we're back to sincerity clothing. That means navy or gray pinstripe suits, white cotton long-collared shirts, pindot, repstripe or refined foulard-design ties, and cap-toe or wing-tip shoes."

Interviewers are also favorably impressed by an applicant who looks them in the eye and shakes hands firmly. Stanley Hyman, who teaches a course at Catholic University in Washington on how to change careers, coaches prospective job seekers in what he calls nonverbals—physical mannerisms that he claims help establish assertiveness and control in the first few minutes of an interview. Hyman has it all worked out: "Place your chair at a 45° angle to the interviewer's desk so that you are almost sitting sideways to it. When you sit down, cross your leg toward the interviewer to indicate strength, and open your jacket to show you're sincere. Pull down your coat collar so that's tight against your shirt, to keep your suit from looking ill fitting. Place your elbow on the chair arm nearest the desk and lean a bit on it. Never put your hands together: that means you're trying to control yourself. If the interviewer tilts backwards, you can back off too—otherwise you'll scare him. Now you can proceed confidently with the interview."

The Rug-and-Jug Rule

Whether you take Hyman's advice literally or not, by this point in the proceedings you should also have been doing what Charles Colenaty of Los Angeles' Management Counselors Associates calls "interviewing the company before it interviews you"—picking up clues form your surroundings as to what sort of firm it is. "When you arrive," says Colenaty, "notice if there are weeds growing in front of the building. When you go in, are you treated indifferently, or does the receptionist act as if they were expecting you? Is she free to chat with you, and do other employees talk to her as though they like her?" If the people are polite and attentive and the housekeeping is good, business probably is too. Adds Eugene L. Mueller, president of Eli Djeddah Associates, a career-planning agency in San Diego: "The job level of the line manager who interviews you may be indicated by whether he has a rug on his floor and a water jug on his desk. Most big corporations have a rug-and-jug rule. If he makes do with vinyl and goes to the drinking fountain, it's a sign of how prestigious *your* job will be."

Interviews often begin with what's called an "open-ended icebreaker": the interviewer's invitation to "tell me all about yourself." Most interviewers hope to elicit a brief, well-organized presentation of your education or recent work history that comes to a logical conclusion (after all, they usually have the biographical facts from your résumé). To avert a disjointed, rambling response, Stanley Hyman's remedy is a polite demurrer: "Your time is valuable and I don't want to waste it. There must be some specifics you want to know."

But members of the 40-Plus Club of Southern California, one of a dozen volunteer groups of unemployed executives in the U.S. and Canada who have banded together to help each other find jobs, are advised to give a softer answer. Their counselors, often out-of-work personnel managers, suggest volunteering only a modicum of information and slipping in a question about the interviewer's company as soon as possible. For example, in talking to a department head, an applicant might interrupt his own recital to say, "In that job, I had my first experience using wholesalers rather than selling directly to retail outlets. I know your company uses wholesalers too. How do you get them to concentrate on your product?"

Hankering for More

From the friendly and general, an interviewer may suddenly switch to a staccato series of probing queries: "Why did you leave your last job?" "What makes you want to work for us?" "Where do you expect to be in five years?" The answers should express a desire for growth and challenge. George Odiorne, dean of the University of Massachusetts' School of Business Administration, suggests: "Faint-praise the firm you left. If you're being interviewed by a fast-moving, sharp outfit, say, 'Well, the company was a fine, old-line, blue-chip conservative corporation.' " Your interviewer will hear in that description the implication that you were an action-oriented person in a stodgy setup that did not offer scope for your abilities—as you assume his company will. For the third question, the wrong answers are: "I want to be secure," or "With a group of people I like." The right response is anything that reveals an aspiration for growth, including, "I want to be earning $10,000 more annually." Indeed, a hankering for more income is generally considered to be synonymous with an interest in achievement. It's a perfectly respectable reason to give for changing jobs.

A Strong Weakness

Interviewers often move on from the probing question to the positively sticky, such as asking an applicant to describe his three greatest weaknesses. "The safest answer," says Odiorne, "is one that presents a weakness that a prospective employer might consider a strength: a confession that you're a work addict or a perfectionist." Stanleigh B. McDonald, author of *Ten Weeks To a Better Job* (1972), disagrees: "If someone told me, 'I'm a workaholic,' I'd say, 'Oh nuts, I've heard that before.' Instead, why not admit a real weakness but emphasize the positive, that you have the character to surmount it? Say, "I hate to do detail work, but I do it thoroughly.'"

Sometimes interviewers will use so-called stress techniques—deliberately abrasive tactics designed to test an applicant's ability to withstand stress without losing his composure. Some of the more familiar ploys include inviting a candidate to smoke but providing him with no ashtray; positioning his chair so that the sun is in his eyes; bombarding him with rapid-fire questions from several people at once; simulating anger at his response; or seating him with other applicants for the same job around a table and asking each to explain in turn why he is the man who should be hired. There is also the pressure interview, in which the employer gets the applicant in his office, puts his feet up on his desk, tilts his chair back and commands, "Talk."

Retired Admiral Hyman G. Rickover, developer of the first atomic submarine, used now-legendary methods to test the mettle of engineers. Seating an applicant on a chair with shortened front legs so that the hapless young man kept sliding forward, he fired questions like, "If you're on a sinking boat with five other men and only one of you can be saved, could you talk the other five into letting you be the one?" When a candidate answered yes, Rickover marched five men into the room, turned to his victim and snapped, "All right son, start talking."

Stress techniques were once a rather common method for interviewing middle- and upper-level executives. Now they're losing favor. As Odiorne explains, "They can't simulate the kind of stress the executive actually meets. Getting through one never proved anything other than that the man could get through a stress interview."

Although applicants used to be advised to keep their cool and endure stress interviews, they are now told to respond assertively. Says Eugene Mueller of Eli Djeddah Associates: "We say to our clients: 'Always preserve your dignity. Nobody should place you in a degrading position. If they do, get up and walk out.'"

Guidelines laid down by the Equal Employment Opportunity Commission can spare applicants other possible indignities. Among the things an interviewer can ask a woman about only if he is prepared to prove that they are job related are her marital status, whether she is pregnant or plans to become so, and even her height and weight (because minimum height and weight requirements have been used to bar women from certain jobs).

The guidelines have taken some of the fun out of interviewing for one midwestern personnel manager. "When I interviewed a woman," he recalls, "I used to say, 'How many kids do you have?' as an area of mutual interest, since I have a family too. It was a way of setting her at ease. Now if I found she had three kids and I hired someone who had none, she could bring a charge."

A Reverse Throw

The candidate's task in an interview is, of course, to persuade his interviewers that his abilities mesh with the company's needs. The problem is to sell himself without making his career sound like an unconvincing litany of successes—especially since he is sitting in an office looking for another job.

According to Carl Boll, who wrote *Executive Jobs Unlimited* (1965), a job-hunting guide that is now in its 16th printing, a good technique is to reverse the interview procedure and throw questions at the interviewer. Says Boll: "Suppose you're a sales manager. You ask the president (I always shoot for the interview with the president), 'Do you have any new products on the line? Are you testing them before they go out? How much are you spending on the tests?' That way you get him talking, and when he mentions a problem in his answer, you say, 'I solved something like that in this way . . .' You have managed to offer him a solution without seeming presumptuous." Boll even suggests taking a notebook into interviews filled with questions about the company to fire at the president. "It impresses him, it's a sign you've done your homework," he insists.

The Pleasantest Ploy

Sometimes it's the interviewer who is inept rather than the interviewee. Robert N. McMurray, a 74-year-old industrial psychologist who studied with Freud and subsequently fashioned interview techniques that have become standard in the curricula of U.S. personnel-management schools, says he has sat in on sessions "where 75% of the interview was the interviewer's autobiography, or overselling the job." Usually an interviewee can do little except wait for a gabby interviewer to pause for breath and then quickly insert a comment of his own. John D. Jordan, a counselor at 40-Plus in Chicago, suggests, "Try asking to see the plant—something that will break his train of thought completely."

No matter how tedious the interviewer or how convinced a candidate is that the job described is not for him, the candidate shouldn't try to end the interview. The company may have another job that will suit him better. Carl Boll thinks a job hunter can salvage something from even the worst interview. "Try to get an offer," he suggests. "Then you can turn it down—and there is nothing so pleasant."

Past problems with mental illness or alcoholism can be a major obstacle for middle-level job hunters. Though many large corporations willingly retain employees who undergo treatment, they are reluctant to hire someone new with such troubles in his past. Generally, employment experts advise an applicant not to volunteer such information. Says Patrick L. Sullivan, who heads his own psychological consulting firm in San Francisco: "I've even advised people to lie. But some people can't, and in that case I've told them, 'Take the chance and somebody may hire you.' It's too bad, but the minute they say, 'I've been a patient in a mental hospital,' they've usually had it."

If the applicant does not volunteer the information and the interviewer uncovers it, perhaps on asking about a gap in his work record caused by hospitalization, the applicant's best recourse is to refer the interviewer to the doctor who treated him and who can testify to his present stability.

Having been fired usually isn't an obstacle to being hired. Says Texas Instruments' Jack Troster: "Naturally it depends on the circumstances, but normally people who have reached middle-level status are not do-nothings." Adds Joe Redmond, PepsiCo's personnel administration manager: "People are often fired because the company is cutting back or there's a personality conflict. If it wasn't that you weren't performing, there probably won't be any problem."

If it was that you weren't performing, some employment counselors advise that you offer a less damning explanation. You stand a good chance of getting away with it, because many companies make it a policy not to give out negative information about former employees for fear of being sued for slander or libel. As a precaution, however, applicants should try to reach an agreement with any boss who fired them so that he will not send in a bad reference. And they should never bad-mouth an ex-boss, for fear of raising an interviewer's suspicion that the applicant will talk the same way about anyone else who hires him.

Wait for the Yeses

Finally, there is the question of money—and most experts on the job interview agree that it should indeed be the final question. If you know your field, you will have a general idea of what companies are paying for your kind of work; salaries are competitive in most industries. In addition, most companies have a salary range, particularly for middle-level jobs, that the personnel manager usually makes known to a candidate in the first interview. Says Carl Boll: "If you start talking salary too early, you'll probably ask either too little or too much. It's easier to negotiate after you've gotten all the yeses."

Salary is only part of the package, of course. Compensation may include other cash incentives like bonuses, plus fringe benefits: profit-sharing, medical and life insurance plans. Almost every firm has these, and they are usually not negotiable. Asking early on about such benefits or about vacations and holidays makes a bad impression. As for the cash, Dudley Darling, a New York executive recruiter, says, "I'd advise the candidate to go for the highest realistic figure: ask for a 15% to 20% raise, and let the interviewer either meet it or make a counter offer." If the rest of the interview has gone well, the chances are he'll meet it.

Discussion Questions

1. How does an applicant interview the company?
2. What is a good strategy to use when an interviewer asks a question such as, "What do you consider your major weaknesses?"
3. When is the appropriate time to discuss the question of money?

Answers:

1. False.
2. False.
3. False.
4. True.
5. True.
6. False.
7. False.

Cases

Women Need Not Apply

William J. Buchholz
Bentley College, Waltham, MA

You can't believe what just happened to you. It had to be positively the worst experience of your life. How can you ever go on another job interview?

You arrive about 10 minutes late for an entry level job interview with Mr. Ripper of Johnston Associates, a management consulting firm. Because Mr. Ripper seemed disturbed to think that you didn't care enough to show up on time, you explained that you had been held up in morning rush-hour traffic. He suggested acidly that morning rush-hour traffic is there *every* morning; interviews with him are not.

As the interview began, you expected Mr. Ripper to ask you a series of questions based on the résumé submitted the week before. Instead, his first comment was this: "Tell me a story."

What the heck does that mean, you thought. You sat there for a few seconds and then replied, "Do you mean you want to know about my personal life?"

He replied, "Well, if you think your personal life story will get you a job here, yes." You got red, and hot, and started to perspire. This is your first interview; what does this guy expect?

Well, you gave it a shot. You told Mr. Ripper about your extracurricular life at college, because that seemed to make the best "story." When you finished, Mr. Ripper just kept looking down at your résumé. In fact, all the while you were telling your story, Mr. Ripper never even looked at you. He did seem a little upset, though, about your college activities. With his eyes on the floor beside you, he rambled off a little speech on women in the work place: how they take good jobs from men who need them to support their families; how they demand to be treated as equals when it is obvious to anyone with half a brain that women are not equal to men. Oh, sure, they can stand more pain and stuff because they need to with childbirth, but that's about it. In fact, that's where women really belong: in the home, rearing children and bringing them up to be God-fearing and responsible people instead of thugs and junkies.

After this little diatribe, Mr. Ripper appeared somewhat agitated; he must have realized he'd let too much slip, so he tried to ease into a question. "Do you have any marriage plans, Miss Johnson?"

You prefer to be called Ms., and what business is it of his anyway? "No, I do not, Mr. Ripper."

"Why not?"

Furious, but controlled, you answered, "Because I'm not in love with anyone right now."

Mr. Ripper raised his brow. "And when you do fall in love, what then, Miss Johnson?" (Ms., Ms., Ms., Ms., you thought to yourself.) "Will you go off and have children and take a 9-month leave? And what about raising your kids? Will you have someone come in and pay them 5 dollars an hour, or will you just plop the kid with a day care center?"

"I don't plan to have children."

"Uhm, hmmm. Miss Johnson, if you were to come to work for us, how much money would you want to start?"

(Ms., Ms., Ms., Ms.) That's a toughie—hadn't really given it much thought; well, you've heard that most of last year's grads started at around 15 thousand so you say, "About 15 thousand, I guess."

"You guess, Miss Johnson?"

(Ms., Ms., Ms., Ms.)

"Don't you *know* what you're worth? Haven't you bothered to check out what our starting salary range is?"

"Well, frankly no, Mr. Ripper. I didn't think we'd be talking salary this early, and I just assumed . . ."

"Never assume, Miss Johnson."

"Mr. Ripper, would you please called me *Ms.* Johnson?"

"Now, I see here that you played soccer, Miss Johnson. Do you think women should engage in contact sports? I mean, isn't that kind of competition more for men? Tell me, Miss Johnson, do you consider yourself competitive? Are you aggressive, Miss Johnson?"

Ah, here it is: Mr. Ripper is going to try to nail you on the petticoats-is-out-to-emasculate-the-male-angle. "Mr. Ripper, I do what I think is right, and I stand up for myself, if that's what you mean. Aggressive? No, I'd say 'assertive' is more accurate."

"Do you think that assertiveness is one of your strengths then, Miss Johnson?"

"Mr. Ripper, a few minutes ago I asked if you would please call me *Ms.* Johnson. Yes, 'assertiveness' is one of my strengths."

"I grant you, Ms. Johnson, you are assertive. Maybe a little *too* assertive? Tell me what you consider to be your weaknesses?"

"I have no significant weaknesses, Mr. Ripper. As you can see from the résumé, I've graduated with highest honors."

"You are very fortunate, indeed, Ms. Johnson, to have no weaknesses. Since you have such a grip on yourself, you certainly must know what you will be doing ten years from now. Please tell me."

"Mr. Ripper, I don't see how I can know that. I'm interviewing for an entry-level management trainee position with you. That's what I'm here for today."

"I see, Ms. Johnson. Then let's go to something that perhaps you do know. What do you consider your greatest accomplishment, and why?"

"I think my greatest accomplishment is my grade point average. Not just anybody can graduate from State with a 3.94 average on a 4.0 scale. I think grades are the best indicator of a person's intellect and of her potential business success."

"I see, Ms. Johnson. Why do you think you would like this particular job?"

"Well, Mr. Ripper, this job would give me a chance to learn a lot about the market and organizational settings. I want to see how a consulting firm really works, and I want to get as much experience as possible and go as far as possible. Eventually maybe I'd even start my own consulting firm—if I learn enough here."

"I see, Ms. Johnson. What then interests you most about our organization?"

"I haven't really had time to find out much about your company, Mr. Ripper. But if it's the same as all the rest of them, I guess what probably interests me most is the chance for advancement in management consulting. As I said before, I'd like to work on my own—I guess."

"One last question, Ms. Johnson. What kinds of people do you find it most difficult to get along with?"

"I'd have to say people like you, Mr. Ripper."

"I see. Thank you, miss. Good day."

Questions

What you have just read is a stress interview, strongly laced with sexism. Both the interviewer and the interviewee have started off on the wrong foot and neither seems able to retrieve the interview. Although this situation may seem far-fetched, it is not. The questions asked are fairly common interview questions; the responses by both parties, unfortunately, are pretty common too.

Analyze this interview. Use the following questions to organize your analysis:

1. What is the first problem you see here? How might that have affected the interview?
2. How would you characterize Mr. Ripper?
3. How would you characterize Ms. Johnson?
4. Are Mr. Ripper's questions fair?
5. Are Ms. Johnson's answers the best ones?
6. How would you have handled Mr. Ripper?

7. Can you trace the emotional pattern of this interview? Plot the peaks and troughs, and see if you can locate the turning point (where Ms. Johnson assumes the attack).

8. Who is the winner here?

After discussing this interview case, role play your own interview. Assume both the interviewer and the interviewee roles if you can. It's a good idea to get the feel for both sides of the desk in interviewing. Perform the role playing in front of a group; you will feel more stress this way, but by practicing under extreme pressure, you will find that your actual interviews will be less frightening (perhaps even easy, by comparison). If you have access to videotaping equipment, tape your interviews and study them carefully. Look for poise and self-control; listen for strong expression and clear articulation. A warning: Do not videotape only once. You may be so disappointed seeing yourself on tape, that you will never actually want to interview. Be prepared for disappointment (nobody ever likes to see that first taping). And interview again and again until you feel reasonably comfortable. Use the interview questions in this case for practice.

Texarkana, Here I Come!

Jack D. Eure

Southwest Texas State University, Sam Marcos, TX

You want that job as Assistant Director of Public Relations for the Texarkana Chamber of Commerce. You were sold on the idea early in your interview with Mr. Robert N. Carter, the organization's manager. But the job won't be easily landed. There's competition—and plenty of it. At least 20 of your classmates were interviewed by Mr. Carter while he was at the University today.

You made a good impression on the man, you think, but you realize that much will depend on the letter of application he asked you to submit for his files and to help in making his recommendations to the Chamber directors. You recall how he stressed the importance of good writing ability in chamber-of-commerce work and told how his own journalistic experience laid the groundwork for his success. That's why, in planning your letter, you are determined to make the quality of your writing stand out. Too, you realize the importance of nonverbal communication in the application letter. Thus, you must pay particular attention to the letter's appearance, thought, attitude, style, and tone.

So that you can interpret your qualifications in terms of what he wants, you begin your preparation by jotting down the more important points stressed in the interview. As well as you can remember, the highlights went something like this:

> "We chamber-of-commerce people have to be rare birds. We should practice and know the meaning of good public relations. We should know and understand businesses and their problems. Our minds should be creative, and we should possess the personality and drive to carry through our ideas. Then we should know the finer points of modern office management. In short, we have to be versatile—Jacks-of-all-trades you might call us.

> "The work won't pay much from the start—about $1100 per month is all I can wring out of the directors. But the job does have possibilities. After two or three years of hard training, the right person will be ready for a managership. I'll help you find that job, too!

> "We don't expect to find someone with experience in this work—not that related experience wouldn't be helpful. Primarily we're interested in finding an individual with the right personality and training—a

257

person who has concentrated on sharpening an ax for the future. We'll teach the person how to swing that ax."

You pick up the clues from his conversation and begin to organize the letter that will help you outstrip your competition. Remember, this is your one big chance to launch your career in the right direction—so don't muff it.

The Across Town Interview

Edward H. Goodin
University of Nevada, Las Vegas, NV

Jody will be graduating with her bachelor's degree in May. During college she has held several part-time jobs. She worked as a bank teller, a salesclerk in a large department store, and as an assistant librarian for an electronics firm. She is currently employed as a credit analyst for a computer firm in Los Angeles.

Beginning in late February, local and out-of-town recruiters visited the university that Jody attends. During March and April, she interviewed with 14 organizations—11 were from the greater metropolitan area of Los Angeles and 3 were from San Diego.

Jody had worked closely with the Career Placement Office in preparing her personal file. She cautiously selected people to write letters of recommendations; the autobiography stressed her academic preparation, work experience, and career objectives; and the file was carefully typewritten and proofread. In addition, the Career Placement Office provided Jody with pamphlets, brochures, and books on interview preparation. She spent hours reading the material and also participated in several "mock" interviews.

Evidently Jody's preparation was worth the time and effort. Five recruiters asked her to come to their company for additional interviews with corporate officials. Jody felt that she would be able to visit all the businesses during the upcoming Spring Recess.

On Tuesday, April 16, Jody scheduled a follow-up interview at 8:30 A.M., with Company K and a second interview at 11 A.M. with Company Y. Jody knew that the on-campus interviews lasted 20 to 30 minutes. She figured that the corporate interviews would be a little longer—1 hour, at the most. She also knew that the travel time between the companies was 35 to 45 minutes—depending upon traffic conditions.

Jody arrived at Company K at 8:20 A.M. She immediately went to the personnel office to meet with Mrs. James, the recruiter she had met at the university. Mrs. James gave Jody a four-page employment application. Jody completed the application before 9:00. Mrs. James reviewed the application with Jody before going into the office of the personnel director. The three of them chatted for about 10 minutes. The recruiter and personnel director were very encouraging—they talked to Jody about salary, fringe benefits, training programs, and a tentative starting date. At 9:35 A.M. the personnel director called the controller and arranged for Jody to visit him at 10 A.M.

259

Jody knew that if the 10 A.M. interview lasted more that 15 or 20 minutes, she would be late for the 11 A.M. interview.

Questions

1. How was it possible for Jody to have four different jobs and not realize that an interview could last 2 to 3 hours, or more?

2. What services are normally performed by a Career Placement Office? Are there other services or agencies that Jody should have used in preparation for job interviews?

3. Was it reasonable for Jody to arrange five interviews during Spring Recess?

4. Should Jody have asked Mrs. James to send the employment application to her home? Should she have returned it by mail or taken it to Mrs. James at the time of the interview? Should applications be handwritten or typewritten?

5. What should Jody have done to prevent overlapping interviews?